CIVIL SERVICES EXAM

UPSC

NEW SYLLABUS

Preliminary & Mains

With Rapid GK 2019 ebook

• **Corporate Office :** 45, 2nd Floor, Maharishi Dayanand Marg, Corner Market, Malviya Nagar, New Delhi-110017

Tel. : 011-49842349 / 49842350

Typeset by Disha DTP Team

How to access the E-book?

INSTRUCTIONS

1. Visit the link given below.
http://bit.ly/rapid-gk-2019
2. You can also scan the QR code provided here.

Note: No login required.

DISHA PUBLICATION

For further information about the books from DISHA,

Log on to **www.dishapublication.com** or email to **info@dishapublication.com**

Contents

Recruitment Process of IAS/ICS Exam

The Union Public Service Commission conducts the Civil Services (Preliminary) Examination which is common for the candidates applying for Civil Services Examination and Indian Forest Service Examination. It acts as a screening mechanism for selection of candidates for the Civil Services (Main) Examination and Indian Forest Service (Main) Examination.

The number of vacancies may undergo change after getting firm number of vacancies from Cadre Controlling Authorities. Reservation will be made for candidates belonging to Scheduled Castes, Scheduled Tribes, Other Backward Classes (OBC) and Physically Disabled Categories in respect of vacancies as may be fixed by the Government.

CSE 201...: Important Dates

- Date of Notification: ... April, 201...
- Last Date to Apply: ... May, 201...
- Exam Date: ... June/July 201...
- Civil Services (Main): ... December, 201...

(A) CENTRES OF EXAMINATION

Examination Centres

(i) Centres for Civil Services (Preliminary) Examination.

Agartala	Gaya	Navi Mumbai
Agra	Ghaziabad	Panaji (Goa)
Ajmer	Gorakhpur	Patna
Ahmedabad	Gurgaon	Port Blair
Aizawl	Gwalior	Puducherry
Aligarh	Hyderabad	Pune
Allahabad	Imphal	Raipur
Ananthapuru	Indore	Rajkot
Aurangabad	Itanagar	Ranchi
Bengaluru	Jabalpur	Sambalpur
Bareilly	Jaipur	Shillong
Bhopal	Jammu	Shimla
Bilaspur	Jodhpur	Siliguri
Chandigarh	Jorhat	Srinagar
Chennai	Kochi	Thane
Coimbatore	Kohima	Thiruvananthapuram

Cuttack	Kolkata	Tiruchirapalli
Dehradun	Kozhikode (Calicut)	Tirupati
Delhi	Lucknow	Udaipur
Dharwar	Ludhiana	Varanasi
Dispur	Madurai	Vellore
Faridabad	Mumbai	Vijayawada
Gangtok	Mysore	Vishakhapatnam
Gautam Buddh Nagar	Nagpur	Warangal

(II) Centres for Civil Services (main) examination

Ahmedabad	Dehradun	Mumbai
Aizawl	Delhi	Patna
Allahabad	Dispur (Guwahati)	Raipur
Bangaluru	Hyderabad	Ranchi
Bhopal	Jaipur	Shillong
Chandigarh	Jammu	Shimla
Chennai	Kolkata	Thiruvananthapuram
Cuttak	Lucknow	Vijayawada

ELIGIBILITY CONDITIONS

(i) Nationality

1. For the Indian Administrative Service and the Indian Police Service, a candidate must be a citizen of India.
2. For other services, a candidate must be either:
   (a) a citizen of India, or
   (b) a subject of Nepal, or
   (c) a subject of Bhutan, or
   (d) a Tibetan refugee who came over to India before 1st January, 1962 with the intention of permanently settling in India,

   or

   (e) a person of Indian origin who has migrated from Pakistan, Burma, Sri Lanka, East African countries of Kenya, Uganda, the United Republic of Tanzania, Zambia, Malawi, Zaire, Ethiopia and Vietnam with the intention of permanently settling in India.

Provided that a candidate belonging to categories (b), (c), (d) and (e) shall be a person in whose favour a certificate of eligibility has been issued by the Government of India. Provided further that candidates belonging to categories (b), (c) and (d) above will not be eligible for appointment to the Indian Foreign Service. A candidate in whose case a certificate of eligibility is necessary, may be admitted to the examination but the offer of appointment may be given only after the necessary eligibility certificate has been issued to him/her by the Government of India.

(ii) Age Limits

(a) A candidate must have attained the age of 21 years and must not have attained the age of 32 years on the 1st of August, 2018, (Prelims exam year) i.e. he/she must have been born not earlier than 2nd August, 1986 and not later than 1st August, 1997.

(b) The upper age limit prescribed above will be relaxable:

- (i) upto a maximum of **five years** if a candidate belongs to a Scheduled Caste or a Scheduled Tribe.
- (ii) upto a maximum of **three years** in the case of candidates belonging to Other Backward Classes who are eligible to avail of reservation applicable to such candidates.
- (iii) upto a maximum of **five years** if a candidate had ordinarily been domiciled in the State of Jammu & Kashmir during the period from the 1st January, 1980 to the 31st December, 1989.
- (iv) upto a maximum of **three years** in the case of Defence Services personnel disabled in operations during hostilities with any foreign country or in a disturbed area and released as a consequence thereof.
- (v) upto a maximum of **five years** in the case of ex-servicemen including Commissioned Officers and ECOs/SSCOs who have rendered at least five years Military Service as on 1st August, 2018 and have been released:
  - (a) on completion of assignment (including those whose assignment is due to be completed within one year from 1st August, 2016) otherwise than by way of dismissal or discharge on account of misconduct or inefficiency, or
  - (b) on account of physical disability attributable to Military Service, or
  - (c) on invalidment.

(vi) Upto a maximum of **five years** in the case of ECOs/SSCOs who have completed an initial period of assignment of five years Military Service as on 1st August, 2018 and whose assignment has been extended beyond five years and in whose case the Ministry of Defence issues a certificate that they can apply for civil employment and that they will be released on three months notice on selection from the date of receipt of offer of appointment.

(vii) upto a maximum of **10 years** in the case of **blind, deaf-mute** and **orthopedically handicapped** persons.

General*	OBC*	SC/ST*	PH*
Minimum: 21 yrs	Minimum: 21 yrs	Minimum: 21 yrs	Minimum: 21 yrs
Maximum: 32 yrs	Maximum: 35 yrs	Maximum: 37 yrs	Maximum: 42 yrs

[For detailed information click the UPSC site: http://upsc.gov.in/sites/default/files/notification]_csp_2018_engl.pdf

(iii) Minimum Educational Qualifications

The candidate must hold a **degree of any of Universities** incorporated by an Act of the Central or State Legislature in India or other educational institutions established by an Act of Parliament or declared to be deemed as a University Under Section-3 of the University Grants Commission Act, 1956, or possess an equivalent qualification.

NOTE I: Candidates who have appeared at an examination the passing of which would render them educationally qualified for the Commission's examination but have not been informed of the results as also the candidates who intend to appear at such a qualifying examination will also be eligible for admission to the Preliminary Examination. All candidates who are declared qualified by the Commission for taking the Civil Services (Main) Examination will be required to produce proof of passing the requisite examination with their application for the Main Examination failing which such candidates will not be admitted to the Main Examination.

NOTE II: In exceptional cases the Union Public Service Commission may treat a candidate who has not any of the foregoing qualifications as a qualified candidate provided that he/she has passed examination conducted by the other Institutions, the standard of which in the opinion of the Commission justifies his/her admission to the examination.

NOTE III: Candidates possessing professional and technical qualifications which are recognised by Government as equivalent to professional and technical degree would also be eligible for admission to the examination.

NOTE IV: Candidates who have passed the final professional M.B.B.S. or any other Medical Examination but have not completed their internship by the time of submission of their applications for the Civil Services (Main) Examination, will be provisionally admitted to the Examination provided they submit along with their application a copy of certificate from the concerned authority of the University/ Institution that they had passed the requisite final professional medical examination. In such cases, the candidates will be required to produce at the time of their interview original Degree or a certificate from the concerned competent authority of the University/Institution that they had completed all requirements (including completion of internship) for the award of the Degree.

(iv) Number of Attempts

General	OBC	SC/ST	PH
6 attempts	9 attempts	No restriction on the number of attempts	General: 9 attempts OBC: 9 attempts SC/ST: No restriction

[For detail information click the UPSC site: http://upsc.gov.in/sites/default/files/ notification]_csp_2018

(v) Physical Standards

Candidates must be physically fit according to physical standards for admission to Civil Services Examination, 201… as per guidelines given in Appendix-III of Rules for Examination published in the Gazette of India Extraordinary dated (notification) … 20…

Fee

Candidates (except Female/SC/ ST/PH Candidates who are exempted from payment of fee) are required to pay fee of ₹ 100/- (Rupees One Hundred only) either by remitting the money in any Branch of SBI by Cash, or by using net banking facility of State Bank of India/etc. for Preliminary Test.

Candidates admitted to the Main Examination will be required to pay a further fee of ₹ 200/-

[For detail information click the UPSC site: http://upsc.gov.in/ exams/notifications]

How to Apply

Candidates are required to apply online using the website http://www.upsconline.nic.in

Detailed instructions for filling up online applications are available on the above mentioned website.

Reservation Criteria

Candidates seeking reservation/ relaxation benefits available for SC/ST/ OBC/PH/ Ex-servicemen must ensure that they are entitled to such reservation/ relaxation as per eligibility prescribed in the Rules/Notice. They should also be in possession of all the requisite certificates in the prescribed format in support of their claim as stipulated in the Rules/ Notice for such benefits, and these certificates should be dated earlier than the due date (closing date) of the application for Civil Services (Prelims) Examination, 2018.

Instructions to the candidates for filling online applications

Candidates must apply Online using the website http://www.upsconline.nic.in/. Salient features of the system of Online Application Form are given hereunder:

- Detailed instructions for filling up online applications are available on the above mentioned website.
- Candidates will be required to complete the Online Application Form containing two stages viz. Part-I and Part-II as per the instructions available in the above mentioned site through drop down menus.
- The candidates are required to pay a fee of Rs. 100/- (Rupees Hundred only) (excepting Female/SC/ST/PH candidates who are exempted from payment of fee) either by remitting the money in any branch of SBI by cash, or by using net banking facility of State Bank of India/State Bank of Bikaner & Jaipur/State Bank of Hyderabad/State Bank of Mysore/State Bank of Patiala/State Bank of Travancore or by using any Visa/Master Credit/Debit Card.
- Before start filling up on Online Application, a candidate must have his photograph and signature duly scanned in the .jpg format in such a manner that each file should not exceed 40 KB and must not be less than 3 KB in size for the photograph and 1 KB for the signature.
- The Online applications (Part I and II) can be filled within the period notified for the purpose, after which link will be disabled.
- Applicants should avoid submitting multiple applications. However, if due to any unavoidable circumstances any applicant submits multiple applications then he must ensure that the applications with higher RID is complete in all respects.
- In case of multiple applications, the applications with higher RID shall be entertained by the Commission and fee paid against one RID shall not be adjusted against any other RID.
- The applicants must ensure that while filling their Application Form, they are providing their valid and active E-mail IDs as the Commission may use electronic mode of communication while contacting them at different stages of examination process.

- The applicants are advised to check their emails at regular intervals and ensure that the email addresses ending with @nic.in are directed to their inbox folder and not to the SPAM folder or any other folder.
- Candidates are strongly advised to apply well in time without waiting for last date for submission of online application.

SECTION-I

PLAN OF EXAMINATION

The competitive examination comprises two successive stages:

(i) Civil Services (Preliminary) Examinations (Objective Type) for the selection of candidates for Main Examination; and

(ii) Civil Services (Main) Examination (Written and Interview) for the selection of candidates for the various services and posts.

The Preliminary Examination will consist of two papers of Objective type (multiple choice questions) and carry a maximum of 400 marks in the subjects set out in subsection (A) of Section-II. This examination is meant to serve as a screening test only; the marks obtained in the Preliminary Examination by the candidates who are declared qualified for admission to the Main Examination will not be counted for determining their final order of merit. The number of candidates to be admitted to the Main Examination will be about twelve to thirteen times the total approximate number of vacancies to be filled in the year in the various Services and Posts. Only those candidates who are declared by the Commission to have qualified in the Preliminary Examination in the year will be eligible for admission to the Main Examination of that year provided they are otherwise eligible for admission to the Main Examination.

Candidates who obtain such minimum qualifying marks in the written part of the Main Examination as may be fixed by the Commission at their discretion, shall be summoned by them for interview for a Personality Test vide sub-section 'C' of Section-II. Marks obtained in the papers will be counted for ranking. The number of candidates to be summoned for interview will be about twice the number of vacancies to be filled. Marks thus obtained by the candidates in the Main Examination (written part as well as interview) would determine their final ranking. Candidates will be allotted to the various Services keeping in view their ranks in the examination and the preferences expressed by them for the various Services and Posts.

SECTION-II

Scheme and subjects for the Preliminary and Main Examinations:

A. PRELIMINARY EXAMINATION

The Examination shall comprise two compulsory papers of 200 marks each.

Prelims Paper	Duration	Questions	Marks
Paper I - General Studies	2 Hours	100	200
Paper II* - Aptitude	2 Hours	80	200
Total			**400**

*[*In General Studies Paper - II, minimum qualifying marks is 33%. You will be selected for Mains Exam based on total marks of General Studies Paper - I.]*

NOTE: (i) Both the question papers will be of the objective type (multiple choice questions).

(ii) The question papers will be set both in Hindi and English. However, questions relating to English Language Comprehension skills of Class X level will be tested through passages from English Language only without providing Hindi translation thereof in the question paper.

(iii) Details of the syllabi are indicated in Part A of Section III.

(iv) Each paper will be of two hours duration. Blind candidates will however; be allowed an extra time of twenty minutes at each paper.

B. MAIN EXAMINATION

Civil Services (Main) Pattern

The pattern has changed from 2015 Main Examination. The new pattern is:

S. No.	Paper	Subject	Marks
1	Paper A	Indian Language (Qualifying)	300
2	Paper B	English (Qualifying)	300
3	Paper I	Essay	250
4	Paper II	General Studies – I	250
5	Paper III	General Studies – II	250
6	Paper IV	General Studies - III	250
7	Paper V	General Studies - IV	250
8	Paper VI	Optional Subject Paper 1	250
9	Paper VII	Optional Subject Paper 2	250
	Total		**1750**
		Interview (Personality Test)	275
	Grand Total		**2025**

Negative Marking in CSAT(PT)

There is negative marking for incorrect answers for all questions except some of the questions where the negative marking will be inbuilt in the form of different marks being awarded to the most appropriate and not-so-appropriate answer for such questions. If you give a wrong answer, one-third of the marks assigned to that question will be deducted as penalty.

Selection for Main

Only those candidates who are declared by the Commission to have qualified in the Preliminary Examination in the year will be eligible for admission to the Main Examination of that year provided they are otherwise eligible for admission to the Main Examination.

Candidates may choose any optional subject from amongst the list of subjects given in para 2 below (Group 1). However, a candidate can opt for the literatures of a language, indicated in Group-2 below para 2, as an optional subject, only if the candidate has graduated in the literature of that particular language as the main subject.

NOTE:

(i) Marks obtained by the candidates for all papers (Paper I-VII) will be counted for merit ranking. However, the Commission will have the discretion to fix qualifying marks in any or all papers of the examination.

(ii) For the Language medium/ literature of languages, the scripts to be used by the candidates will be as under:

Language	Script	Language	Script
Assamese	Assamese	Oriya	Oriya
Bengali	Bengali	Punjabi	Gurumukhi
Gujarati	Gujarati	Sanskrit	Devanagari
Hindi	Devanagari	Sindhi	Devanagari or Arabic
Kannada	Kannada	Tamil	Tamil
Kashmiri	Persian	Telugu	Telugu
Konkani	Devanagari	Urdu	Persian
Malayalam	Malayalam	Bodo	Devanagari
Manipuri	Bengali	Dogri	Devanagari
Marathi	Devanagari	Maithilli	Devanagari
Nepali	Devanagari	Santhali	Devanagari or Olchiki

Note: For Santhali language, question paper will be printed in Devanagari script; but candidates will be free to answer either in Devanagari script or in Olchiki.

2. List of optional subjects for Main Examination:

Group-1

(i) Agriculture
(ii) Animal Husbandry and Veterinary Science
(iii) Anthropology
(iv) Botany
(v) Chemistry
(vi) Civil Engineering
(vii) Commerce and Accountancy
(viii) Economics
(ix) Electrical Engineering
(x) Geography
(xi) Geology
(xii) History
(xiii) Law
(xiv) Management
(xv) Mathematics
(xvi) Mechanical Engineering
(xvii) Medical Science
(xviii) Philosophy
(xix) Physics
(xx) Political Science and International Relations
(xxi) Psychology
(xxii) Public Administration
(xxiii) Sociology
(xxiv) Statistics
(xxv) Zoology

Group-2

Literature of any one of the following languages:

Assamese, Bengali, Bodo, Dogri, Gujarati, Hindi, Kannada, Kashmiri, Konkani, Maithili, Malayalam, Manipuri, Marathi, Nepali, Oriya, Punjabi, Sanskrit, Santhali, Sindhi, Tamil, Telugu, Urdu, English.

NOTE:

(i) The question papers for the examination will be of conventional (essay) type.

(ii) Each paper will be of 3 hours duration.

(iii) Candidates will have the option to answer all the question papers, except Section 2 of the Paper-I (English comprehension and English précis) in English or Hindi. If the candidate has had his/ her graduation in any of the following language mediums using the particular language medium for qualifying the graduate level examination, then he/she may opt for that particular language medium to answer all the question papers, except Section 2 of the Paper-I (English comprehension and English précis).

Assamese, Bengali, Bodo, Dogri, Gujarati, Kannada, Kashmiri, Konkani, Maithili, Malayalam, Manipuri, Marathi, Nepali, Oriya, Punjabi, Sanskrit, Santhali, Sindhi, Tamil, Telugu, and Urdu

(iv) Candidates exercising the option to answer Papers in any one of the languages mentioned above may, if they so desire, give English version within brackets of only the description of the technical terms, if any, in addition to the version in the language opted by them. Candidates should, however, note that if they misuse the above rule, a deduction will be made on this account from the total marks otherwise accruing to them and in extreme cases; their script(s) will not be valued for being in an unauthorized medium.

The question papers (other than the literature of language papers) will be set in Hindi and English only.

(vi) The details of the syllabi are set out in Part B of Section III.

General Instructions (Preliminary as well as Main Examination):

(i) Candidates must write the papers in their own hand. In no circumstances will they be allowed the help of a scribe to write the answers for them. However, blind candidates and candidates with Locomotor Disability and Cerebral Pasly where dominant (writing) extremity is affected to the extent of slowing the performance of function (minimum of 40% impairment) will be allowed to write the examination with the help of a scribe in both the civil Service (Preliminary) as well as in the Civil Services (Main) Examination.

(ii) Compensatory time of twenty minutes per hour shall be permitted for the Blind candidates and the candidates with locomotor disability and cerebral palsy where dominant (writing) extremity is affected to the extent of slowing the performance of function (minimum of 40% impairment) in both the civil Services (Preliminary) as well as in the Civil Services (Main) Examination. However, no scribe shall be permitted to such candidates.

NOTE 1: The eligibility conditions of a scribe, his/her conduct inside the examination hall and the manner in which and extent to which he/she can help the blind candidate in writing the Civil Services Examination shall be governed by the instructions issued by the UPSC in this regard. Violation of all or any of the said instructions shall entail the cancellation of the candidature of the blind candidate in addition to any other action that the UPSC may take against the scribe.

NOTE 2: For purpose of these rules the candidate shall be deemed to be a blind candidate if the percentage of visual impairment is 40% or more. The criteria for determining the percentage of visual impairment shall be as follows:

All with corrections

Category	Better eye	Worse eye	Percentage
Category 0	6/9-6/18	6/24 to 6/36	20%
Category I	6/18-6/36	6/60 to nil	40%
Category II	6/60-4/60 or field of vision 10-20°	3/60 to nil	75%
Category III	3/60-1/60 or field of to nil vision 10°	F.C. at 1 ft to nil	100%
Category IV	FC. at 1 ft to nil field of vision 100°	F.C. at 1 ft to nil field of vision 100°	100%
One eyed person	6/6	F.C. at 1 ft to nil	30%

NOTE 3: For availing of the concession admissible to a blind candidate, the candidate concerned shall produce a certificate in the prescribed proforma from a Medical Board constituted by the Central/State Governments alongwith his application for the Main Examination.

NOTE 4:

(i) The concession admissible to blind candidates shall not be admissible to those suffering from Myopia.

(ii) The Commission have discretion to fix qualifying marks in any or all the subjects of the examination.

(iii) If a candidate's handwriting is not easily legible, a deduction will be made on this account from the total marks otherwise accruing to him.

(iv) Marks will not be allotted for mere superficial knowledge.

(v) Credit will be given for orderly, effective and exact expression combined with due economy of words in all subjects of the examination.

(vi) In the question papers, wherever required, SI units will be used.

(vii) Candidates should use only international form of Indian numerals (i.e. 1, 2, 3, 4, 5, 6, etc.) while answering question papers.

(viii) Candidates will be allowed the use of Scientific (Non-Programmable type) Calculators at the conventional (Essay) type examination of UPSC. Programmable type calculators will however not be allowed and the use of such calculators shall tantamount to resorting to unfair means by the candidates. Loaning or interchanging of calculators in the Examination Hall is not permitted.

It is also important to note that candidates are not permitted to use calculators for answering objective type papers (Test Booklets). They should not therefore, bring the same inside the Examination Hall.

C. INTERVIEW TEST

The candidate will be interviewed by a Board who will have before them a record of his/her career. He/she will be asked questions on matters of general interest. The object of the interview is to assess the personal suitability of the candidate for a career in public service by a Board of competent and unbiased observers. The test is intended to judge the mental calibre of a candidate. In broad terms this is really an assessment of not only his/her intellectual qualities but also social traits and his/her interest in current affairs. Some of the qualities to be judged are mental alertness, critical powers of assimilation, clear and logical exposition, balance of judgement, variety and depth of interest, ability for social cohesion and leadership, intellectual and moral integrity.

The technique of the interview is not that of a strict cross-examination but of a natural, though directed and purposive conversation which is intended to reveal the mental qualities of the candidate.

The interview test is not intended to be a test either of the specialised or general knowledge of the candidates which has been already tested through their written papers. Candidates are expected to have taken an intelligent interest not only in their special subjects of academic study but also in the events which are happening around them both within and outside their own state or country as well as in modern currents of thought and in new discoveries which should rouse the curiosity of well educated youth.

SECTION-III

SYLLABUS

A. Syllabus for Civil Services (Preliminary) Examinations

Paper I - General Studies: (200 marks/duration : 2 hours)

- **Current Affairs:** events of national and international importance.
- **History of India** and Indian National Movement.
- **Indian and World Geography:** Physical, Social, Economic Geography of India and the World.
- **Indian Polity and Governance:** Constitution, Political System, Panchayati Raj, Public Policy, Rights Issues, etc.
- **Economic and Social Development:** Sustainable Development, Poverty, Inclusion, Demographics, Social Sector initiatives, etc.
- **General issues on Environmental** Ecology, Bio-diversity and Climate Change (that do not require subject specialization).
- **General Science.**

Paper II – Aptitude: (200 marks/duration : 2 hours)

- Comprehension
- Interpersonal skills including communication skills
- Logical reasoning and analytical ability
- Decision-making and problem-solving
- General mental ability
- Basic numeracy (numbers and their relations, orders of magnitude, etc.) (Class X level),
- Data interpretation (charts, graphs, tables, data sufficiency etc. - Class X level)

*[Note: **Paper-II** of the Civil Services (Preliminary) Examination will be a qualifying paper with minimum qualifying marks fixed at 33%]*

B. Syllabus for Civil Services (Main) Examinations

Paper-A and B:

There will be two qualifying papers in any Indian language and English each of 300 marks.

The aim of the paper is to test the candidates ability to read and understand serious discursive prose, and how they express their ideas clearly and correctly, in English and Indian Language concerned.

The pattern of questions would be broadly as follows:

Paper-A: Indian Languages:

(i) Comprehension of given passages

(ii) Precis Writing

(iii) Usage and Vocabulary

(iv) Short Essays

(v) Translation from English to the Indian language and vice-versa.

Paper-B: English

(i) Comprehension of given passages

(ii) Precis Writing

(iii) Usage and Vocabulary

(iv) Short Essays

*[**Note 1:** The Papers on Indian Languages and English will be of Matriculation or equivalent standard and will be of qualifying nature only. The marks obtained in these papers will not be counted for ranking.*

***Note 2:** The candidates will have to answer the English and Indian Languages papers in English and the respective Indian language (except where translation is involved].*

Paper-I : Essay-250 Marks

Candidates are required to write two essays on a specific topic. The choice of subjects will be given. They are expected to keep closely to the subject of the essay to arrange their ideas in orderly fashion, and to write concisely. Credit will be given for effective and exact expression.

Paper-II

General Studies-I: Indian Heritage and Culture, History and Geography of the World and Society (250 marks).

- Indian culture covers the salient aspects of Art Forms, Literature and Architecture from ancient to modern times.
- Modern Indian history from about the middle of the eighteenth century until the present- significant events, personalities, issues.
- The Freedom Struggle - its various stages and important contributors / contributions from different parts of the country.

- Post-independence consolidation and reorganization within the country. History of the world will include events from 18th century such as industrial revolution, world wars, redrawal of national boundaries, colonization, decolonization, political philosophies like communism, capitalism, socialism, etc. and their forms and effect on the society.
- Salient features of Indian Society, Diversity of India.
- Role of women and women's organizations, population and associated issues, poverty and developmental issues, urbanization, their problems and their remedies; Effects of globalization on Indian society.
- Social empowerment, communalism, regionalism & secularism.
- Salient features of world's physical geography.
- Distribution of key natural resources across the world (including South Asia and the Indian subcontinent); factors responsible for the location of primary, secondary, and tertiary sector industries in various parts of the world (including India).
- Important Geophysical phenomena such as earthquakes, Tsunami, Volcanic activity, cyclone, etc. geographical features and their location- changes in critical geographical features (including water bodies and ice-caps) and in flora and fauna and the effects of such changes.

Paper-III

General Studies-II: Governance, Constitution, Polity, Social Justice and International relations (250 marks).

- **Indian Constitution:** historical underpinnings, evolution, features, amendments, significant provisions and basic structure.
- Functions and responsibilities of the Union and the States, issues and challenges pertaining to the federal structure, devolution of powers and finances up to local levels and challenges therein.
- Separation of powers between various organs dispute redressal mechanisms and institutions.
- Comparison of the Indian constitutional scheme with that of other countries
- **Parliament and State Legislatures:** structure, functioning, conduct of business, powers & privileges and issues arising out of these.
- Structure, organization and functioning of the Executive and the Judiciary Ministries and Departments of the Government; pressure groups and formal/ informal associations and their role in the Polity.
- Salient features of the Representation of People's Act.
- Appointment to various Constitutional posts, powers, functions and responsibilities of various Constitutional Bodies; Statutory, regulatory and various quasi-judicial bodies

- Government policies and interventions for development in various sectors and issues arising out of their design and implementation.
- Development processes and the development industry- the role of NGOs, SHGs, various groups and associations, donors, charities, institutional and other stakeholders
- Welfare schemes for vulnerable sections of the population by the Centre and States and the performance of these schemes; mechanisms, laws, institutions and Bodies constituted for the protection and betterment of these vulnerable sections.
- Issues relating to development and management of Social Sector/Services relating to Health, Education, Human Resources.
- Issues relating to poverty and hunger.
- Important aspects of governance, transparency and accountability, e-governance- applications, models, successes, limitations, and potential; citizens charters, transparency & accountability and institutional and other measures.
- Role of civil services in a democracy.
- India and its neighbourhood- relations.
- Bilateral, regional and global groupings and agreements involving India and/or affecting India's interests
- Effect of policies and politics of developed and developing countries on India's interests, Indian diaspora. Important International institutions, agencies and fora- their structure, mandate.

Paper-IV

General Studies-III (Technology, Economic Development, Bio-diversity, Environment, Security and Disaster Management) of 250 marks which may include following topics:

- Indian Economy and issues relating to planning, mobilization of resources, growth, development and employment.
- Inclusive growth and issues arising from it.
- Government Budgeting.
- Major crops, cropping patterns in various parts of the country, different types of irrigation and irrigation systems storage, transport and marketing of agricultural produce and issues and related constraints; e-technology in the aid of farmers

- Issues related to direct and indirect farm subsidies and minimum support prices; Public Distribution System- objectives, functioning, limitations, revamping; issues of buffer stocks and food security; Technology missions; economics of animal-rearing.
- Food processing and related industries in India- scope and significance, location, upstream and downstream requirements, supply chain management.
- Land reforms in India.
- Effects of liberalization on the economy, changes in industrial policy and their effects on industrial growth.
- Infrastructure: Energy, Ports, Roads, Airports, Railways etc.
- Investment models.
- Science and Technology- developments and their applications and effects in everyday life
- Achievements of Indians in science & technology; indigenization of technology and developing new technology.
- Awareness in the fields of IT, Space, Computers, robotics, nano-technology, bio-technology and issues relating to intellectual property rights.
- Conservation, environmental pollution and degradation, environmental impact assessment
- Disaster and disaster management.
- Linkages between development and spread of extremism.
- Role of external state and non-state actors in creating challenges to internal security.
- Challenges to internal security through communication networks, role of media and social networking sites in internal security challenges, basics of cyber security; money-laundering and its prevention
- Security challenges and their management in border areas; linkages of organized crime with terrorism
- Various Security forces and agencies and their mandate

Paper-V

General Studies -IV (Ethics, Integrity and Aptitude) of 250 marks which may include following topics:

This paper will include questions to test the candidates' attitude and approach to issues relating to integrity, probity in public life and his problem solving approach to various issues and conflicts faced by him in dealing with society. Questions may utilise the case study approach to determine these aspects. The following broad areas will be covered.

- **Ethics and Human Interface:** Essence, determinants and consequences of Ethics in human actions; dimensions of ethics; ethics in private and public relationships. Human Values - lessons from the lives and teachings of great leaders, reformers and administrators; role of family, society and educational institutions in inculcating values.
- **Attitude:** content, structure, functions; its influence and relation with thought and behaviour; moral and political attitudes; social influence and persuasion. Aptitude and foundational values for Civil Service , integrity, impartiality and non-partisanship, objectivity, dedication to public service, empathy, tolerance and compassion towards the weaker sections.
- Emotional intelligence-concepts, and their utilities and application in administration and governance.
- Contributions of moral thinkers and philosophers from India and the world.
- **Public/Civil service values and Ethics in Public administration:** Status and problems; ethical concerns and dilemmas in government and private institutions; laws, rules, regulations and conscience as sources of ethical guidance; accountability and ethical governance; strengthening of ethical and moral values in governance; ethical issues in international relations and funding; corporate governance.
- **Probity in Governance:** Concept of public service; Philosophical basis of governance and probity; Information sharing and transparency in government, Right to Information, Codes of Ethics, Codes of Conduct, Citizen's Charters, Work culture, Quality of service delivery, Utilization of public funds, challenges of corruption.
- Case Studies on above issues.

PAPER-VI & PAPER VII

Optional Subject Papers I & II

List of optional subjects for Main Examination:

Agriculture, Animal Husbandry and Veterinary Science, Anthropology, Botany, Chemistry, Civil Engineering, Commerce and Accountancy, Economics, Electrical Engineering, Geography, Geology, History, Law, Management; Mathematics, Mechanical Engineering, Medical Science, Philosophy, Physics, Political Science and International Relations, Psychology, Public Administration, Sociology, Statistics and Zoology.

Literature of any one of the following languages:

Assamese, Bengali, Bodo, Dogri, Gujarati, Hindi, Kannada, Kashmiri, Konkani, Maithili, Malayalam, Manipuri, Marathi, Nepali, Oriya, Punjabi, Sanskrit, Santhali, Sindhi, Tamil, Telugu, Urdu, English.

Candidates may choose any optional subject from the list of subjects.

*[**Note:** The candidates would be allowed to use any one language from the Eighth Schedule of the Constitution or English as the medium of writing the examination.]*

OPTIONAL SUBJECTS

AGRICULTURE

PAPER - I

Ecology and its relevance to man, natural resources, their sustainable management and conservation. Physical and social environment as factors of crop distribution and production. Agro ecology; cropping pattern as indicators of environments. Environmental pollution and associated hazards to crops, animals and humans.

Climate change – International conventions and global initiatives. Green house effect and global warming. Advance tools for ecosystem analysis – Remote Sensing (RS) and Geographic Information Systems (GIS). Cropping patterns in different agro-climatic zones of the country. Impact of high-yielding and short-duration varieties on shifts in cropping patterns. Concepts of various cropping and farming systems. Organic and Precision farming. Package of practices for production of important cereals, pulses, oil seeds, fibres, sugar, commercial and fodder crops. Important features and scope of various types of forestry plantations such as social forestry, agro-forestry, and natural forests.

Propagation of forest plants. Forest products. Agro forestry and value addition. Conservation of forest flora and fauna. Weeds, their characteristics, dissemination and association with various crops; their multiplications; cultural, biological, and chemical control of weeds. Soil- physical, chemical and biological properties. Processes and factors of soil formation. Soils of India. Mineral and organic constituents of soils and their role in maintaining soil productivity. Essential plant nutrients and other beneficial elements in soils and plants. Principles of soil fertility, soil testing and fertilizer recommendations, integrated nutrient management. Biofertilizers. Losses of nitrogen in soil, nitrogen-use efficiency in submerged rice soils, nitrogen fixation in soils. Efficient phosphorus and potassium use. Problem soils and their reclamation. Soil factors affecting greenhouse gas emission.

Soil conservation, integrated watershed management. Soil erosion and its management. Dry land agriculture and its problems. Technology for stabilizing agriculture production in rain fed areas. Water-use efficiency in relation to crop production, criteria for scheduling irrigations, ways and means of reducing run-off losses of irrigation water. Rainwater harvesting. Drip and sprinkler irrigation. Drainage of waterlogged soils, quality of irrigation water, effect of industrial effluents on soil and water pollution. Irrigation projects in India. Farm management, scope, importance and characteristics, farm planning. Optimum resource use and budgeting. Economics of different types of farming systems. Marketing management – strategies for development, market intelligence. Price fluctuations and their cost; role of co-operatives in agricultural economy; types and systems of farming and factors affecting them. Agricultural price policy. Crop Insurance.

Agricultural extension, its importance and role, methods of evaluation of extension programmes, socioeconomic survey and status of big, small and marginal farmers and landless agricultural labourers. Training programmes for extension workers. Role of Krishi Vigyan Kendra's (KVK) in dissemination of Agricultural technologies. Non Government Organization (NGO) and self-help group approach for rural development.

PAPER - II

Cell structure, function and cell cycle. Synthesis, structure and function of genetic material. Laws of heredity. Chromosome structure, chromosomal aberrations, linkage and cross-over, and their significance in recombination breeding. Polyploidy, euploids and aneuploids. Mutations – and their role in crop improvement.

Heritability, sterility and incompatibility, classification and their application in crop improvement. Cytoplasmic inheritance, sex-linked, sex-influenced and sex-limited characters. History of plant breeding. Modes of reproduction, selfing and crossing techniques. Origin, evolution and domestication of crop plants, center of origin, law of homologous series, crop genetic resources- conservation and utilization. Application of principles of plant breeding, improvement of crop plants. Molecular markers and their application in plant improvement. Pure-line selection, pedigree, mass and recurrent selections, combining ability, its significance in plant breeding. Heterosis and its exploitation. Somatic hybridization.

Breeding for disease and pest resistance. Role of interspecific and intergeneric hybridization. Role of genetic engineering and biotechnology in crop improvement. Genetically modified crop plants. Seed production and processing technologies. Seed certification, seed testing and storage. DNA finger printing and seed registration. Role of public and private sectors in seed production and marketing. Intellectual Property Rights (IPR) issues, WTO issues and its impact on Agriculture. Principles of Plant Physiology with reference to plant nutrition, absorption, translocation and metabolism of nutrients. Soil water-plant relationship.

Enzymes and plant pigments; photosynthesis-modern concepts and factors affecting the process, aerobic and anaerobic respiration; C3, C4 and CAM mechanisms. Carbohydrate, protein and fat metabolism. Growth and development; photoperiodism and vernalilzation. Plant growth substances and their role in crop production. Physiology of seed development and germination; dormancy. Stress physiology – draught, salt and water stress. Major fruits, plantation crops, vegetables, spices and flower crops. Package practices of major horticultural crops. Protected cultivation and high tech horticulture. Post harvest technology and value addition of fruits and vegetables. Landscaping and commercial floriculture. Medicinal and aromatic plants. Role of fruits and vegetables in human nutrition.

Diagnosis of pests and diseases of field crops, vegetables, orchard and plantation crops and their economic importance. Classification of pests and diseases and their management. Integrated pest and disease management. Storage pests and their management. Biological control of pests and diseases. Epidemiology and forecasting of major crop pests and diseases. Plant quarantine measures. Pesticides, their formulation and modes of action.

Food production and consumption trends in India. Food security and growing population – vision 2020. Reasons for grain surplus. National and international food policies. Production, procurement, distribution constraints. Availability of food grains, per capita expenditure on food. Trends in poverty, Public Distribution System and Below Poverty Line population, Targeted Public Distribution System (PDS), policy implementation in context to globalization. Processing constraints. Relation of food production to National Dietary Guidelines and food consumption pattern. Food based dietary approaches to eliminate hunger. Nutrient deficiency – Micro nutrient deficiency : Protein Energy Malnutrition or Protein Calorie Malnutrition (PEM or PCM), Micro nutrient deficiency and HRD in context of work capacity of women and children. Food grain productivity and food security.

ANIMAL HUSBANDRY AND VETERINARY SCIENCE

PAPER – I

1. Animal Nutrition

1.1 Partitioning of food energy within the animal. Direct and indirect calorimetry. Carbon – nitrogen balance and comparative slaughter methods. Systems for expressing energy value of foods in ruminants, pigs and poultry. Energy requirements for maintenance, growth, pregnancy, lactation, egg, wool, and meat production.

1.2 Latest advances in protein nutrition. Energy protein interrelationships. Evaluation of protein quality. Use of NPN compounds in ruminant diets. Protein requirements for maintenance, growth, pregnancy, lactation, egg, wool and meat production.

1.3 Major and trace minerals – Their sources, physiological functions and deficiency symptoms. Toxic minerals. Mineral interactions. Role of fat-soluble and water – soluble vitamins in the body, their sources and deficiency symptoms.

1.4 Feed additives – methane inhibitors, probiotics, enzymes, antibiotics, hormones, oligosaccharides, antioxidants, emulsifiers, mould inhibitors, buffers etc. Use and abuse of growth promoters like hormones and antibiotics – latest concepts.

1.5 Conservation of fodders. Storage of feeds and feed ingredients. Recent advances in feed technology and feed processing. Anti – nutritional and toxic factors present in livestock feeds. Feed analysis and quality control. Digestibility trials – direct, indirect and indicator methods. Predicting feed intake in grazing animals.

1.6 Advances in ruminant nutrition. Nutrient requirements. Balanced rations. Feeding of calves, pregnant, work animals and breeding bulls. Strategies for feeding milch animals during different stages of lactation cycle.

Effect of feeding on milk composition. Feeding of goats for meat and milk production. Feeding of sheep for meat and wool production.

1.7 Swine Nutrition. Nutrient requirements. Creep, starter, grower and finisher rations. Feeding of pigs for lean meat production. Low cost rations for swine.

1.8 Poultry nutrition. Special features of poultry nutrition. Nutrient requirements for meat and egg production. Formulation of rations for different classes of layers and broilers.

2. Animal Physiology

2.1 Physiology of blood and its circulation, respiration; excretion. Endocrine glands in health and disease.

2.2 Blood constituents - Properties and functions-blood cell formation-Haemoglobin synthesis and chemistryplasma proteins production, classification and properties, coagulation of blood; Haemorrhagic disorders anticoagulants-blood groups-Blood volume-Plasma expanders-Buffer systems in blood. Biochemical tests and their significance in disease diagnosis.

2.3 Circulation - Physiology of heart, cardiac cycle, heart sounds, heart beat, electrocardiograms. Work and efficiency of heart-effect of ions on heart function-metabolism of cardiac muscle, nervous and chemical regulation of heart, effect of temperature and stress on heart, blood pressure and hypertension, osmotic regulation, arterial pulse, vasomotor regulation of circulation, shock. Coronary and pulmonary circulation, Blood-Brain barrier- Cerebrospinal fluid- circulation in birds.

2.4 Respiration - Mechanism of respiration, Transport and exchange of gases – neural control of respirationchemo- receptors-hypoxia-respiration in birds.

2.5 Excretion-Structure and function of kidney-formation of urine-methods of studying renal function-renal regulation of acidbase balance: physiological constituents of urine-renal failure-passive venous congestion-Urinary secretion in chicken-Sweat glands and their function. Bio-chemical test for urinary dysfunction.

2.6 Endocrine glands - Functional disorders their symptoms and diagnosis. Synthesis of hormones, mechanism and control of secretion- hormonal receptors-classification and function.

2.7 Growth and Animal Production- Prenatal and postnatal growth, maturation, growth curves, measures of growth, factors affecting growth, conformation, body composition, meat quality.

2.8 Physiology of Milk Production, Reproduction and Digestion- Current status of hormonal control of mammary development, milk secretion and milk ejection, Male and Female reproductive organs, their components and functions. Digestive organs and their functions.

2.9 Environmental Physiology- Physiological relations and their regulation; mechanisms of adaptation, environmental factors and regulatory mechanisms involved in animal behaviour, climatology – various parameters and their importance. Animal ecology. Physiology of behaviour. Effect of stress on health and production.

3. Animal Reproduction

Semen quality- Preservation and Artificial Insemination- Components of semen, composition of spermatozoa, chemical and physical properties of ejaculated semen, factors affecting semen in vivo and in vitro. Factors affecting semen production and quality, preservation, composition of diluents, sperm concentration, transport of diluted semen. Deep freezing techniques in cows, sheep, goats, swine and poultry. Detection of oestrus and time of insemination for better conception. Anoestrus and repeat breeding.

4. Livestock Production and Management

4.1 Commercial Dairy Farming- Comparison of dairy farming in India with advanced countries. Dairying under mixed farming and as specialized farming, economic dairy farming. Starting of a dairy farm, Capital and land requirement, organization of the dairy farm. Opportunities in dairy farming, factors determining the efficiency of dairy animal. Herd recording, budgeting, cost of milk production, pricing policy; Personnel Management. Developing Practical and Economic rations for dairy cattle; supply of greens throughout the year, feed and fodder requirements of Dairy Farm. Feeding regimes for young stock and bulls, heifers and breeding animals; new trends in feeding young and adult stock; Feeding records.

4.2 Commercial meat, egg and wool production-Development of practical and economic rations for sheep, goats, pigs, rabbits and poultry. Supply of greens, fodder, feeding regimes for young and mature stock. New trends in enhancing production and management. Capital and land requirements and socio-economic concept.

4.3 Feeding and management of animals under drought, flood and other natural calamities.

5. Genetics and Animal Breeding

History of animal genetics. Mitosis and Meiosis: Mendelian inheritance; deviations to Mendelian genetics; Expression of genes; Linkage and crossing over; Sex determination, sex influenced and sex limited characters; Blood groups and polymorphism; Chromosome aberrations; Cytoplasmic inheritance. Gene and its structure; DNA as a genetic material; Genetic code and protein synthesis; Recombinant DNA technology. Mutations, types of mutations, methods for detecting mutations and mutation rate. Trans-genesis.

5.1 Population Genetics applied to Animal Breeding- Quantitative Vs. qualitative traits; Hardy Weinberg Law; Population Vs. individual; Gene and genotypic frequency; Forces changing gene frequency; Random drift and small populations; Theory of path coefficient; Inbreeding, methods of estimating inbreeding coefficient, systems of inbreeding, Effective population size; Breeding value, estimation of breeding value, dominance and epistatic deviation; Partitioning of variation; Genotype X environment correlation and genotype X environment interaction; role of multiple measurements; Resemblance between relatives.

5.2 Breeding Systems- Breeds of live-stock and Poultry. Heritability, repeatability and genetic and phenotypic correlations, their methods of estimation and precision of estimates; Aids to selection and their relative merits; Individual, pedigree, family and within family selection; Progeny testing; Methods of selection; Construction of selection indices and their uses; Comparative evaluation of genetic gains through various selection methods;

Indirect selection and correlated response; Inbreeding, out breeding, upgrading, cross-breeding and synthesis of breeds; Crossing of inbred lines for commercial production; Selection for general and specific combining ability; Breeding for threshold characters. Sire index.

6. Extension

Basic philosophy, objectives, concept and principles of extension. Different Methods adopted to educate farmers under rural conditions. Generation of technology, its transfer and feedback. Problems and constraints in transfer of technology. Animal husbandry programmes for rural development.

PAPER–II

1. Anatomy, Pharmacology and Hygiene

1.1 Histology and Histological Techniques: Paraffin embedding technique of tissue processing and H.E. staining – Freezing microtomy- Microscopy-Bright field microscope and electron microscope. Cytology structure of cell, organells and inclusions; cell division-cell types- Tissues and their classification-embryonic and adult tissues Comparative histology of organs-Vascular, Nervous, digestive, respiratory, musculo- skeletal and urogenital systems Endocrine glands -Integuments-sense organs.

1.2 Embryology – Embryology of vertebrates with special reference to aves and domestic mammals gametogenesis-fertilization-germ layers- foetal membranes and placentation-types of placenta in domestic mammals-Teratology-twins and twinning-organogenesis -germ layer derivatives-endodermal, mesodermal and ectodermal derivates.

1.3 Bovine Anatomy- Regional Anatomy: Para-nasal sinuses of OX- surface anatomy of salivary glands. Regional anatomy of infraorbital, maxillary, mandibuloalveolar, mental and cornual nerve block. Regional anatomy of paravertebral nerves, pudendal nerve, median ulnar and radial nerves-tibial,fibular and digital nerves-Cranial nerves-structures involved in epidural anaesthesia-superficial lymph nodes-surface anatomy of visceral organs of thoracic, abdominal and pelvic cavities-comparative features of locomotor apparatus and their application in the biomechanics of mammalian body.

1.4 Anatomy of Fowl- Musculo-skeletal system-functional anatomy in relation to respiration and flying, digestion and egg production.

1.5 Pharmacology and therapeutic drugs Cellular level of pharmacodynamics and pharmacokinetics. Drugs acting on fluids and electrolyte balance. Drugs acting on Autonomic nervous system. Modern concepts of anaesthesia and dissociative anaesthetics. Autacoids. Antimicrobials and principles of chemotherapy in microbial infections. Use of hormones in therapeutics-chemotherapy of parasitic infections. Drug and economic concerns in the Edible tissues of animals-chemotherapy of Neoplastic diseases. Toxicity due to insecticides, plants, metals, non-metals, zootoxins and mycotoxins.

1.6 Veterinary Hygiene with reference to water, air and habitation - Assessment of pollution of water, air and soil-Importance of climate in animal health-effect of environment on animal function and performance relationship between industrialization and animal agriculture- animal housing requirements for specific categories of domestic animals viz. pregnant cows and cows, milking cows, broiler birds- stress, strain and productivity in relation to animal habitation.

2. Animal Diseases

2.1 Etiology, epidemiology pathogenesis, symptoms, postmortem lesions, diagnosis, and control of infectious diseases of cattle, sheep and goat, horses, pigs and poultry.

2.2 Etiology, epidemiology, symptoms, diagnosis, treatment of production diseases of cattle, horse, pig and poultry.

2.3 Deficiency diseases of domestic animals and birds.

2.4 Diagnosis and treatment of non-specific conditions like impaction, Bloat, Diarrhoea, Indigestion, dehydration, stroke, poisoning.

2.5 Diagnosis and treatment of neurological disorders.

2.6 Principles and methods of immunization of animals against specific diseases herd immunity- disease free zones- 'zero' disease concept-chemoprophylaxis.

2.7 Anaesthesia- local, regional and general-preanesthetic medication. Symptoms and surgical interference in fractures and dislocation. Hernia, choking abomasal displacement- Caesarian operations. Rumenotomy-Castrations.

2.8 Disease investigation techniques. Materials for laboratory investigation-Establishment of Animal Health Centers- Disease free zone.

3. Veterinary Public Health

3.1 Zoonoses. - Classification, definition, role of animals and birds in prevalence and transmission of zoonotic diseases- occupational zoonotic diseases.

3.2 Epidemiology- Principle, definition of epidemiological terms, application of epidemiological measures in the study of diseases and disease control. Epidemiological features of air, water and food borne infections. OIE regulations, WTO, sanitary and phytosanitary measures.

3.3 Veterinary Jurisprudence- Rules and Regulations for improvement of animal quality and prevention of animal diseases - State and central rules for prevention of animal and animal product borne diseases-S P C A Veterolegal cases- Certificates Materials and Methods of collection of samples for veterolegal investigation.

4. Milk and Milk Products Technology

4.1 Market Milk: Quality, testing and grading of raw milk. Processing, packaging, storing, distribution, marketing, defects and their control. Preparation of the following milks: Pasteurized, standardized, toned, double toned, sterilized, homogenized, reconstituted, recombined and flavoured milks. Preparation of cultured milks, cultures and their management, yoghurt, Dahi, Lassi and Srikhand. Preparation of flavoured and sterilized milks. Legal standards. Sanitation requirement for clean and safe milk and for the milk plant equipment.

4.2 Milk Products Technology: Selection of raw materials, processing, storing, distributing and marketing milk products such as Cream, Butter, Ghee, Khoa, Channa, Cheese, condensed, evaporated, dried milk and baby food, Ice cream and Kulfi; by-products, whey products, butter milk, lactose and casein. Testing, grading, judging milk products- BIS and Agmark specifications, legal standards, quality control and nutritive properties. Packaging, processing and operational control. Costing of dairy products.

5. Meat Hygiene and Technology

5.1 Meat Hygiene

5.1.1 Ante mortem care and management of food animals, stunning, slaughter and dressing operations; abattoir requirements and designs; Meat inspection procedures and judgment of carcass meat cuts- grading of carcass meat cuts- duties and functions of Veterinarians in wholesome meat production.

5.1.2 Hygienic methods of handling production of meat- Spoilage of meat and control measures- Post -slaughter physicochemical changes in meat and factors that influence them- Quality improvement methods –Adulteration of meat and detection Regulatory provisions in Meat trade and Industry.

5.2 Meat Technology

5.2.1 Physical and chemical characteristics of meat- Meat emulsions- Methods of preservation of meat- Curing, canning, irradiation, packaging of meat and meat products, processing and formulations.

5.3 By- products- Slaughter house by- products and their utilization- Edible and inedible by products- Social and economic implications of proper utilization of slaughter house by-products- Organ products for food and pharmaceuticals.

5.4 Poultry Products Technology- Chemical composition and nutritive value of poultry meat, pre - slaughter care and management. Slaughtering techniques, inspection, preservation of poultry meat and products. Legal and BIS standards. Structure, composition and nutritive value of eggs. Microbial spoilage. Preservation and maintenance. Marketing of poultry meat, eggs and products. Value added meat products.

5.5 Rabbit/Fur Animal farming – Rabbit meat production. Disposal and utilization of fur and wool and recycling of waste by products. Grading of wool.

ANTHROPOLOGY

PAPER-I

1.1 Meaning, scope and development of Anthropology.

1.2 Relationships with other disciplines: Social Sciences, Behavioural Sciences, Life Sciences, Medical Sciences, Earth Sciences and Humanities.

1.3 Main branches of Anthropology, their scope and relevance:
 (a) Social- cultural Anthropology.
 (b) Biological Anthropology.
 (c) Archaeological Anthropology.
 (d) Linguistic Anthropology.

1.4 Human Evolution and emergence of Man:
 (a) Biological and Cultural factors in human evolution.
 (b) Theories of Organic Evolution (PreDarwinian, Darwinian and Post-Darwinian).
 (c) Synthetic theory of evolution; Brief outline of terms and concepts of evolutionary biology (Doll's rule, Cope's rule, Gause's rule, parallelism, convergence, adaptive radiation, and mosaic evolution).

1.5 Characteristics of Primates; Evolutionary Trend and Primate Taxonomy; Primate Adaptations; (Arboreal and Terrestrial) Primate Taxonomy; Primate Behaviour; Tertiary and Quaternary fossil primates; Living Major Primates; Comparative Anatomy of Man and Apes; Skeletal changes due to erect posture and its implications.

1.6 Phylogenetic status, characteristics and geographical distribution of the following:
 (a) Plio-pleistocene hominids in South and East Africa - Australopithecines.
 (b) Homo erectus: Africa (Paranthropus), Europe (Homo erectus heidelbergensis), Asia (Homo erectus javanicus, Homo erectus pekinensis).
 (c) Neanderthal Man- La-Chapelle-auxsaints (Classical type), Mt. Carmel (Progressive type).
 (d) Rhodesian man.
 (e) Homo sapiens — Cromagnon, Grimaldi and Chancelede.

1.7 The biological basis of life: The Cell, DNA structure and replication, Protein Synthesis, Gene, Mutation, Chromosomes, and Cell Division.

1.8 (a) Principles of Prehistoric Archaeology. Chronology: Relative and Absolute Dating methods.
 (b) Cultural Evolution- Broad Outlines of Prehistoric cultures:
 (i) Paleolithic
 (ii) Mesolithic
 (iii) Neolithic
 (iv) Chalcolithic
 (v) Copper-Bronze Age
 (vi) Iron Age

2.1 **The Nature of Culture:** The concept and characteristics of culture and civilization; Ethnocentrism vis-àvis cultural Relativism.

2.2 **The Nature of Society:** Concept of Society; Society and Culture; Social Institutions; Social groups; and Social stratification.

2.3 **Marriage:** Definition and universality; Laws of marriage (endogamy, exogamy, hypergamy, hypogamy, incest taboo); Types of marriage (monogamy, polygamy, polyandry, group marriage). Functions of marriage; Marriage regulations (preferential, prescriptive and proscriptive); Marriage payments (bride wealth and dowry).

2.4 **Family:** Definition and universality; Family, household and domestic groups; functions of family; Types of family (from the perspectives of structure, blood relation, marriage, residence and succession); Impact of urbanization, industrialization and feminist movements on family.

2.5 **Kinship:** Consanguinity and Affinity; Principles and types of descent (Unilineal, Double, Bilateral, Ambilineal); Forms of descent groups (lineage, clan, phratry, moiety and kindred); Kinship terminology (descriptive and classificatory); Descent, Filiation and Complimentary Filiation; Descent and Alliance.

3. **Economic organization:** Meaning, scope and relevance of economic anthropology; Formalist and Substantivist debate; Principles governing production, distribution and exchange (reciprocity, redistribution and market), in communities, subsisting on hunting and gathering, fishing, swiddening, pastoralism, horticulture, and agriculture; globalization and indigenous economic systems.

4. **Political organization and Social Control:** Band, tribe, chiefdom, kingdom and state; concepts of power, authority and legitimacy; social control, law and justice in simple societies.

5. **Religion:** Anthropological approaches to the study of religion (evolutionary, psychological and functional); monotheism and polytheism; sacred and profane; myths and rituals; forms of religion in tribal and peasant societies (animism, animatism, fetishism, naturism and totemism); religion, magic and science distinguished; magicoreligious functionaries (priest, shaman, medicine man, sorcerer and witch).

6. **Anthropological theories:**

(a) Classical evolutionism (Tylor, Morgan and Frazer)

(b) Historical particularism (Boas); Diffusionism (British, German and American)

(c) Functionalism (Malinowski); Structural-functionlism (Radcliffe-Brown)

(d) Structuralism (L'evi - Strauss and E.Leach)

(e) Culture and personality (Benedict, Mead, Linton, Kardiner and Cora – du Bois).

(f) Neo - evolutionism (Childe, White, Steward, Sahlins and Service)

(g) Cultural materialism (Harris)

(h) Symbolic and interpretive theories (Turner, Schneider and Geertz)

(i) Cognitive theories (Tyler, Conklin)

(j) Post- modernism in anthropology

7. Culture, language and communication: Nature, origin and characteristics of language; verbal and nonverbal communication; social context of language use.

8. Research methods in anthropology:

(a) Fieldwork tradition in anthropology

(b) Distinction between technique, method and methodology

(c) Tools of data collection: observation, interview, schedules, questionnaire, Case study, genealogy, lifehistory, oral history, secondary sources of information, participatory methods.

(d) Analysis, interpretation and presentation of data.

9.1 Human Genetics: Methods and Application: Methods for study of genetic principles in man-family study (pedigree analysis, twin study, foster child, co-twin method, cytogenetic method, chromosomal and karyo-type analysis), biochemical methods, immunological methods, D.N.A. technology and recombinant technologies.

9.2 Mendelian genetics in man-family study, single factor, multifactor, lethal, sublethal and polygenic inheritance in man.

9.3 Concept of genetic polymorphism and selection, Mendelian population, HardyWeinberg law; causes and changes which bring down frequency – mutation, isolation, migration, selection, inbreeding and genetic drift. Consanguineous and non-consanguineous mating, genetic load, genetic effect of consanguineous and cousin marriages.

9.4 Chromosomes and chromosomal aberrations in man, methodology.

(a) Numerical and structural aberrations (disorders).

(b) Sex chromosomal aberrations – Klinefelter (XXY), Turner (XO), Super female (XXX), intersex and other syndromic disorders.

(c) Autosomal aberrations – Down syndrome, Patau, Edward and Cri-du-chat syndromes.

(d) Genetic imprints in human disease, genetic screening, genetic counseling, human DNA profiling, gene mapping and genome study.

9.5 Race and racism, biological basis of morphological variation of non-metric and metric characters. Racial criteria, racial traits in relation to heredity and environment; biological basis of racial classification, racial differentiation and race crossing in man.

9.6 Age, sex and population variation as genetic marker- ABO, Rh blood groups, HLA Hp, transferring, Gm, blood enzymes. Physiological characteristics-

Hb level, body fat, pulse rate, respiratory functions and sensory perceptions in different cultural and socio-economic groups.

9.7 Concepts and methods of Ecological Anthropology. Bio-cultural Adaptations – Genetic and Non- genetic factors. Man's physiological responses to environmental stresses: hot desert, cold, high altitude climate.

9.8 Epidemiological Anthropology: Health and disease. Infectious and non-infectious diseases. Nutritional deficiency related diseases.

10. Concept of human growth and development: stages of growth - pre-natal, natal, infant, childhood, adolescence, maturity, senescence.
    - Factors affecting growth and development genetic, environmental, biochemical, nutritional, cultural and socio-economic.
    - Ageing and senescence. Theories and observations - biological and chronological longevity. Human physique and somatotypes. Methodologies for growth studies.

11.1 Relevance of menarche, menopause and other bioevents to fertility. Fertility patterns and differentials.

11.2 Demographic theories- biological, social and cultural.

11.3 Biological and socio-ecological factors influencing fecundity, fertility, natality and mortality.

12. Applications of Anthropology: Anthropology of sports, Nutritional anthropology, Anthropology in designing of defence and other equipments, Forensic Anthropology, Methods and principles of personal identification and reconstruction, Applied human genetics – Paternity diagnosis, genetic counseling and eugenics, DNA technology in diseases and medicine, serogenetics and cytogenetics in reproductive biology.

PAPER–II

1.1 Evolution of the Indian Culture and Civilization — Prehistoric (Palaeolithic, Mesolithic, Neolithic and Neolithic Chalcolithic). Protohistoric (Indus Civilization): Pre- Harappan, Harappan and postHarappan cultures. Contributions of tribal cultures to Indian civilization.

1.2 Palaeo – anthropological evidences from India with special reference to Siwaliks and Narmada basin (Ramapithecus, Sivapithecus and Narmada Man).

1.3 Ethno-archaeology in India : The concept of ethno-archaeology; Survivals and Parallels among the hunting, foraging, fishing, pastoral and peasant communities including arts and crafts producing communities.

2. Demographic profile of India — Ethnic and linguistic elements in the Indian population and their distribution. Indian population – factors influencing its structure and growth.

3.1 The structure and nature of traditional Indian social system — Varnashram, Purushartha, Karma, Rina and Rebirth.

3.2 Caste system in India- structure and characteristics, Varna and caste, Theories of origin of caste system, Dominant caste, Caste mobility, Future of caste system, Jajmani system, Tribe- caste continuum.

3.3 Sacred Complex and Nature- Man-Spirit Complex.

3.4 Impact of Buddhism, Jainism, Islam and Christianity on Indian society.

4. Emergence and growth of anthropology in India-Contributions of the 18th, 19th and early 20th Century scholar-administrators. Contributions of Indian anthropologists to tribal and caste studies.

5.1 Indian Village: Significance of village study in India; Indian village as a social system; Traditional and changing patterns of settlement and inter-caste relations; Agrarian relations in Indian villages; Impact of globalization on Indian villages.

5.2 Linguistic and religious minorities and their social, political and economic status.

5.3 Indigenous and exogenous processes of socio-cultural change in Indian society: Sanskritization, Westernization, Modernization; Inter-play of little and great traditions; Panchayati raj and social change; Media and social change.

6.1 Tribal situation in India – Bio-genetic variability, linguistic and socio-economic characteristics of tribal populations and their distribution.

6.2 Problems of the tribal Communities — land alienation, poverty, indebtedness, low literacy, poor educational facilities, unemployment, underemployment, health and nutrition.

6.3 Developmental projects and their impact on tribal displacement and problems of rehabilitation. Development of forest policy and tribals. Impact of urbanization and industrialization on tribal populations.

7.1 Problems of exploitation and deprivation of Scheduled Castes, Scheduled Tribes and Other Backward Classes. Constitutional safeguards for Scheduled Tribes and Scheduled Castes.

7.2 Social change and contemporary tribal societies: Impact of modern democratic institutions, development programmes and welfare measures on tribals and weaker sections.

7.3 The concept of ethnicity; Ethnic conflicts and political developments; Unrest among tribal communities; Regionalism and demand for autonomy; Pseudo-tribalism; Social change among the tribes during colonial and post-Independent India.

8.1 Impact of Hinduism, Buddhism, Christianity, Islam and other religions on tribal societies.

8.2 Tribe and nation state — a comparative study of tribal communities in India and other countries.

9.1 History of administration of tribal areas, tribal policies, plans, programmes of tribal development and their implementation. The concept of PTGs (Primitive Tribal Groups), their distribution, special programmes for their development. Role of N.G.O.s in tribal development.

9.2 Role of anthropology in tribal and rural development.

9.3 Contributions of anthropology to the understanding of regionalism, communalism, and ethnic and political movements.

BOTANY

PAPER–I

1. Microbiology and Plant Pathology

Structure and reproduction/multiplication of viruses, viroids, bacteria, fungi and mycoplasma; Applications of microbiology in agriculture, industry, medicine and in control of soil and water pollution; Prion and Prion hypothesis.

Important crop diseases caused by viruses, bacteria, mycoplasma, fungi and nematodes; Modes of infection and dissemination; Molecular basis of infection and disease resistance/defence; Physiology of parasitism and control measures; Fungal toxins; Modelling and disease forecasting; Plant quarantine.

2. Cryptogams

Algae, fungi, lichens, bryophytes, pteridophytes - structure and reproduction from evolutionary viewpoint; Distribution of Cryptogams in India and their ecological and economic importance.

3. Phanerogams

Gymnosperms: Concept of Progymnosperms; Classification and distribution of gymnosperms; Salient features of Cycadales, Ginkgoales, Coniferales and Gnetales, their structure and reproduction; General account of Cycadofilicales, Bennettitales and Cordaitales; Geological time scale; Type of fossils and their study techniques. Angiosperms: Systematics, anatomy, embryology, palynology and phylogeny.

Taxonomic hierarchy; International Code of Botanical Nomenclature; Numerical taxonomy and chemotaxonomy; Evidence from anatomy, embryology and palynology. Origin and evolution of angiosperms; Comparative account of various systems of classification of angiosperms; Study of angiospermic families – Mangnoliaceae, Ranunculaceae, Brassicaceae, Rosaceae, Fabaceae, Euphorbiaceae, Malvaceae, Dipterocarpaceae, Apiaceae, Asclepiadaceae,

Verbenaceae, Solanaceae, Rubiaceae, Cucurbitaceae, Asteraceae, Poaceae, Arecaceae, Liliaceae, Musaceae and Orchidaceae.

Stomata and their types; Glandular and non-glandular trichomes; Unusual secondary growth; Anatomy of C3 and C4 plants; Xylem and phloem differentiation; Wood anatomy.

Development of male and female gametophytes, pollination, fertilization; Endosperm - its development and function; Patterns of embryo development; Polyembroyony and apomixes; Applications of palynology; Experimental embryology including pollen storage and test-tube fertilization.

4. Plant Resource Development

Domestication and introduction of plants; Origin of cultivated plants; Vavilov's centres of origin; Plants as sources for food, fodder, fibre, spices, beverages, edible oils, drugs, narcotics, insecticides, timber, gums, resins and dyes, latex, cellulose, starch and its products; Perfumery; Importance of Ethnobotany in Indian context; Energy plantations; Botanical Gardens and Herbaria.

5. Morphogenesis

Totipotency, polarity, symmetry and dfferentiation; Cell, tissue, organ and protoplast culture; Somatic hybrids and Cybrids; Micropropagation; Somaclonal variation and its applications; Pollen haploids, embryo rescue methods and their applications.

PAPER–II

1. Cell Biology

Techniques of cell biology; Prokaryotic and eukaryotic cells - structural and ultra-structural details; Structure and function of extra-cellular matrix (cell wall), membranes-cell adhesion, membrane transport and vesicular transport; Structure and function of cell organelles (chloroplasts, mitochondria, ER, dictyo-somes ribosomes, endosomes, lysosomes, peroxisomes); Cytoskelaton and microtubules; Nucleus, nucleolus, nuclear pore complex; Chromatin and nucleosome; Cell signalling and cell receptors; Signal transduction; Mitosis and meiosis; Molecular basis of cell cycle; Numerical and structural variations in chromosomes and their significance; Chromatin organization and packaging of genome; Polytene chromosomes; B-chromosomes – structure, behaviour and significance.

2. Genetics, Molecular Biology and Evolution

Development of genetics; Gene versus allele concepts (Pseudoalleles); Quantitative genetics and multiple factors; Incomplete dominance, polygenic inheritance, multiple alleles; Linkage and crossing over; Methods of gene mapping, including molecular maps (idea of mapping function); Sex chromosomes and sex-linked inheritance, sex determination and molecular basis of sex differentiation; Mutations (biochemical and molecular basis); Cytoplasmic inheritance and cytoplasmic genes (including genetics of male sterility). Structure and synthesis of nucleic acids and proteins; Genetic code and regulation of gene expression; Gene silencing; Multigene families; Organic evolution – evidences, mechanism and theories. Role of RNA in origin and evolution.

3. Plant Breeding, Biotechnology and Biostatistics

Methods of plant breeding – introduction, selection and hybridization (pedigree, backcross, mass selection, bulk method); Mutation, polyploidy, male sterility and heterosis breeding; Use of apomixes in plant breeding; DNA sequencing; Genetic engineering – methods of transfer of genes; Transgenic crops and biosafety aspects; Development and use of molecular markers in plant breeding; Tools and techniques - probe, southern blotting, DNA fingerprinting, PCR and FISH. Standard deviation and coefficient of variation (CV); Tests of significance (Z-test, t-test and chi-square test); Probability and distributions (normal, binomial and Poisson); Correlation and regression.

4. Physiology and Biochemistry

Water relations, mineral nutrition and ion transport, mineral deficiencies; Photosynthesis – photochemical reactions; photo-phosphorylation and carbon fixation pathways; C3, C4 and CAM pathways; Mechanism of phloem transport; Respiration (anerobic and aerobic, including fermentation) – electron transport chain and oxidative phosphorylation; Photorespiration; Chemiosmotic theory and ATP synthesis; Lipid metabolism; Nitrogen fixation and nitrogen metabolism; Enzymes, coenzymes; Energy transfer and energy conservation

Importance of secondary metabolites; Pigments as photoreceptors (plastidial pigments and phytochrome); Plant movements; Photoperiodism and flowering, vernalization, senescence; Growth substances – their chemical nature, role and applications in agri-horticulture; Growth indices, growth movements; Stress physiology (heat, water, salinity, metal); Fruit and seed physiology; Dormancy, storage and germination of seed; Fruit ripening – its molecular basis and manipulation.

5. Ecology and Plant Geography

Concept of ecosystem; Ecological factors; Concepts and dynamics of community; Plant succession; Concept of biosphere; Ecosystems; Conservation; Pollution and its control (including phytoremediation); Plant indicators; Environment (Protection) Act.

Forest types of India - Ecological and economic importance of forests, afforestation, deforestation and social forestry; Endangered plants, endemism, IUCN categories, Red Data Books; Biodiversity and its conservation; Protected Area Network; Convention on Biological Diversity; Farmers' Rights and Intellectual Property Rights; Concept of Sustainable Development; Biogeochemical cycles; Global warming and climatic change; Invasive species; Environmental Impact Assessment; Phytogeo-graphical regions of India.

CHEMISTRY

PAPER–I

1. Atomic Structure

Heisenberg's uncertainty principle, Schrodinger wave equation (time independent); Interpretation of wave function, particle in one-dimensional box, quantum numbers, hydrogen atom wave functions; Shapes of s, p and d orbitals.

2. Chemical Bonding

Ionic bond, characteristics of ionic compounds, lattice energy, Born-Haber cycle; covalent bond and its general characteristics, polarities of bonds in molecules and their dipole moments; Valence bond theory, concept of resonance and resonance energy; Molecular orbital theory (LCAO method); bonding in H_2+, H_2, He_2+ to Ne_2, NO, CO, HF, and CN–; Comparison of valence bond and molecular orbital theories, bond order, bond strength and bond length.

3. Solid State

Crystal systems; Designation of crystal faces, lattice structures and unit cell; Bragg's law; X-ray diffraction by crystals; Close packing, radius ratio rules, calculation of some limiting radius ratio values; Structures of NaCl, ZnS, CsCl and CaF2; Stoichiometric and nonstoichiometric defects, impurity defects, semi-conductors.

4. The Gaseous State and Transport Phenomenon

Equation of state for real gases, inter-molecular interactions and critical phenomena and liquefaction of gases, Maxwell's distribution of speeds, intermolecular collisions, collisions on the wall and effusion; Thermal conductivity and viscosity of ideal gases.

5. Liquid State

Kelvin equation; Surface tension and surface energy, wetting and contact angle, interfacial tension and capillary action.

6. Thermodynamics

Work, heat and internal energy; first law of thermodynamics. Second law of thermodynamics; entropy as a state function, entropy changes in various processes, entropy– reversibility and irreversibility, Free energy functions; Thermodynamic equation of state; Maxwell relations; Temperature, volume and pressure dependence of U, H, A, G, Cp and Cvá and â; J-T effect and inversion temperature; criteria for equilibrium, relation between equilibrium constant and thermodynamic quantities; Nernst heat theorem, introductory idea of third law of thermodynamics.

7. Phase Equilibria and Solutions

Clausius-Clapeyron equation; phase diagram for a pure substance; phase equilibria in binary systems, partially miscible liquids–upper and lower critical solution temperatures; partial molar quantities, their significance and determination; excess thermodynamic functions and their determination.

8. Electrochemistry

Debye-Huckel theory of strong electrolytes and Debye-Huckel limiting Law for various equilibrium and transport properties. Galvanic cells, concentration cells; electrochemical series, measurement of e.m.f. of cells and its applications fuel cells and batteries.

Processes at electrodes; double layer at the interface; rate of charge transfer, current density; over-potential; electro-analytical techniques: Polarography, amperometry, ion selective electrodes and their uses.

9. Chemical Kinetics

Differential and integral rate equations for zeroth, first, second and fractional order reactions; Rate equations involving reverse, parallel, consecutive and chain reactions; branching chain and explosions; effect of temperature and pressure on rate constant; Study of fast reactions by stopflow and relaxation methods; Collisions and transition state theories.

10. Photochemistry

Absorption of light; decay of excited state by different routes; photochemical reactions between hydrogen and halogens and their quantum yields.

11. Surface Phenomena and Catalysis

Absorption from gases and solutions on solid adsorbents, Langmuir and B.E.T. adsorption isotherms; determination of surface area, characteristics and mechanism of reaction on heterogeneous catalysts.

12. Bio-inorganic Chemistry

Metal ions in biological systems and their role in ion transport across the membranes (molecular mechanism), oxygen-uptake proteins, cytochromes and ferredoxins.

13. Coordination Compounds

(i) Bonding theories of metal complexes; Valence bond theory, crystal field theory and its modifications; applications of theories in the explanation of magnetism and electronic spectra of metal complexes.

(ii) Isomerism in coordination compounds; IUPAC nomenclature of coordination compounds; stereochemistry of complexes with 4 and 6 coordination numbers; chelate effect and polynuclear complexes; trans effect and its theories; kinetics of substitution reactions in square-planer complexes; thermodynamic and kinetic stability of complexes.

(iii) EAN rule, Synthesis structure and reactivity of metal carbonyls; carboxylate anions, carbonyl hydrides and metal nitrosyl compounds.

(iv) Complexes with aromatic systems, synthesis, structure and bonding in metal olefin complexes, alkyne complexes and cyclopentadienyl complexes; coordinative unsaturation, oxidative addition reactions, insertion reactions, fluxional molecules and their characterization; Compounds with metal-metal bonds and metal atom clusters.

14. Main Group Chemistry

Boranes, borazines, phosphazenes and cyclic phosphazene, silicates and silicones, Interhalogen compounds; Sulphur – nitrogen compounds, noble gas compounds.

15. General Chemistry of 'f' Block Elements

Lanthanides and actinides; separation, oxidation states, magnetic and spectral properties; lanthanide contraction.

PAPER-II

1. Delocalised Covalent Bonding

Aromaticity, anti-aromaticity; annulenes, azulenes, tropolones, fulvenes, sydnones.

2.

(i) Reaction Mechanisms: General methods (both kinetic and non-kinetic) of study of mechanism of organic reactions: isotopic method, cross-over experiment, intermediate trapping, stereochemistry; energy of activation; thermodynamic control and kinetic control of reactions.

(ii) Reactive Intermediates: Generation, geometry, stability and reactions of carbonium ions and carbanions, free radicals, carbenes, benzynes and nitrenes.

(iii) Substitution Reactions: S_N1, S_N2 and S_Ni mechanisms; neighbouring group participation; electrophilic and nucleophilic reactions of aromatic compounds including heterocyclic compounds–pyrrole, furan, thiophene and indole.

(iv) Elimination Reactions: E1, E2 and E1cb mechanisms; orientation in E2 reactions–Saytzeff and Hoffmann; pyrolytic syn elimination – Chugaev and Cope eliminations.

(v) Addition Reactions: Electrophilic addition to C=C and C=C; nucleophilic addition to C=0, C=N, conjugated olefins and carbonyls.

(vi) Reactions and Rearrangements:

(a) Pinacol-pinacolone, Hoffmann, Beckmann, Baeyer–Villiger, Favorskii, Fries, Claisen, Cope, Stevens and Wagner-Meerwein rearrangements.

(b) Aldol condensation, Claisen condensation, Dieckmann, Perkin, Knoevenagel, Witting, Clemmensen, Wolff-Kishner, Cannizzaro and von Richter reactions; Stobbe, benzoin and acyloin condensations; Fischer indole synthesis, Skraup synthesis, Bischler-Napieralski, Sandmeyer, Reimer-Tiemann and Reformatsky reactions.

3. Pericyclic Reactions

Classification and examples; Woodward-Hoffmann rules – electrocyclic reactions, cycloaddition reactions [2+2 and 4+2] and sigmatropic shifts [1, 3; 3, 3 and 1, 5] FMO approach.

4. (i) **Preparation and Properties of Polymers:** Organic polymers–polyethy-lene, polystyrene, polyvinyl chloride, teflon, nylon, terylene, synthetic and natural rubber.

(ii) **Biopolymers:** Structure of proteins, DNA and RNA.

5. Synthetic Uses of Reagents

OsO_4, HIO_4, CrO_3, $Pb(OAc)_4$, SeO_2, NBS, B_2H_6, Na-Liquid NH_3, $LiAlH_4$, $NaBH_4$, n-BuLi and MCPBA.

6. Photochemistry

Photochemical reactions of simple organic compounds, excited and ground states, singlet and triplet states, Norrish-Type I and Type II reactions.

7. Spectroscopy

Principle and applications in structure elucidation:

(i) **Rotational:** Diatomic molecules; isotopic substitution and rotational constants.

(ii) **Vibrational:** Diatomic molecules, linear triatomic molecules, specific frequencies of functional groups in polyatomic molecules.

(iii) **Electronic:** Singlet and triplet states; n □π* and π π* transitions; application to conjugated double bonds and conjugated carbonyls–Woodward-Fieser rules; Charge transfer spectra.

(iv) **Nuclear Magnetic Resonance (^{1}H NMR):** Basic principle; chemical shift and spin-spin interaction and coupling constants.

(v) **Mass Spectrometry:** Parent peak, base peak, metastable peak, McLafferty rearrangement.

CIVIL ENGINEERING

PAPER–I

1. Engineering Mechanics, Strength of Materials and Structural Analysis

1.1 Engineering Mechanics: Units and Dimensions, SI Units, Vectors, Concept of Force, Concept of particle and rigid body. Concurrent, Non Concurrent and parallel forces in a plane, moment of force, free body diagram, conditions of equilibrium, Principle of virtual work, equivalent force system. First and Second Moment of area, Mass moment of Inertia. Static Friction.

Kinematics and Kinetics: Kinematics in Cartesian Co-ordinates, motion under uniform and non-uniform acceleration, motion under gravity. Kinetics of particle: Momentum and Energy principles, collision of elastic bodies, rotation of rigid bodies.

1.2 Strength of Materials: Simple Stress and Strain, Elastic constants, axially loaded compression members, Shear force and bending moment, theory of simple bending, Shear Stress distribution across cross sections, Beams of uniform strength. Deflection of beams: Macaulay's method, Mohr's Moment area method, Conjugate beam method, unit load method. Torsion of Shafts, Elastic stability of columns, Euler's Rankine's and Secant formulae.

1.3 Structural Analysis: Castiglianio's theorems I and II, unit load method of consistent deformation applied to beams and pin jointed trusses. Slopedeflection, moment distribution, Rolling loads and Influences lines: Influences lines for Shear Force and Bending moment at a section of beam. Criteria for maximum shear force and bending Moment in beams traversed by a system of moving loads. Influences lines for simply supported plane pin jointed trusses.

Arches: Three hinged, two hinged and fixed arches, rib shortening and temperature effects.

Matrix methods of analysis: Force method and displacement method of analysis of indeterminate beams and rigid frames.

Plastic Analysis of beams and frames: Theory of plastic bending, plastic analysis, statical method, Mechanism method.

Unsymmetrical bending: Moment of inertia, product of inertia, position of Neutral Axis and Principle axes, calculation of bending stresses.

2. Design of Structures: Steel, Concrete and Masonry Structures

2.1 Structural Steel Design

Structural Steel: Factors of safety and load factors. Riveted, bolted and welded joints and connections. Design of tension and compression member, beams of built up section, riveted and welded plate girders, gantry girders, stancheons with battens and lacings.

2.2 Design of Concrete and Masonry Structures

Concept of mix design. Reinforced Concrete: Working Stress and Limit State method of design– Recommendations of I.S. codes Design of one way and two way slabs, stair-case slabs, simple and continuous beams of rectangular, T and L sections. Compression members under direct load with or without eccentricity, Cantilever and Counter fort type retaining walls. Water tanks: Design requirements for Rectangular and circular tanks resting on ground.

Prestressed concrete: Methods and systems of prestressing, anchorages, Analysis and design of sections for flexure based on working stress, loss of prestress. Design of brick masonry as per I.S. Codes.

3. Fluid Mechanics, Open Channel Flow and Hydraulic Machines

3.1 Fluid Mechanics

Fluid properties and their role in fluid motion, fluid statics including forces acting on plane and curved surfaces.

Kinematics and Dynamics of Fluid flow: Velocity and accelerations, stream lines, equation of continuity, irrotational and rotational flow, velocity potential and stream functions.

Continuity, momentum and energy equation, Navier-Stokes equation, Euler's equation of motion, application to fluid flow problems, pipe flow, sluice gates, weirs.

3.2 Dimensional Analysis and Similitude

Buckingham's Pi-theorem, dimensionless parameters.

3.3 Laminar Flow

Laminar flow between parallel, stationary and moving plates, flow through tube.

3.4 Boundary layer

Laminar and turbulent boundary layer on a flat plate, laminar sub layer, smooth and rough boundaries, drag and lift.

Turbulent flow through pipes: Characteristics of turbulent flow, velocity distribution and variation of pipe friction factor, hydraulic grade line and total energy line.

3.5 Open channel flow

Uniform and non-uniform flows, momentum and energy correction factors, specific energy and specific force, critical depth, rapidly varied flow, hydraulic jump, gradually varied flow, classification of surface profiles, control section, step method of integration of varied flow equation.

3.6 Hydraulic Machines and Hydropower

Hydraulic turbines, types classification, Choice of turbines, performance parameters, controls, characteristics, specific speed. Principles of hydropower development.

4. Geotechnical Engineering

Soil Type and structure – gradation and particle size distribution – consistency limits. Water in soil – capillary and structural – effective stress and pore water pressure – permeability concept – field and laboratory determination of permeability – Seepage pressure – quick sand conditions – Shear strength determination – Mohr Coulomb concept.

Compaction of soil – Laboratory and field tests.

Compressibility and consolidation concept – consolidation theory – consolidation settlement analysis.

Earth pressure theory and analysis for retaining walls, Application for sheet piles and Braced excavation. Bearing capacity of soil – approaches for analysis – Field tests – settlement analysis – stability of slope of earth walk.

Subsurface exploration of soils – methods Foundation – Type and selection criteria for foundation of structures – Design criteria for foundation – Analysis of distribution of stress for footings and pile – pile group actionpile load test. Ground improvement techniques.

PAPER-II

1. Construction Technology, Equipment, Planning and Management

1.1 Construction Technology:

Engineering Materials: Physical properties of construction materials with respect to their use in construction - Stones, Bricks and Tiles; Lime, Cement, different types of Mortars and Concrete. Specific use of ferro cement, fibre reinforced C.C, High strength concrete.

Timber, properties and defects – common preservation treatments.

Use and selection of materials for specific use like Low Cost Housing, Mass Housing, High Rise Buildings.

1.2 Construction

Masonry principles using Brick, stone, Blocks – construction detailing and strength characteristics.

Types of plastering, pointing, flooring, roofing and construction features.

Common repairs in buildings. Principles of functional planning of building for residents and specific use – Building code provisions. Basic principles of detailed and approximate estimating - specification writing and rate analysis – principles of valuation of real property.

Machinery for earthwork, concreting and their specific uses – Factors affecting selection of equipments – operating cost of Equipments.

1.3 Construction Planning and Management

Construction activity – schedules- organization for construction industry – Quality assurance principles.

Use of Basic principles of network – analysis in form of CPM and PERT – their use in construction monitoring, Cost optimization and resource allocation.

Basic principles of Economic analysis and methods.

Project profitability – Basic principles of Boot approach to financial planning – simple toll fixation criterions.

2. Surveying and Transportation Engineering

2.1 Surveying

Common methods and instruments for distance and angle measurement for CE work – their use in plane table, traverse survey, leveling work, triangulation, contouring and topographical map. Basic principles of photogrammetry and remote sensing.

2.2 Railway Engineering

Permanent way – components, types and their functions – Functions and Design constituents of turn and crossings – Necessity of geometric design of track – Design of station and yards.

2.3 Highway Engineering

Principles of Highway alignments – classification and geometrical design elements and standards for Roads.

Pavement structure for flexible and rigid pavements - Design principles and methodology of pavements.

Typical construction methods and standards of materials for stabilized soil, WBM, Bituminous works and CC roads.

Surface and sub-surface drainage arrangements for roads - culvert structures.

Pavement distresses and strengthening by overlays. Traffic surveys and their applications in traffic planning - Typical design features for channelized, intersection, rotary etc – signal designs – standard Traffic signs and markings.

3. Hydrology, Water Resources and Engineering

3.1 Hydrology

Hydrological cycle, precipitation, evaporation, transpiration, infiltration, overland flow, hydrograph, flood frequency analysis, flood routing through a reservoir, channel flow routing-Muskingam method.

3.2 Ground water flow

Specific yield, storage coefficient, coefficient of permeability, confined and unconfined equifers, aquifers, aquitards, radial flow into a well under confined and unconfined conditions.

3.3 Water Resources Engineering

Ground and surface water resource, single and multipurpose projects, storage capacity of reservoirs, reservoir losses, reservoir sedimentation.

3.4 Irrigation Engineering

(i) **Water requirements of crops:** consumptive use, duty and delta, irrigation methods and their efficiencies.

(ii) **Canals:** Distribution systems for canal irrigation, canal capacity, canal losses, alignment of main and distributory canals, most efficient section, lined canals, their design, regime theory, critical shear stress, bed load.

(iii) **Water logging:** causes and control, salinity.

(iv) **Canal structures:** Design of head regulators, canal falls, aqueducts, metering flumes and canal outlets.

(v) **Diversion headwork:** Principles and design of weirs of permeable and impermeable foundation, Khosla's theory, energy dissipation.

(vi) **Storage works:** Types of dams, design, principles of rigid gravity, stability analysis.

(vii) **Spillways:** Spillway types, energy dissipation.

(viii) **River training:** Objectives of river training, methods of river training.

4. Environmental Engineering

4.1 Water Supply

Predicting demand for water, impurities of water and their significance, physical, chemical and bacteriological analysis, waterborne diseases, standards for potable water.

4.2 Intake of water

Water treatment: principles of coagulation, flocculation and sedimentation; slow; rapid-, pressure-, filters; chlorination, softening, removal of taste, odour and salinity.

4.3 Sewerage systems

Domestic and industrial wastes, storm sewage–separate and combined systems, flow through sewers, design of sewers.

4.4 Sewage characterization

BOD, COD, solids, dissolved oxygen, nitrogen and TOC. Standards of disposal in normal watercourse and on land.

4.5 Sewage treatment

Working principles, units, chambers, sedimentation tanks, trickling filters, oxidation ponds, activated sludge process, septic tank, disposal of sludge, recycling of wastewater.

4.6 Solid waste

Collection and disposal in rural and urban contexts, management of long-term ill effects.

5. Environmental pollution

Sustainable development. Radioactive wastes and disposal. Environmental impact assessment for thermal power plants, mines, river valley projects. Air pollution. Pollution control acts.

COMMERCE AND ACCOUNTANCY

PAPER-I

Accounting and Finance

Accounting, Taxation & Auditing

1. Financial Accounting

Accounting as a Financial Information System; Impact of Behavioural Sciences. Accounting Standards e.g., Accounting for Depreciation, Inventories, Research and Development Costs, Long-term Construction Contracts, Revenue Recognition, Fixed Assets, Contingencies, Foreign Exchange Transactions, Investments and Government Grants, Cash Flow Statement, Earnings Per Share.

Accounting for Share Capital Transactions including Bonus Shares, Right Shares, Employees Stock Option and Buy- Back of Securities.

Preparation and Presentation of Company Final Accounts.

Amalgamation, Absorption and Reconstruction of Companies.

2. Cost Accounting

Nature and Functions of Cost Accounting. Installation of Cost Accounting System. Cost Concepts related to Income Measurement, Profit Planning, Cost Control and Decision Making.

Methods of Costing: Job Costing, Process Costing, Activity Based Costing. Volume – cost – Profit Relationship as a tool of Profit Planning.

Incremental Analysis/ Differential Costing as a Tool of Pricing Decisions, Product Decisions, Make or Buy Decisions, Shut-Down Decisions etc.

Techniques of Cost Control and Cost Reduction: Budgeting as a Tool of Planning and Control. Standard Costing and Variance Analysis.

Responsibility Accounting and Divisional Performance Measurement.

3. Taxation

Income Tax: Definitions; Basis of Charge; Incomes which do not form Part of Total Income. Simple problems of Computation of Income (of Individuals only) under Various Heads, i.e., Salaries, Income from House Property, Profits and Gains from Business or Profession, Capital Gains, Income from other sources, Income of other Persons included in Assessee's Total Income.

Set - Off and Carry Forward of Loss.

Deductions from Gross Total Income. Salient Features/Provisions Related to VAT and Services Tax.

4. Auditing

Company Audit: Audit related to Divisible Profits, Dividends, Special investigations, Tax audit.

Audit of Banking, Insurance, Non-Profit Organizations and Charitable Societies/ Trusts/Organizations.

Financial Management, Financial Institutions and Markets

1. Financial Management

Finance Function: Nature, Scope and Objectives of Financial Management: Risk and Return Relationship.

Tools of Financial Analysis: Ratio Analysis, Funds-Flow and Cash-Flow Statement.

Capital Budgeting Decisions: Process, Procedures and Appraisal Methods. Risk and Uncertainty Analysis and Methods.

Cost of capital: Concept, Computation of Specific Costs and Weighted Average Cost of Capital. CAPM as a Tool of Determining Cost of Equity Capital.

Financing Decisions: Theories of Capital Structure - Net Income (NI) Approach, Net Operating Income (NOI) Approach, MM Approach and Traditional Approach. Designing of Capital structure: Types of Leverages (Operating, Financial and Combined), EBIT- EPS Analysis, and other Factors.

Dividend Decisions and Valuation of Firm: Walter's Model, MM Thesis, Gordan's Model Lintner's Model.

Factors Affecting Dividend Policy.

Working Capital Management: Planning of Working Capital. Determinants of Working Capital. Components of Working Capital Cash, Inventory and Receivables. Corporate Restructuring with focus on Mergers and Acquisitions (Financial aspects only).

2. Financial Markets and Institutions

Indian Financial System: An Overview Money Markets: Participants, Structure and Instruments. Commercial Banks. Reforms in Banking sector. Monetary and Credit Policy of RBI. RBI as a Regulator.

Capital Market: Primary and Secondary Market. Financial Market Instruments and Innovative Debt Instruments; SEBI as a Regulator.

Financial Services: Mutual Funds, Venture Capital, Credit Rating Agencies, Insurance and IRDA.

PAPER–II

Organisation Theory and Behaviour, Human Resource Management and Industrial Relations. Organisation Theory and Behaviour

1. Organisation Theory

Nature and Concept of Organisation; External Environment of Organizations -Technological, Social, Political, Economical and Legal; Organizational Goals - Primary and Secondary goals, Single and Multiple Goals; Management by Objectives.

Evolution of Organisation Theory: Classical, Neo-classical and Systems Approach.

Modern Concepts of Organisation Theory: Organisational Design, Organisational Structure and Organisational Culture.

Organisational Design–Basic Challenges; Differentiation and Integration Process; Centralization and Decentralization Process; Standardization / Formalization and Mutual Adjustment. Coordinating Formal and Informal Organizations. Mechanistic and Organic Structures.

Designing Organizational structures–Authority and Control; Line and Staff Functions, Specialization and Coordination. Types of Organization Structure –Functional. Matrix Structure, Project Structure. Nature and Basis of Power, Sources of Power, Power Structure and Politics. Impact of Information Technology on Organizational Design and Structure. Managing Organizational Culture.

2. Organisation Behaviour

Meaning and Concept; Individual in organizations: Personality, Theories, and Determinants; Perception - Meaning and Process.

Motivation: Concepts, Theories and Applications. Leadership-Theories and Styles. Quality of Work Life (QWL): Meaning and its impact on Performance, Ways of its Enhancement. Quality Circles (QC) – Meaning

and their Importance. Management of Conflicts in Organizations. Transactional Analysis, Organizational Effectiveness, Management of Change.

Human Resources Management and Industrial Relations

1. Human Resources Management (HRM)

Meaning, Nature and Scope of HRM, Human Resource Planning, Job Analysis, Job Description, Job Specification, Recruitment Process, Selection Process,

Orientation and Placement, Training and Development Process, Performance Appraisal and 360° Feed Back, Salary and Wage Administration, Job Evaluation,

Employee Welfare, Promotions, Transfers and Separations.

2. Industrial Relations (IR)

Meaning, Nature, Importance and Scope of IR, Formation of Trade Unions, Trade Union Legislation, Trade Union Movement in India. Recognition of Trade Unions, Problems of Trade Unions in India. Impact of Liberalization on Trade Union Movement.

Nature of Industrial Disputes: Strikes and Lockouts, Causes of Disputes, Prevention and Settlement of Disputes.

Worker's Participation in Management: Philosophy, Rationale, Present Day Status and Future Prospects.

Adjudication and Collective Bargaining.

Industrial Relations in Public Enterprises, Absenteeism and Labour Turnover in Indian Industries and their Causes and Remedies.

ILO and its Functions.

ECONOMICS

PAPER–I

1. Advanced Micro Economics

(a) Marshallian and Walrasiam Approaches to Price determination.

(b) Alternative Distribution Theories: Ricardo, Kaldor, Kaleeki.

(c) Markets Structure: Monopolistic Competition, Duopoly, Oligopoly.

(d) Modern Welfare Criteria: Pareto Hicks & Scitovsky, Arrow's Impossibility Theorem, A.K. Sen's Social Welfare Function.

2. Advanced Macro Economics

Approaches to Employment Income and Interest Rate determination: Classical, Keynes (IS-LM) curve, Neo classical synthesis and New classical, Theories of Interest Rate determination and Interest Rate Structure.

3. Money - Banking and Finance

(a) Demand for and Supply of Money: Money Multiplier Quantity Theory of Money (Fisher, Pique and Friedman) and Keyne's Theory on Demand for Money, Goals and Instruments of Monetary Management in Closed and Open Economies. Relation between the Central Bank and the Treasury. Proposal for ceiling on growth rate of money.

(b) Public Finance and its Role in Market Economy: In stabilization of supply, allocation of resources and in distribution and development. Sources of Govt. revenue, forms of Taxes and Subsidies, their incidence and effects. Limits to taxation, loans, crowding-out effects and limits to borrowings. Public Expenditure and its effects.

4. International Economics

(a) Old and New Theories of International Trade
   (i) Comparative Advantage
   (ii) Terms of Trade and Offer Curve.
   (iii) Product Cycle and Strategic Trade Theories.
   (iv) Trade as an engine of growth and theories of under development in an open economy.

(b) Forms of Protection: Tariff and quota.

(c) Balance of Payments Adjustments: Alternative Approaches.
   (i) Price versus income, income adjustments under fixed exchange rates.
   (ii) Theories of Policy Mix.
   (iii) Exchange rate adjustments under capital mobility.
   (iv) Floating Rates and their Implications for Developing Countries: Currency Boards.
   (v) Trade Policy and Developing Countries.
   (vi) BOP, adjustments and Policy Coordination in open economy macro-model.
   (vii) Speculative attacks.
   (viii) Trade Blocks and Monetary Unions.
   (ix) WTO: TRIMS, TRIPS, Domestic Measures, Different Rounds of WTO talks.

5. Growth and Development

(a) (i) Theories of growth: Harrod's model,
   (ii) Lewis model of development with surplus labour,
   (iii) Balanced and Unbalanced growth,
   (iv) Human Capital and Economic Growth.
   (v) Research and Development and Economic Growth

(b) Process of Economic Development of Less developed countries: Myrdal and Kuzments on economic development and structural change: Role of Agriculture in Economic Development of less developed countries.

(c) Economic development and International Trade and Investment, Role of Multinationals.

(d) Planning and Economic Development: changing role of Markets and Planning, Private- Public Partnership.

(e) Welfare indicators and measures of growth – Human Development Indices. The basic needs approach.

(f) Development and Environmental Sustainability – Renewable and Non Renewable Resources, Environmental Degradation, Intergenerational equity development.

PAPER–II

1. Indian Economy in Pre-Independence Era

Land System and its changes, Commercialization of agriculture, Drain theory, Laissez faire theory and critique. Manufacture and Transport: Jute, Cotton, Railways, Money and Credit.

2. Indian Economy after Independence

(A) The Pre Liberalization Era

(i) Contribution of Vakil, Gadgil and V.K.R.V. Rao.

(ii) Agriculture: Land Reforms and land tenure system, Green Revolution and capital formation in agriculture.

(iii) Industry Trends in composition and growth, Role of public and private sector, Small scale and cottage industries.

(iv) National and Per capita income: patterns, trends, aggregate and Sectoral composition and changes their in.

(v) Broad factors determining National Income and distribution, Measures of poverty, Trends in poverty and inequality.

(B) The Post Liberalization Era

(i) New Economic Reform and Agriculture: Agriculture and WTO, Food processing, Subsidies, Agricultural prices and public distribution system, Impact of public expenditure on agricultural growth.

(ii) New Economic Policy and Industry: Strategy of industrialization, Privatization, Disinvestments, Role of foreign direct investment and multinationals.

(iii) New Economic Policy and Trade: Intellectual property rights: Implications of TRIPS, TRIMS, GATS and new EXIM policy.

(iv) New Exchange Rate Regime: Partial and full convertibility, Capital account convertibility.

(v) New Economic Policy and Public Finance: Fiscal Responsibility Act, Twelfth Finance Commission and Fiscal Federalism and Fiscal Consolidation.

(vi) New Economic Policy and Monetary system. Role of RBI under the new regime.

(vii) Planning: From central Planning to indicative planning, Relation between planning and markets for growth and decentralized planning: 73rd and 74th Constitutional amendments.

(viii) New Economic Policy and Employment: Employment and poverty, Rural wages, Employment Generation, Poverty alleviation schemes, New Rural, Employment Guarantee Scheme.

ELECTRICAL ENGINEERING

PAPER-I

1. Circuit Theory

Circuit components; network graphs; KCL, KVL; circuit analysis methods: nodal analysis, mesh analysis; basic network theorems and applications; transient analysis: RL, RC and RLC circuits; sinusoidal steady state analysis; resonant circuits; coupled circuits; balanced 3-phase circuits; Two-port networks.

2. Signals & Systems

Representation of continuous–time and discrete-time signals & systems; LTI systems; convolution; impulse response; time-domain analysis of LTI systems based on convolution and differential/difference equations. Fourier transform, Laplace transform, Z-transform, Transfer function. Sampling and recovery of signals DFT, FFT Processing of analog signals through discrete-time systems.

3. E.M. Theory

Maxwell's equations, wave propagation in bounded media. Boundary conditions, reflection and refraction of plane waves. Transmission line: travelling and standing waves, impedance matching, Smith chart.

4. Analog Electronics

Characteristics and equivalent circuits (large and small-signal) of Diode, BJT, JFET and MOSFET. Diode circuits: clipping, clamping, rectifier. Biasing and bias stability. FET amplifiers. Current mirror; Amplifiers; single and multi-stage, differential, operational, feedback and power. Analysis of amplifiers; frequency response of amplifiers. OPAMP circuits. Filters; sinusoidal oscillators: criterion for oscillation; single-transistor and OPAMP configurations. Function generators and wave-shaping circuits. Linear and switching power supplies.

5. Digital Electronics

Boolean algebra; minimization of Boolean functions; logic gates; digital IC families (DTL, TTL, ECL, MOS, CMOS). Combinational circuits: arithmetic circuits, code converters, multiplexers and decoders. Sequential circuits: latches and flip-flops, counters and shift-registers. Comparators, timers, multi-vibrators. Sample and hold circuits, ADCs and DACs. Semiconductor memories. Logic implementation using programmable devices (ROM, PLA, FPGA).

6. Energy Conversion

Principles of electromechanical energy conversion: Torque and emf in rotating machines. DC machines: characteristics and performance analysis; starting and speed control of motors; Transformers: principles of operation and analysis; regulation, efficiency; 3-phase transformers. 3-phase induction machines and synchronous machines: characteristics and performance analysis; speed control.

7. Power Electronics and Electric Drives

Semiconductor power devices: diode, transistor, thyristor, triac, GTO and MOSFET–static characteristics and principles of operation; triggering circuits; phase control rectifiers; bridge converters: fully-controlled and halfcontrolled; principles of thyristor choppers and inverters; DC-DC converters; Switch mode inverter; basic concepts of speed control of DC and AC Motor drives applications of variable-speed drives.

8. Analog Communication

Random variables: continuous, discrete; probability, probability functions. Statistical averages; probability models; Random signals and noise: white noise, noise equivalent bandwidth; signal transmission with noise; signal to noise ratio. Linear CW modulation: Amplitude modulation: DSB, DSB-SC and SSB. Modulators and Demodulators; Phase and Frequency modulation: PM & FM signals; narrowband FM; generation & detection of FM and PM, Deemphasis, Preemphasis. CW modulation system: Superhetrodyne receivers, AM receivers, communication receivers, FM receivers, phase locked loop, SSB receiver Signal to noise ratio calculation for AM and FM receivers.

PAPER-II

1. Control Systems

Elements of control systems; block-diagram representation; open-loop & closed-loop systems; principles and applications of feed-back. Control system components. LTI systems: time-domain and transform-domain analysis. Stability: Routh Hurwitz criterion, root-loci, Bodeplots and polar plots, Nyquist's criterion; Design of lead-lad compensators. Proportional, PI, PID controllers. State-variable representation and analysis of control systems.

2. Microprocessors and Microcomputers

PC organisation; CPU, instruction set, register set, timing diagram, programming, interrupts, memory interfacing, I/O interfacing, programmable peripheral devices.

3. Measurement and Instrumentation

Error analysis; measurement of current, voltage, power, energy, power-factor, resistance, inductance, capacitance and frequency; bridge measurement. Signal conditioning circuit; Electronic measuring instruments: multimeter, CRO, digital voltmeter, frequency counter, Q-meter, spectrum-analyzer, distortionmeter. Transducers: thermocouple, thermistor, LVDT, strain-gauge, piezo-electric crystal.

4. Power Systems: Analysis and Control

Steady-state performance of overhead transmission lines and cables; principles of active and reactive power transfer and distribution; per-unit quantities; bus admittance and impedance matrices; load flow; voltage control and power factor correction; economic operation; symmetrical components, analysis of symmetrical and unsymmetrical faults. Concept of system stability: swing curves and equal area criterion. Static VAR system. Basic concepts of HVDC transmission.

5. Power System Protection

Principles of overcurrent, differential and distance protection. Concept of solid state relays. Circuit breakers. Computer aided protection: Introduction; line bus, generator, transformer protection; numeric relays and application of DSP to protection.

6. Digital Communication

Pulse code modulation (PCM), differential pulse code modulation (DPCM), delta modulation (DM), Digital modulation and demodulation schemes: amplitude, phase and frequency keying schemes (ASK, PSK, FSK). Error control coding: error detection and correction, linear block codes, convolution codes. Information measure and source coding. Data networks, 7-layer architecture.

GEOGRAPHY

PAPER-I

Principles of Geography

Physical Geography

1. **Geomorphology:** actors controlling landform development; endogenetic and exogenetic forces; Origin and evolution of the earth's crust; Fundamentals of geomagnetism; Physical conditions of the earth's interior; Geosynclines; Continental drift; Isostasy; Plate tectonics; Recent views on mountain building; Vulcanicity; Earthquakes and Tsunamis; Concepts of geomorphic cycles and Landscape development ; Denudation chronology; Channel morphology; Erosion surfaces; Slope development; Applied Geomorphology: Geohydrology, economic geology and environment.

2. **Climatology:** Temperature and pressure belts of the world; Heat budget of the earth; Atmospheric circulation; atmospheric stability and instability.

Planetary and local winds; Monsoons and jet streams; Air masses and fronto genesis, Temperate and tropical cyclones; Types and distribution of precipitation; Weather and Climate; Koppen's, Thornthwaite's and Trewartha's classification of world climates; Hydrological cycle; Global climatic change and role and response of man in climatic changes, Applied climatology and Urban climate.

3. **Oceanography:** Bottom topography of the Atlantic, Indian and Pacific Oceans; Temperature and salinity of the oceans; Heat and salt budgets, Ocean deposits; Waves, currents and tides; Marine resources: biotic, mineral and energy resources; Coral reefs, coral bleaching; sealevel changes; law of the sea and marine pollution.

4. **Biogeography:** Genesis of soils; Classification and distribution of soils; Soil profile; Soil erosion, Degradation and conservation; Factors influencing world distribution of plants and animals; Problems of deforestation and conservation measures; Social forestry; agro-forestry; Wild life; Major gene pool centres.

5. **Environmental Geography:** Principle of ecology; Human ecological adaptations; Influence of man on ecology and environment; Global and regional ecological changes and imbalances; Ecosystem their management and conservation; Environmental degradation, management and conservation; Biodiversity and sustainable development; Environmental policy; Environmental hazards and remedial measures; Environmental education and legislation.

Human Geography

1. **Perspectives in Human Geography:** Areal differentiation; regional synthesis; Dichotomy and dualism; Environmentalism; Quantitative revolution and locational analysis; radical, behavioural, human and welfare approaches; Languages, religions and secularisation; Cultural regions of the world; Human development index.

2. **Economic Geography:** World economic development: measurement and problems; World resources and their distribution; Energy crisis; the limits to growth; World agriculture: typology of agricultural regions; agricultural inputs and productivity; Food and nutrition problems; Food security; famine: causes, effects and remedies; World industries: locational patterns and problems; patterns of world trade.

3. **Population and Settlement Geography:** Growth and distribution of world population; demographic attributes; Causes and consequences of migration; concepts of over-under-and optimum population; Population theories, world population problems and policies, Social well-being and quality of life; Population as social capital. Types and patterns of rural settlements;

Environmental issues in rural settlements; Hierarchy of urban settlements; Urban morphology: Concepts of primate city and rank-size rule; Functional classification of towns; Sphere of urban influence; Rural urban fringe; Satellite towns; Problems and remedies of urbanization; Sustainable development of cities.

4. **Regional Planning:** Concept of a region; Types of regions and methods of regionalisation; Growth centres and growth poles; Regional imbalances; regional development strategies; environmental issues in regional planning; Planning for sustainable development.

5. **Models, Theories and Laws in Human Geography:** Systems analysis in Human geography; Malthusian, Marxian and demographic transition models; Central Place theories of Christaller and Losch;Perroux and Boudeville; Von Thunen's model of agricultural location; Weber's model of industrial location; Ostov's model of stages of growth. Heartland and Rimland theories; Laws of international boundaries and frontiers.

PAPER–II

Geography of India

1. **Physical Setting:** Space relationship of India with neighboring countries; Structure and relief; Drainage system and watersheds; Physiographic regions; Mechanism of Indian monsoons and rainfall patterns, Tropical cyclones and western disturbances; Floods and droughts; Climatic regions; Natural vegetation; Soil types and their distributions.

2. **Resources:** Land, surface and ground water, energy, minerals, biotic and marine resources; Forest and wild life resources and their conservation; Energy crisis.

3. **Agriculture:** Infrastructure: irrigation, seeds, fertilizers, power; Institutional factors: land holdings, land tenure and land reforms; Cropping pattern, agricultural productivity, agricultural intensity, crop combination, land capability; Agro and social-forestry; Green revolution and its socio-economic and ecological implications; Significance of dry farming; Livestock resources and white revolution; aqua - culture; sericulture, apiculture and poultry; agricultural regionalisation; agro-climatic zones; agro- ecological regions.

4. **Industry:** Evolution of industries; Locational factors of cotton, jute, textile, iron and steel, aluminium, fertilizer, paper, chemical and pharmaceutical, automobile, cottage and agro-based industries; Industrial houses and complexes including public sector undertakings; Industrial regionalisation; New industrial policies; Multinationals and liberalization; Special Economic Zones; Tourism including eco-tourism.

5. **Transport, Communication and Trade:** Road, railway, waterway, airway and pipeline networks and their complementary roles in regional development; Growing importance of ports on national and foreign trade; Trade balance; Trade Policy; Export processing zones; Developments in communication and information technology and their impacts on economy and society; Indian space programme.
6. **Cultural Setting:** Historical Perspective of Indian Society; Racial, linguistic and ethnic diversities; religious minorities; major tribes, tribal areas and their problems; cultural regions; Growth, distribution and density of population; Demographic attributes: sex-ratio, age structure, literacy rate, work-force, dependency ratio, longevity; migration (inter-regional, intra-regional and international) and associated problems; Population problems and policies; Health indicators.
7. **Settlements:** Types, patterns and morphology of rural settlements; Urban developments; Morphology of Indian cities; Functional classification of Indian cities; Conurbations and metropolitan regions; urban sprawl; Slums and associated problems; town planning; Problems of urbanization and remedies.
8. **Regional Development and Planning:** Experience of regional planning in India; Five Year Plans; Integrated rural development programmes; Panchayati Raj and decentralised planning; Command area development; Watershed management; Planning for backward area, desert, drought prone, hill, tribal area development; multi-level planning; Regional planning and development of island territories.
9. **Political Aspects:** Geographical basis of Indian federalism; State reorganisation; Emergence of new states; Regional consciousness and inter state issues; international boundary of India and related issues; Cross border terrorism; India's role in world affairs; Geopolitics of South Asia and Indian Ocean realm.
10. **Contemporary Issues:** Ecological issues: Environmental hazards: landslides, earthquakes, Tsunamis, floods and droughts, epidemics; Issues relating to environmental pollution; Changes in patterns of land use; Principles of environmental impact assessment and environmental management; Population explosion and food security; Environmental degradation; Deforestation, desertification and soil erosion; Problems of agrarian and industrial unrest; Regional disparities in economic development; Concept of sustainable growth and development; Environmental awareness; Linkage of rivers; Globalisation and Indian economy.

Note: Candidates will be required to answer one compulsory map question pertinent to subjects covered by this paper.

GEOLOGY

PAPER - I

1. General Geology

The Solar System, Meteorites, Origin and interior of the earth and age of earth; Volcanoes- causes and products, Volcanic belts; Earthquakes-causes, effects, Seismic zones of India; Island arcs, trenches and midocean ridges; Continental drifts; Seafloor spreading, Plate tectonics; Isostasy.

2. Geomorphology and Remote Sensing

Basic concepts of geomorphology; Weathering and soil formations; Landforms, slopes and drainage; Geomorphic cycles and their interpretation; Morphology and its relation to structures and lithology; Coastal geomorphology; Applications of geomorphology in mineral prospecting, civil engineering; Hydrology and environmental studies; Geomorphology of Indian subcontinent.

Aerial photographs and their interpretation-merits and limitations; The Electromagnetic spectrum; Orbiting satellites and sensor systems; Indian Remote Sensing Satellites; Satellites data products; Applications of remote sensing in geology; The Geographic Information Systems (GIS) and Global Positioning System (GPS) – its applications.

3. Structural Geology

Principles of geologic mapping and map reading, Projection diagrams, Stress and strain ellipsoid and stress-strain relationships of elastic, plastic and viscous materials; Strain markers in deformed rocks; Behaviour of minerals and rocks under deformation conditions; Folds and faults classification and mechanics; Structural analysis of folds, foliations, lineations, joints and faults, unconformities; Timerelationship between crystallization and deformation.

4. Paleontology

Species- definition and nomenclature; Megafossils and Microfossils; Modes of preservation of fossils; Different kinds of microfossils; Application of microfossils in correlation, petroleum exploration, paleoclimatic and paleoceanographic studies; Evolutionary trend in Hominidae, Equidae and Proboscidae; Siwalik fauna; Gondwana flora and fauna and its importance; Index fossils and their significance.

5. Indian Stratigraphy

Classification of stratigraphic sequences: lithostratigraphic, biostratigraphic, chronostratigraphic and magnetostratigraphic and their interrelationships; Distribution and classification of Precambrian rocks of India; Study of stratigraphic distribution and lithology of Phanerozoic rocks of India with reference to fauna, flora and economic importance; Major boundary problemsCambrian/Precambrian, Permian/Triassic, Cretaceous/Tertiary and Pliocene/Pleistocene; Study of climatic conditions, paleogeography and igneous activity in the Indian subcontinent in the geological past; Tectonic framework of India; Evolution of the Himalayas.

6. Hydrogeology and Engineering Geology

Hydrologic cycle and genetic classification of water; Movement of subsurface water; Springs; Porosity, permeability, hydraulic conductivity, transmissivity and storage coefficient, classification of aquifers; Waterbearing characteristics of rocks; Groundwater chemistry; Salt water intrusion; Types of wells; Drainage basin morphometry; Exploration for groundwater; Ground-water recharge; Problems and management of groundwater; Rainwater harvesting; Engineering properties of rocks; Geological investigations for dams, tunnels highways, railway and bridges; Rock as construction material; Landslides-causes, prevention and rehabilitation; Earthquake-resistant structures.

PAPER-II

1. Mineralogy

Classification of crystals into systems and classes of symmetry; International system of crystallographic notation; Use of projection diagrams to represent crystal symmetry; Elements of X-ray crystallography. Physical and chemical characters of rock forming silicate mineral groups; Structural classification of silicates; Common minerals of igneous and metamorphic rocks; Minerals of the carbonate, phosphate, sulphide and halide groups; Clay minerals. Optical properties of common rock forming minerals; Pleochroism, extinction angle, double refraction, birefringence, twinning and dispersion in minerals.

2. Igneous and Metamorphic Petrology

Generation and crystallization of magmas; Crystallization of albite-anorthite, diopside-anorthite and diopsidewollastonite- silica systems; Bowen's Reaction Principle; Magmatic differentation and assimilation; Petrogenetic significance of the textures and structures of igneous rocks; Petrography and petrogenesis of granite, syenite, diorite, basic and ultrabasic groups, charnockite, anorthosite and alkaline rocks; Carbonatites; Deccan volcanic province.

Types and agents of metamorphism; Metamorphic grades and zones; Phase rule; Facies of regional and contact metamorphism; ACF and AKF diagrams; Textures and structures of metamorphic rocks; Metamorphism of arenaceous, argillaceous and basic rocks; Minerals assemblages Retrograde metamorphism; Metasomatism and granitisation, migmatites, Granulite terrains of India.

3. Sedimentary Petrology

Sediments and Sedimentary rocks: Processes of formation; digenesis and lithification; Clastic and non-clastic rocks-their classification, petrography and depositional environment; Sedimentary facies and provenance; Sedimentary structures and their significance; Heavy minerals and their significance; Sedimentary basins of India.

4. Economic Geology

Ore, ore minerals and gangue, tenor of ore, classification of ore deposits; Process of formation of minerals deposits; Controls of ore localization; Ore textures and structures; Metallogenic epochs and provinces; Geology of the important Indian deposits of aluminium, chromium, copper, gold, iron, lead zinc, manganese, titanium, uranium and thorium and industrial minerals; Deposits of coal and petroleum in India; National Mineral Policy; Conservation and utilization of mineral resources; Marine mineral resources and Law of Sea.

5. Mining Geology

Methods of prospecting-geological, geophysical, geochemical and geobotanical; Techniques of sampling; Estimation of reserves or ore; Methods of exploration and mining metallic ores, industrial minerals, marine mineral resources and building stones; Mineral beneficiation and ore dressing.

6. Geochemistry and Environmental Geology

Cosmic abundance of elements; Composition of the planets and meteorites; Structure and composition of Earth and distribution of elements; Trace elements; Elements of crystal chemistry-types of chemical bonds, coordination number; Isomorphism and polymorphism; Elementary thermodynamics. Natural hazards-floods, mass wasting, costal hazards, earthquakes and volcanic activity and mitigation; Environmental impact of urbanization, mining, industrial and radioactive waste disposal, use of fertilizers, dumping of mine waste and fly ash; Pollution of ground and surface water, marine pollution; Environment protection legislative measures in India; Sea level changes: causes and impact.

HISTORY

PAPER-I

1. Sources

Archaeological sources: Exploration, excavation, epigraphy, numismatics, monuments Literary sources: Indigenous: Primary and secondary; poetry, scientific literature, literature, literature in regional languages, religious literature.

Foreign accounts: Greek, Chinese and Arab writers.

2. Pre-history and Proto-history

Geographical factors; hunting and gathering (paleolithic and mesolithic); Beginning of agriculture (neolithic and chalcolithic).

3. Indus Valley Civilization

Origin, date, extent, characteristics, decline, survival and significance, art and architecture.

4. Megalithic Cultures

Distribution of pastoral and farming cultures outside the Indus, Development of community life, Settlements, Development of agriculture, Crafts, Pottery, and Iron industry.

5. Aryans and Vedic Period

Expansions of Aryans in India. Vedic Period: Religious and philosophic literature; Transformation from Rig Vedic period to the later Vedic period; Political, social and economical life; Significance of the Vedic Age; Evolution of Monarchy and Varna system.

6. Period of Mahajanapadas

Formation of States (Mahajanapada) : Republics and monarchies; Rise of urban centres; Trade routes; Economic growth; Introduction of coinage; Spread of Jainism and Buddhism; Rise of Magadha and Nandas. Iranian and Macedonian invasions and their impact.

7. Mauryan Empire

Foundation of the Mauryan Empire, Chandragupta, Kautilya and Arthashastra; Ashoka; Concept of Dharma; Edicts; Polity, Administration; Economy; Art, architecture and sculpture; External contacts; Religion; Spread of religion; Literature. Disintegration of the empire; Sungas and Kanvas.

8. Post-Mauryan Period (Indo-Greeks, Sakas, Kushanas, Western Kshatrapas)

Contact with outside world; growth of urban centres, economy, coinage, development of religions, Mahayana, social conditions, art, architecture, culture, literature and science.

9. Early State and Society in Eastern India, Deccan and South India

Kharavela, The Satavahanas, Tamil States of the Sangam Age; Administration, economy, land grants, coinage, trade guilds and urban centres; Buddhist centres; Sangam literature and culture; Art and architecture.

10. Guptas, Vakatakas and Vardhanas

Polity and administration, Economic conditions, Coinage of the Guptas, Land grants, Decline of urban centres, Indian feudalism, Caste system, Position of women, Education and educational institutions; Nalanda, Vikramshila and Vallabhi, Literature, scientific literature, art and architecture.

11. Regional States during Gupta Era

The Kadambas, Pallavas, Chalukyas of Badami; Polity and Administration, Trade guilds, Literature; growth of Vaishnava and Saiva religions. Tamil Bhakti movement, Shankaracharya; Vedanta; Institutions of temple and temple architecture; Palas, Senas, Rashtrakutas, Paramaras, Polity and administration; Cultural aspects. Arab conquest of Sind; Alberuni, The Chalukyas of Kalyana, Cholas, Hoysalas, Pandyas; Polity and Administration; local Government; Growth of art and architecture, religious sects, Institution of temple and Mathas, Agraharas, education and literature, economy and society.

12. Themes in Early Indian Cultural History

Languages and texts, major stages in the evolution of art and architecture, major philosophical thinkers and schools, ideas in Science and Mathematics.

13. Early Medieval India, 750-1200

- Polity: Major political developments in Northern India and the Peninsula, origin and the rise of Rajputs - The Cholas: administration, village economy and society
- "Indian Feudalism"
- Agrarian economy and urban settlements
- Trade and commerce
- Society: the status of the Brahman and the new social order
- Condition of women
- Indian science and technology

14. Cultural Traditions in India, 750-1200

- Philosophy: Skankaracharya and Vedanta, Ramanuja and Vishishtadvaita, Madhva and Brahma-Mimansa
- Religion: Forms and features of religion, Tamil devotional cult, growth of Bhakti, Islam and its arrival in India, Sufism
- Literature: Literature in Sanskrit, growth of Tamil literature, literature in the newly developing languages, Kalhan's Rajtarangini, Alberuni's India
- Art and Architecture: Temple architecture, sculpture, painting

15. The Thirteenth Century

- Establishment of the Delhi Sultanate: The Ghurian invasions – factors behind Ghurian success
- Economic, social and cultural consequences
- Foundation of Delhi Sultanate and early Turkish Sultans
- Consolidation: The rule of Iltutmish and Balban

16. The Fourteenth Century

- "The Khalji Revolution"
- Alauddin Khalji: Conquests and territtorial expansion, agrarian and economic measures
- Muhammad Tughluq: Major projects, agrarian measures, bureaucracy of Muhammad Tughluq
- Firuz Tughluq: Agrarian measures, achievements in civil engineering and public works, decline of the Sultanate, foreign contacts and Ibn Battuta's account

17. Society, Culture and Economy in the Thirteenth and Fourteenth Centuries

- Society: composition of rural society, ruling classes, town dwellers, women, religious classes, caste and slavery under the Sultanate, Bhakti movement, Sufi movement
- Culture: Persian literature, literature in the regional languages of North India, literature in the languages of South India, Sultanate architecture and new structural forms, painting, evolution of a composite culture
- Economy: Agricultural production, rise of urban economy and non-agricultural production, trade and commerce

18. The Fifteenth and Early Sixteenth Century – Political Developments and Economy

- Rise of Provincial Dynasties: Bengal, Kashmir (Zainul Abedin), Gujarat, Malwa, Bahmanids
- The Vijayanagara Empire
- Lodis
- Mughal Empire, First phase: Babur and Humayun
- The Sur Empire: Sher Shah's administration
- Portuguese Colonial enterprise
- Bhakti and Sufi Movements

19. The Fifteenth and early Sixteenth Century – Society and Culture

- Regional cultural specificities
- Literary traditions
- Provincial architecture
- Society, culture, literature and the arts in Vijayanagara Empire.

20. Akbar

- Conquests and consolidation of the Empire
- Establishment of Jagir and Mansab systems
- Rajput policy
- Evolution of religious and social outlook, theory of Sulh-i-kul and religious policy
- Court patronage of art and technology

21. Mughal Empire in the Seventeenth Century

- Major administrative policies of Jahangir, Shahjahan and Aurangzeb
- The Empire and the Zamindars
- Religious policies of Jahangir, Shahjahan and Aurangzeb
- Nature of the Mughal State
- Late Seventeenth century crisis and the revolts
- The Ahom Kingdom
- Shivaji and the early Maratha Kingdom.

22. Economy and Society in the Sixteenth and Seventeenth Centuries

- Population, agricultural production, craft production
- Towns, commerce with Europe through Dutch, English and French companies : a trade revolution
- Indian mercantile classes, banking, insurance and credit systems
- Condition of peasants, condition of women
- Evolution of the Sikh community and the Khalsa Panth

23. Culture in the Mughal Empire

- Persian histories and other literature
- Hindi and other religious literature
- Mughal architecture
- Mughal painting
- Provincial architecture and painting - Classical music
- Science and technology

24. The Eighteenth Century

- Factors for the decline of the Mughal Empire
- The regional principalities: Nizam's Deccan, Bengal, Awadh
- Maratha ascendancy under the Peshwas

- The Maratha fiscal and financial system
- Emergence of Afghan Power, Battle of Panipat:1761
- State of politics, culture and economy on the eve of the British conquest

PAPER-II

1. European Penetration into India

The Early European Settlements; The Portuguese and the Dutch; The English and the French East India Companies; Their struggle for supremacy; Carnatic Wars; Bengal -The conflict between the English and the Nawabs of Bengal; Siraj and the English; The Battle of Plassey; Significance of Plassey.

2. British Expansion in India

Bengal – Mir Jafar and Mir Kasim; The Battle of Buxar; Mysore; The Marathas; The three Anglo-Maratha Wars; The Punjab.

3. Early Structure of the British Raj

The early administrative structure; From diarchy to direct control; The Regulating Act (1773); The Pitt's India Act (1784); The Charter Act (1833); The voice of free trade and the changing character of British colonial rule; The English utilitarian and India.

4. Economic Impact of British Colonial Rule

(a) Land revenue settlements in British India; The Permanent Settlement; Ryotwari Settlement; Mahalwari Settlement; Economic impact of the revenue arrangements; Commercialization of agriculture; Rise of landless agrarian labourers; Impoverishment of the rural society.

(b) Dislocation of traditional trade and commerce; De-industrialisation; Decline of traditional crafts; Drain of wealth; Economic transformation of India; Railroad and communication network including telegraph and postal services; Famine and poverty in the rural interior; European business enterprise and its limitations.

5. Social and Cultural Developments

The state of indigenous education, its dislocation; Orientalist-Anglicist controversy, The introduction of western education in India; The rise of press, literature and public opinion; The rise of modern vernacular literature; Progress of science; Christian missionary activities in India.

6. Social and Religious Reform movements in Bengal and Other Areas

Ram Mohan Roy, The Brahmo Movement; Devendranath Tagore; Iswarchandra Vidyasagar; The Young Bengal Movement; Dayanada Saraswati; The social reform movements in India including Sati, widow remarriage, child marriage etc.;

The contribution of Indian renaissance to the growth of modern India; Islamic revivalism – the Feraizi and Wahabi Movements.

7. Indian Response to British Rule

Peasant movements and tribal uprisings in the 18th and 19th centuries including the Rangpur Dhing (1783), the Kol Rebellion (1832), the Mopla Rebellion in Malabar (1841-1920), the Santal Hul (1855), Indigo Rebellion (1859-60), Deccan Uprising (1875) and the Munda Ulgulan (18991900); The Great Revolt of 1857 - Origin, character, causes of failure, the consequences; The shift in the character of peasant uprisings in the post-1857 period; the peasant movements of the 1920s and 1930s.

8. Factors leading to the birth of Indian Nationalism; Politics of Association; The Foundation of the Indian National Congress; The Safety-valve thesis relating to the birth of the Congress; Programme and objectives of Early Congress; the social composition of early Congress leadership; the Moderates and Extremists; The Partition of Bengal (1905); The Swadeshi Movement in Bengal; the economic and political aspects of Swadeshi Movement; The beginning of revolutionary extremism in India.

9. Rise of Gandhi; Character of Gandhian nationalism; Gandhi's popular appeal; Rowlatt Satyagraha; the Khilafat Movement; the Non-cooperation Movement; National politics from the end of the Non-cooperation movement to the beginning of the Civil Disobedience movement; the two phases of the Civil Disobedience Movement; Simon Commission; The Nehru Report; the Round Table Conferences; Nationalism and the Peasant Movements; Nationalism and Working class movements; Women and Indian youth and students in Indian politics (1885-1947); the election of 1937 and the formation of ministries; Cripps Mission; the Quit India Movement; the Wavell Plan; The Cabinet Mission.

10. Constitutional Developments in the Colonial India between 1858 and 1935.

11. Other strands in the National Movement.

The Revolutionaries: Bengal, the Punjab, Maharashtra, U.P, the Madras Presidency, Outside India. The Left; The Left within the Congress: Jawaharlal Nehru, Subhas Chandra Bose, the Congress Socialist Party; the Communist Party of India, other left parties.

12. Politics of Separatism; the Muslim League; the Hindu Mahasabha; Communalism and the politics of partition; Transfer of power; Independence.

13. Consolidation as a Nation; Nehru's Foreign Policy; India and her neighbours (1947-1964); The linguistic reorganization of States (1935-1947); Regionalism and regional inequality; Integration of Princely States; Princes in electoral politics; the Question of National Language.

14. Caste and Ethnicity after 1947; Backward castes and tribes in postcolonial electoral politics; Dalit movements.

15. Economic development and political change; Land reforms; the politics of planning and rural reconstruction; Ecology and environmental policy in post – colonial India; Progress of science.

16. Enlightenment and Modern ideas

(i) Major ideas of Enlightenment: Kant, Rousseau

(ii) Spread of Enlightenment in the colonies

(iii) Rise of socialist ideas (up to Marx); spread of Marxian Socialism.

17. Origins of Modern Politics

(i) European States System.

(ii) American Revolution and the Constitution.

(iii) French revolution and aftermath, 1789-1815.

(iv) American Civil War with reference to Abraham Lincoln and the abolition of slavery.

(v) British Democratic Politics, 1815-1850; Parliamentary Reformers, Free Traders, Chartists.

18. Industrialization

(i) English Industrial Revolution: Causes and Impact on Society

(ii) Industrialization in other countries: USA, Germany, Russia, Japan

(iii) Industrialization and Globalization.

19. Nation-State System

(i) Rise of Nationalism in 19th century

(ii) Nationalism: state-building in Germany and Italy

(iii) Disintegration of Empires in the face of the emergence of nationalities across the world.

20. Imperialism and Colonialism

(i) South and South-East Asia

(ii) Latin America and South Africa

(iii) Australia

(iv) Imperialism and free trade: Rise of neo-imperialism.

21. Revolution and Counter-Revolution

(i) 19th Century European revolutions

(ii) The Russian Revolution of 1917-1921

(iii) Fascist Counter-Revolution, Italy and Germany.

(iv) The Chinese Revolution of 1949

22. World Wars

(i) 1st and 2nd World Wars as Total Wars: Societal implications

(ii) World War I: Causes and consequences

(iii) World War II: Causes and consequence

23. The World after World War II

(i) Emergence of two power blocs

(ii) Emergence of Third World and non-alignment

(iii) UNO and the global disputes.

24. Liberation from Colonial Rule

(i) Latin America-Bolivar

(ii) Arab World-Egypt

(iii) Africa-Apartheid to Democracy

(iv) South-East Asia-Vietnam

25. Decolonization and Underdevelopment

(i) Factors constraining development: Latin America, Africa

26. Unification of Europe

(i) Post War Foundations: NATO and European Community

(ii) Consolidation and Expansion of European Community

(iii) European Union.

27. Disintegration of Soviet Union and the Rise of the Unipolar World

(i) Factors leading to the collapse of Soviet communism and the Soviet Union, 1985-1991

(ii) Political Changes in Eastern Europe 1989-2001.

(iii) End of the cold war and US ascendancy in the World as the lone superpower.

LAW

PAPER-I

Constitutional and Administrative Law

1. Constitution and Constitutionalism: The distinctive features of the Constitution.
2. Fundamental rights – Public interest litigation; Legal Aid; Legal services authority.

3. Relationship between fundamental rights, directive principles and fundamental duties.
4. Constitutional position of the President and relation with the Council of Ministers.
5. Governor and his powers.
6. Supreme Court and High Courts:
   (a) Appointments and transfer.
   (b) Powers, functions and jurisdiction.
7. Centre, States and local bodies:
   (a) Distribution of legislative powers between the Union and the States.
   (b) Local bodies.
   (c) Administrative relationship among Union, State and Local Bodies.
   (d) Eminent domain – State property – common property – community property.
8. Legislative powers, privileges and immunities.
9. Services under the Union and the States:
   (a) Recruitment and conditions of services; Constitutional safeguards; Administrative tribunals.
   (b) Union Public Service Commission and State Public Service Commissions – Power and functions
   (c) Election Commission – Power and functions.
10. Emergency provisions.
11. Amendment of the Constitution.
12. Principles of natural justice – Emerging trends and judicial approach.
13. Delegated legislation and its constitutionality.
14. Separation of powers and constitutional governance.
15. Judicial review of administrative action.
16. Ombudsman: Lokayukta, Lokpal etc.

International Law

1. Nature and definition of international law.
2. Relationship between international law and municipal law.
3. State recognition and state succession.
4. Law of the sea: Inland waters, territorial sea, contiguous zone, continental shelf, exclusive economic zone, high seas.
5. Individuals: Nationality, statelessness; Human rights and procedures available for their enforcement.
6. Territorial jurisdiction of States, extradition and asylum.
7. Treaties: Formation, application, termination and reservation.

8. United Nations: Its principal organs, powers, functions and reform.
9. Peaceful settlement of disputes – different modes.
10. Lawful recourse to force: aggression, self-defence, intervention.
11. Fundamental principles of international humanitarian law – International conventions and contemporary developments.
12. Legality of the use of nuclear weapons; ban on testing of nuclear weapons; Nuclear – non proliferation treaty, CTBT.
13. International terrorism, state sponsored terrorism, hijacking, international criminal court.
14. New international economic order and monetary law: WTO, TRIPS, GATT, IMF, World Bank.
15. Protection and improvement of the human environment: International efforts.

PAPER-II

Law of Crimes

1. General principles of criminal liability: Mens rea and actus reus, mens rea in statutory offences.
2. Kinds of punishment and emerging trends as to abolition of capital punishment.
3. Preparation and criminal attempt.
4. General exceptions.
5. Joint and constructive liability.
6. Abetment.
7. Criminal conspiracy.
8. Offences against the State.
9. Offences against public tranquility.
10. Offences against human body.
11. Offences against property.
12. Offences against women.
13. Defamation.
14. Prevention of Corruption Act, 1988.
15. Protection of Civil Rights Act 1955 and subsequent legislative developments.
16. Plea bargaining.

Law of Torts

1. Nature and definition.
2. Liability based upon fault and strict liability; Absolute liability.

3. Vicarious liability including State liability.
4. General defences.
5. Joint tort feasors.
6. Remedies.
7. Negligence.
8. Defamation.
9. Nuisance.
10. Conspiracy.
11. False imprisonment.
12. Malicious prosecution.
13. Consumer Protection Act, 1986.

Law of Contracts and Mercantile Law

1. Nature and formation of contract/Econtract.
2. Factors vitiating free consent.
3. Void, voidable, illegal and unenforceable agreements.
4. Performance and discharge of contracts.
5. Quasi- Contracts.
6. Consequences of breach of contract.
7. Contract of indemnity, guarantee and insurance.
8. Contract of agency.
9. Sale of goods and hire purchase.
10. Formation and dissolution of partnership.
11. Negotiable Instruments Act, 1881.
12. Arbitration and Conciliation Act, 1996.
13. Standard form contracts.

Contemporary Legal Developments

1. Public Interest Litigation.
2. Intellectual property rights – Concept, types/prospects.
3. Information Technology Law including Cyber Laws – Concept, purpose/prospects.
4. Competition Law- Concept, purpose/prospects.
5. Alternate Dispute Resolution – Concept, types/prospects.
6. Major statutes concerning environmental law.
7. Right to Information Act.
8. Trial by media.

Literature of the following languages

Note (i): A candidate may be required to answer some or all the questions in the language concerned.

Note (ii): In regard to the languages included in the Eighth Schedule to Constitution, the scripts will be the same as indicated in Section-II (B) of Appendix I relating to Main Examination.

Note (iii): Candidates should note that the questions not required to be answered in a specific language will have to be answered in the language medium indicated by them for answering papers on Essay, General Studies and Optional Subjects.

ASSAMESE

PAPER-I

(Answers must be written in Assamese)

Section-A

Language

(a) History of the origin and development of the Assamese language-its position among the Indo-Aryan Languages - periods in its history.

(b) Developments of Assamese prose.

(c) Vowels and consonants of the Assamese languages-rules of phonetic changes with stress on Assamese coming down from Old Indo-Aryan.

(d) Assamese vocabulary-and its sources.

(e) Morphology of the language-conjugation-enclitic definitives and pleonastic suffixes.

(f) Dilectical divergences-the standard colloquial and the Kamrupi dialect in particulars.

(g) Assamese scripts-its evolution through the ages till 19th century A.D.

Section-B

Literary Criticism and Literary History

(a) Principles of Literary criticism upto New criticism.

(b) Different literary genres.

(c) Development of literary forms in Assamese.

(d) Development of literary criticism in Assamese.

(e) Periods of the literary history of Assam from the earliest beginnings, i.e. from the period of the charyyageets with their socio-cultural background : the proto Assamese-Pre-Sankaradeva - Sankaradeva-post Sankaradeva – Modern period (from the coming of the Britishers)-Post-Independence period. Special emphasis is to be given on the Vaisnavite period, the gonaki and the post-Independence period.

PAPER-II

This paper will require first-hand reading of the texts prescribed and will be designed to test the candidates' critical ability.

(Answers must be written in Assamese)

Section-A

Rãmãyana (Ayodhya Kãnda only) - by Madhava Kandali.

Pãrijãt-Harana - by Sankaradeva.

Rãsakrïdã - by Sankaradeva (From Kirtana Ghosa).

Bargeet - by Madhavadeva

Rãjasûya - by Madhavadeva.

Kãthã-Bhãgavata (Books I and II) - by Baikunthanath Bhattacharyya.

Gurucarit-Kathã (Sankaradeva's Part only) - ed. by Maheswar Neog

Section-B

Mor Jeevan Soñwaran - by Lakshminath Bezbaroa.

Kripãbar Barbaruãr Kãkatar Topola - by Lakshminath Bezbaroa.

Pratimã - by Chandra Kumar Agarwalla.

Gãoñburhã - by Padmanath Gohain Barua.

Monamatî - by Rajanikanta Bordoloi.

Purani Asamîyã Sãhitya - by Banikanta Kakati.

Kãrengar Ligirî - by Jyotiprasad Agarwalla

Jeevanar Bãtat - by Bina Barwa (Birinchi Kumar Barua)

Mrityunjoy - by Birendrakumar Bhattacharyya

Samrãt - by Navakanta Barua.

BENGALI

PAPER-I

History of Language and Literature.

Answers must be written in Bengali.

Section-A

Topics from the History of Bangla language

1. The chronological track from Proto Indo-European to Bangla (Family tree with branches and approximate dates).
2. Historical stages of Bangla (Old, Middle, New) and their linguistic features.
3. Dialects of Bangla and their distinguishing characteristics.
4. Elements of Bangla Vocabulary.

5. Forms of Bangla Literary Prose-Sadhu and Chalit.
6. Processes of language change relevant for Bangla: Apinihiti (Anaptyxis), Abhishruti (umlaut), Murdhanyibhavan (cerebralization), Nasikyibhavan (Nasalization), Samibhavan (Assimilation), Sadrishya (Analogy), Svaragama (Vowel insertion)-Adi Svaragama, Madhya Svaragama or Svarabhakti, Antya Svaragama, Svarasangati (Vowel hormony), y-shruti and w-shruti.
7. Problems of standardization and reform of alphabet and spelling, and those of transliteration and Romanization.
8. Phonology, Morphology and Syntax of Modern Bangla. (Sounds of Modern Bangla, Conjuncts; word formations, compounds; basic sentence patterns.)

Section-B

Topics from the History of Bangla Literature.

1. Periodization of Bangla Literature : Old Bangla and Middle Bangla.
2. Points of difference between modern and pre-modern Bangla Literature.
3. Roots and reasons behind the emergence of modernity in Bangla Literature.
4. Evolution of various Middle Bangla forms : Mangal kavyas, Vaishnava lyrics, Adapted narratives (Ramayana, Mahabharata, Bhagavata) and religious biographies.
5. Secular forms in middle Bangla literature.
6. Narrative and lyric trends in the nineteenth century Bangla poetry.
7. Development of prose.
8. Bangla dramatic literature (nineteenth century, Tagore, Post-1944 Bangla drama).
9. Tagore and post-Tagoreans.
10. Fiction, major authors: (Bankimchandra, Tagore, Saratchandra, Bibhutibusan, Tarasankar, Manik).
11. Women and Bangla literature : creators and created.

PAPER-II

Prescribed texts for close study.

Answers must be written in Bengali.

Section-A

1. **Vaishnava Padavali** (Calcutta University) Poems of Vidyapati, Chandidas, Jnanadas, Govindadas and Balaramdas.
2. **Chandimangal** Kalketu episode by Mukunda (Sahitya Akademi).
3. **Chaitanya Charitamrita** Madya Lila, by Krishnadas Kaviraj (Sahitya Akademi).
4. **Meghnadbadh Kavya** by Madhusudan Dutta.

5. **Kapalkundala** by Bankimchandra Chattarjee.
6. **Samya** and **Bangadesher Krishak** by Bankimchandra Chatterjee.
7. **Sonar Tari** by Rabindranath Tagore.
8. **Chhinnapatravali** by Rabindranath Tagore.

Section-B

9. **Raktakarabi** by Rabindranath Tagore.
10. **Nabajatak** by Rabindranath Tagore.
11. **Grihadaha** by Saratchandra Chatterjee.
12. **Prabandha Samgraha** Vol. 1, by Pramatha Choudhuri.
13. **Aranyak** by Bibhutibhusan Banerjee
14. **Short stories** by Manik Bandyopadhyay : Atashi Mami, Pragaitihasik, Holud-Pora, Sarisrip, Haraner Natjamai, Chhoto-Bokulpurer Jatri, Kustharogir Bou, Jakey Ghush Ditey Hoy.
15. **Shrestha Kavita** by Jibanananda Das.
16. **Jagori** by Satinath Bhaduri.
17. **Ebam Indrajit** by Badal Sircar.

BODO

PAPER-I

History of Bodo Language and Literature

(Answers must be written in Bodo)

Section-A

History of Bodo Language

1. Homeland, language family, its present status and its mutual contact with Assamese.
2. (a) Phonemes : Vowel and Consonant Phonemes

   (b) Tones.
3. Morphology : Gender, Case & Case endings, Plural suffix, Definitives, Verbal suffix.
4. Vocabulary and its sources.
5. Syntax : Types of sentences, Word Order.
6. History of Scripts used in writing Bodo Language since inception.

Section-B

History of Bodo Literature

1. General introduction of Bodo folk literature.
2. Contribution of the Missionaries.

3. Periodization of Bodo Literature.
4. Critical analysis of different genre (Poetry, Novel, Short Story and Drama)
5. Translation Literature.

PAPER-II

The Paper will require first-hand reading of the texts prescribed and will be designed to test the critical ability of the candidates.

(Answers must be written in Bodo)

Section-A

(a) Khonthai-Methai (Edited by Madaram Brahma & Rupnath Brahma).
(b) Hathorkhi-Hala (Edited by Pramod Chandra Brahma)
(c) Boroni Gudi Sibsa Arw Aroz : Madaram Brahma.
(d) Raja Nilambar : Dwarendra Nath Basumatary.
(e) Bibar (Prose section) (Edited by Satish Chandra Basumatary)

Section-B

(a) Gibi Bithai (Aida Nwi) : Bihuram Boro
(b) Radab : Samar Brahma Chaudhury
(c) Okhrang Gongse Nangou : Brajendra Kumar Brahma
(d) Baisagu Arw Harimu : Laksheswar Brahma.
(e) Gwdan Boro : Manoranjan Lahary
(f) Jujaini Or : Chittaranjan Muchahary
(g) Mwihoor : Dharanidhar Wary
(h) Hor Badi Khwmsi : Kamal Kumar Brahma
(i) Jaolia Dewan : Mangal Singh Hozowary
(j) Hagra Guduni Mwi : Nilkamal Brahma.

DOGRI

PAPER-I

History of Dogri Language and Literature

(Answers must be written in Dogri)

Section-A

History of Dogri Language

1. Dogri language : Origin and development through different stages.
2. Linguistic boundaries of Dogri and its dialects.
3. Characteristic features of Dogri language.

4. Structure of Dogri Language :
   (a) Sound Structure : Segmental : Vowels and Consonants Non-Segmental: Length, Stress, Nasalization, Tone and Juncture.
   (b) Morphology of Dogri :
      (i) Inflection Categories: Gender, Number, Case, Person, Tense and Voice.
      (ii) Word Formation : use of prefixes, infixes and suffixes.
      (iii) Vocabulary : Tatsam, tadbhav, foreign and regional.
   (c) Sentence Structure: Major Sentence - types and their constituents, agreement and concord in Dogri syntax.
5. Dogri Language and Scripts : Dogre/Dogra Akkhar, Devanagari and Persian.

Section-B

History of Dogri Literature

1. A brief account of Pre-independence Dogri Literature : Poetry & Prose.
2. Development of modern Dogri Poetry and main trends in Dogri Poetry.
3. Development of Dogri short-story, main trends & prominent short-story writers.
4. Development of Dogri Novel, main trends & contribution of Dogri Novelists.
5. Development of Dogri Drama & contribution of prominent Playwrights.
6. Development of Dogri Prose : Essays, Memoirs & Travelogues.
7. An introduction to Dogri Folk literature - Folk songs, Folk tales & Ballads.

PAPER-II

Textual Cristisim of Dogri Literature

(Answers must be written in Dogri)

Section-A

Poetry

1. Azadi Paihle Di Dogri Kavita.

   The following poets: Devi Ditta, Lakkhu, Ganga Ram, Ramdhan, Hardutt, Pahari Gandhi Baba Kanshi Ram & Permanand Almast.
2. Modern Dogri Poetry

   Azadi Bad Di Dogri Kavita

   The following poets: Kishan Smailpuri, Tara Smailpuri, Mohan Lal Sapolia, Yash Sharma, K.S. Madhukar, Padma Sachdev, Jitendra Udhampuri, Charan Singh and Prakash Premi.
3. Sheeraza Dogri Number 102, Ghazal Ank.

   The following poets: Ram Lal Sharma, Ved Pal Deep, N.D. Jamwal, Shiv

Ram Deep, Ashwini Magotra and Virendra Kesar.

4. Sheeraza Dogri Number 147, Ghazal Ank

   The following poets: R.N. Shastri, Jitendra Udhampuri, Champa Sharma and Darshan Darshi.

5. Ramayan (Epic) by Shambhu Nath Sharma (upto Ayodhya Kand)

6. Veer Gulab (Khand Kavya) by Dinoo Bhai Pant.

Section-B

Prose

1. Ajakani Dogri Kahani

   The following short story writers: Madan Mohan Sharma, Narendra Khajuria and B.P. Sathe.

2. Ajakani Dogri Kahani Part-II

   The following Short Story writters: Ved Rahi, Narsingh Dev Jamwal, Om Goswami, Chhattrapal, Lalit Magotra, Chaman Arora and Ratan Kesar.

3. Khatha Kunj Bhag II

   The following Story writters: Om Vidyarthi, Champa Sharma and Krishan Sharma.

4. Meel Patthar (collection of short stories) by Bandhu Sharma

5. Kaiddi (Novel) by Desh Bandhu Dogra Nutan

6. Nanga Rukkh (Novel) by O.P. Sharma Sarathi.

7. Nayaan (Drama) by Mohan Singh.

8. Satrang (A collection of one act plays)

   The following pay wrights: Vishwa Nath Khajuria, Ram Nath Shastri, Jitendra Sharma, Lalit Magotra and Madan Mohan Sharma.

9. Dogri Lalit Nibandh

   The following authors: Vishwa Nath Khajuria, Narayan Mishra, Balkrishan Shastri, Shiv Nath, Shyam Lal Sharma, Lakshmi Narayan.

   D.C. Prashant, Ved Ghai, Kunwar Viyogi.

ENGLISH

The syllabus consists of two papers, designed to test a first-hand and critical reading of texts prescribed from the following periods in English Literature: Paper I: 1600-1900 and Paper II : 1900-1990.

There will be two compulsory questions in each paper:

(a) A short-notes question related to the topics for general study, and

(b) A critical analysis of UNSEEN passages both in prose and verse.

PAPER-I

Answers must be written in English.

Texts for detailed study are listed below.

Candidates will also be required to show adequate knowledge of the following topics and movements:

The Renaissance : Elizabethan and Jacobean Drama; Metaphysical Poetry; The Epic and the Mock-epic; Neoclassicism; Satire; The Romantic Movement; The Rise of the Novel; The Victorian Age.

Section-A

1. William Shakespeare : **King Lear and The Tempest.**
2. John Donne. The following poems :
   - Canonization;
   - Death be not proud;
   - The Good Morrow;
   - On his Mistress going to bed;
   - The Relic;
3. John Milton : **Paradise Lost, I, II, IV, IX**
4. Alexander Pope. **The Rape of the Lock.**
5. William Wordsworth. The following poems:
   - Ode on Intimations of Immortality.
   - Tintern Abbey.
   - Three years she grew.
   - She dwelt among untrodden ways.
   - Michael.
   - Resolution and Independence.
   - The World is too much with us.
   - Milton, thou shouldst be living at this hour.
   - Upon Westminster Bridge.
6. Alfred Tennyson : **In Memoriam.**
7. Henrik Ibsen : **A Doll's House.**

Section-B

1. Jonathan Swift. **Gulliver's Travels.**
2. Jane Austen. **Pride and Prejudice.**
3. Henry Fielding. **Tom Jones.**
4. Charles Dickens. **Hard Times.**
5. George Eliot. **The Mill on the Floss.**
6. Thomas Hardy. **Tess of the d'Urbervilles.**
7. Mark Twain. **The Adventures of Huckleberry Finn.**

PAPER-II

Answers must be written in English.

Texts for detailed study are listed below.

Candidates will also be required to show adequate knowledge of the following topics and movements:

Modernism; Poets of the Thirties; The stream-of-consciousness Novel; Absurd Drama; Colonialism and Post-Colonialism; Indian Writing in English; Marxist, Psychoanalytical and Feminist approaches to literature; Post-Modernism.

Section-A

1. William Butler Yeats. The following poems:
   - Easter 1916
   - The Second Coming
   - A Prayer for my daughter.
   - Sailing to Byzantium.
   - The Tower.
   - Among School Children.
   - Leda and the Swan.
   - Meru
   - Lapis Lazuli
   - The Second Coming
   - Byzantium.
2. T.S. Eliot. The following poems :
   - The Love Song of J.Alfred Prufrock
   - Journey of the Magi.
   - Burnt Norton.
3. W.H. Auden. The following poems :
   - Partition
   - Musee des Beaux Arts
   - in Memory of W.B. Yeats
   - Lay your sleeping head, my love
   - The Unknown Citizen
   - Consider
   - Mundus Et Infans
   - The Shield of Achilles
   - September 1, 1939
   - Petition.
4. John Osborne : **Look Back in Anger.**

5. Samuel Beckett. **Waiting for Godot.**
6. Philip Larkin. The following poems :
   - Next
   - Please
   - Deceptions
   - Afternoons
   - Days
   - Mr. Bleaney
7. A.K. Ramanujan. The following poems :
   - Looking for a Causim on a Swing
   - A River
   - Of Mothers, among other Things
   - Love Poem for a Wife 1
   - Small-Scale Reflections on a Great House
   - Obituary

   (All these poems are available in the anthology Ten Twentieth Century Indian Poets, edited by R. Parthasarthy, published by Oxford University Press, New Delhi).

Section-B

1. Joseph Conrad. **Lord Jim.**
2. James Joyce. **Portrait of the Artist as a Young Man.**
3. D.H. Lawrence. **Sons and Lovers.**
4. E.M. Forster. **A Passage to India**.
5. Virginia Woolf. **Mrs Dalloway.**
6. Raja Rao. **Kanthapura.**
7. V.S. Naipal. **A House for Mr. Biswas.**

GUJARATI

PAPER-I

Answers must be written in Gujarati

Section-A

Gujarati Language : Form and history

1. History of Gujarati Language with special reference to New Indo-Aryan i.e. last one thousand years.
2. Significant features of the Gujarati language: Phonology, morphology and syntax.

3. Major dialects: Surti, Pattani, charotari and Saurashtri.

History of Gujarati Literature

Medieval:

4. Jaina tradition
5. Bhakti tradition: Sagun and Nirgun (Jnanmargi)
6. Non-sectarian tradition (Laukik parampara)

Modern:

7. Sudharak yug
8. Pandit yug
9. Gandhi yug
10. Anu-Gandhi yug
11. Adhunik yug

Section-B

Literary Forms: (Salient features, history and development of the following literary forms):

(a) Medieval

(i) Narratives: Rasa, Akhyan and Padyavarta

(ii) Lyrical: Pada

(b) Folk

(iii) Bhavai

(c) Modern

(iv) Fiction: Novel and short story

(v) Drama

(vi) Literary Essay

(vii) Lyrical Poetry

(d) Criticism

(viii) History of theoretical Gujarati criticism

(ix) Recent research in folk tradition.

PAPER-II

Answers must be written in Gujarati

The paper will require first hand reading of the texts prescribed and will be designed to test the critical abilityof the candidate.

Section-A

1. Medieval

(i) Vasantvilas phagu-**Ajnatkrut**

(ii) Kadambari-**Bhalan**

(iii) Sudamacharitra-**Premanand**

(iv) Chandrachandravatini Varta-**Shamal**

(v) Akhegeeta-**Akho**

2. **Sudharakyug & Pandityug**

(vi) Mari Hakikat-**Narmadashankar Dave**

(vii) Farbasveerah- **Dalpatram**

(viii) Saraswatichandra-Part-I **Govardhanram Tripathi**

(ix) Purvalap- 'Kant' **(Manishankar Ratnaji Bhatt)**

(x) Raino Parvat-**Ramanbhai Neelkanth**

Section-B

1. **Gandhiyug & Anu Gandhiyug**

(i) Hind Swaraj-**Mohandas Karmachand Gandhi**

(ii) Patanni Prabhuta- **Kanhaiyalal Munshi**

(iii) Kavyani Shakti- **Ramnarayan Vish-Wanath Pathak**

(iv) Saurashtrani Rasdhar Part 1- **Zaverchand Meghani**

(v) Manvini Bhavai-**Pannalal Patel**

(vi) Dhvani-**Rajendra Shah**

2. **Adhunik Yug**

(vii) Saptapadi-**Umashankar Joshi**

(viii) Janantike- **Suresh Joshi**

(ix) Ashwatthama- **Sitanshu Yashaschandra**

HINDI

PAPER-I

Answers must be written in Hindi

Section-A

1. History of Hindi Language and Nagari Lipi.

(i) Grammatical and applied forms of Apbhransh, Awahatta & Arambhik Hindi.

(ii) Development of Braj and Awadhi as literary language during medieval period.

(iii) Early form of Khari-boli in Siddha-Nath Sahitya, Khusero, Sant Sahitaya, Rahim etc. and Dakhni Hindi.

(iv) Development of Khari-boli and Nagari Lipi during 19th Century.

(v) Standardisation of Hindi Bhasha & Nagari Lipi.

(vi) Development of Hindi as national Language during freedom movement.

(vii) The development of Hindi as a National Language of Union of India.

(viii) Scientific & Technical development of Hindi Language.

(ix) Prominent dialects of Hindi and their inter- relationship.

(x) Salient features of Nagari Lipi and the efforts for its reform & Standard form of Hindi.

(xi) Grammatical structure of Standard Hindi.

Section-B

2. History of Hindi Literature

I. The relevance and importance of Hindi literature and tradition of writing History of Hindi Literature.

II. Literary trends of the following four periods of history of Hindi Literature.

(a) Adikal-Sidh, Nath and Raso Sahitya.

Prominent poets - Chandvardai, Khusaro, Hemchandra, Vidyapati.

(b) Bhaktikal - Sant Kavyadhara, Sufi Kavyadhara, Krishna Bhaktidhara and Ram Bhaktidhara.

Prominent Poets - Kabir, Jayasi, Sur & Tulsi.

(c) Ritikal-Ritikavya, Ritibaddhakavya & Riti Mukta Kavya.

Prominent Poets-Keshav, Bihari, Padmakar and Ghananand.

(d) Adhunik Kal

(i) Renaissance, the development of Prose, Bharatendu Mandal.

(ii) Prominent Writers : Bharatendu, Bal Krishna Bhatt & Pratap Narain Mishra.

(iii) Prominent trends of modern Hindi Poetry : Chhayavad, Pragativad, Proyogvad, Nai Kavita, Navgeet and Contemporary poetry and Janvadi Kavita.

Prominent Poets : Maithili Sharan Gupta, Prasad, Nirala, Mahadevi, Dinkar, Agyeya, Muktibodh, Nagarjun.

III. Katha Sahitya

(a) Upanyas & Realism

(b) The origin and development of Hindi Novels.

(c) Prominent Novelists : Premchand, Jainendra, Yashpal, Renu and Bhism Sahani.

(d) The origin and development of Hindi short story.

(e) Prominent short Story Writers : Premchand, Prasad, Agyeya, Mohan Rakesh & Krishna Shobti.

IV. Drama & Theatre

(a) The origin & Development of Hindi Drama.

(b) Prominent Dramatists : Bharatendu, Prasad, Jagdish Chandra Mathur, Ram Kumar Verma, Mohan Rakesh.

(c) The development of Hindi Theatre.

V. Criticism

(a) The origin and development of Hindi criticism : Saiddhantik, Vyavharik, Pragativadi, Manovishleshanvadi & Nai Alochana.

(b) Prominent critics : Ramchandra Shukla, Hajari Prasad Dwivedi, Ram Vilas Sharma & Nagendra.

VI. The other forms of Hindi prose-Lalit Nibandh, Rekhachitra, Sansmaran, Yatravrittant.

PAPER-II

Answers must be written in Hindi

This paper will require first hand reading of prescribed texts and will test the critical ability of the candidates.

Section-A

1. Kabir : Kabir Granthawali, Ed., Shyam Sundar Das (First hundred Sakhis.)
2. Surdas : Bhramar Gitsar, Ed. Ramchandra Shukla (First hundred Padas)
3. Tulsidas : Ramchrit Manas (Sundar Kand) Kavitawali (Uttar Kand).
4. Jayasi : Padmawat Ed. Shyam Sundar Das (Sinhal Dwip Khand & Nagmativiyog Khand)
5. Bihari : Bihari Ratnakar Ed. Jagnnath Prasad Ratnakar (First 100 Dohas)
6. Maithili : Bharat Bharati Sharan Gupta
7. Prasad : Kamayani (Chinta and Sharddha Sarg)
8. Nirala : Rag-Virag, Ed. Ram Vilas Sharma (Ram Ki Shakti Puja & Kukurmutta).
9. Dinkar : Kurushetra 10. Agyeya : Angan Ke Par Dwar (Asadhya Vina)
10. Muktiboth: Brahma Rakshas
11. Nagarjun: Badal Ko Ghirte Dekha Hai, Akal Ke Bad, Harijan Gatha.

Section-B

1. Bharatendu : Bharat Durdasha
2. Mohan Rakesh : Ashad Ka Ek Din
3. Ramchandra Shukla : Chintamani (Part I) (Kavita Kya Hai Shraddha Aur Bhakti)
4. Dr. Satyendra : Nibandh Nilaya-Bal Krishna Bhatt, Premchand, Gulab Rai, Hajari Prasad Dwivedi, Ram Vilas Sharma, Agyeya, Kuber Nath Rai.

5. Premchand : Godan, Premchand ki Sarvashreshtha Kahaniyan, Ed. Amrit Rai/Manjusha - Prem Chand ki Sarvashreshtha Kahaniyan, Ed. Amrit Rai.
6. Prasad : Skandgupta
7. Yashpal : Divya
8. Phaniswar Nath Renu : Maila Anchal
9. Mannu Bhandari : Mahabhoj
10. Rajendra Yadav : Ek Dunia Samanantar (All Stories)

KANNADA

PAPER-I

Answers must be written in Kannada

Section-A

A. History of Kannada Language

What is Language? General characteristics of Language. Dravidian Family of Languages and its specific features, Antiquity of Kannada Language, Different Phases of its Development.

Dialects of Kannada Language: Regional and Social Various aspects of development of Kannada Language: phonological and Semantic changes. Language borrowing.

B. History of Kannada Literature

Ancient Kannada literature : Influence and Trends. Poets for study : Specified poets from Pampa to Ratnakara Varni are to be studied in the light of contents, form and expression : Pampa, Janna, Nagachandra.

Medieval Kannada literature : Influence and Trends.

Vachana literature : Basavanna, Akka Mahadevi.

Medieval Poets : Harihara, Ragha-vanka, Kumar-Vyasa.

Dasa literature : Purandra and Kanaka.

Sangataya : Ratnakaravarni

C. Modern Kannada literature

Influence, trends and idealogies, Navodaya, Pragatishila, Navya, Dalita and Bandaya.

Section-B

A. Poetics and literary criticism

Definition and concepts of poetry : Word, Meaning, Alankara, Reeti, Rasa, Dhwani, Auchitya. Interpretations of Rasa Sutra.

Modern Trends of literary criticism : Formalist, Historical, Marxist, Feminist, Post-colonial criticism.

B. Cultural History of Karnataka

Contribution of Dynasties to the culture of Karnataka : Chalukyas of Badami and Kalyani, Rashtrakutas,

Hoysalas, Vijayanagara rulers, in literary context. Major religions of Karnataka and their cultural contributions.

Arts of Karnataka : Sculpture, Architecture, Painting, Music, Dance-in the literary context. Unification of Karnataka and its impact on Kannada literature.

PAPER-II

Answers must be written in Kannada

The paper will require first-hand reading of the Texts prescribed and will be designed to test the critical ability of the candidates.

Section-A

A. Old Kannada Literature

1. Vikramaarjuna Vijaya of Pampa (cantos 12 & 13), (Mysore University Pub.)
2. Vaddaraadhane (Sukumaraswamyia Kathe, Vidyutchorana Kathe)

B. Medieval Kannada Literature

1. Vachana Kammata, Ed: K. Marulasiddappa K.R. Nagaraj (Bangalore University Pub.)
2. Janapriya Kanakasamputa, Ed. D. Javare Gowda (Kannada and Culture Directorate, Bangalore)
3. Nambiyannana Ragale, Ed., T.N. Sreekantaiah (Ta.Vem. Smaraka Grantha Male, Mysore)
4. Kumaravyasa Bharata : Karna Parva (Mysore University)
5. Bharatesha Vaibhava Sangraha Ed. Ta. Su. Shama Rao (Mysore University)

Section-B

A. Modern Kannada Literature

1. Poetry : Hosagannada Kavite, Ed : G.H. Nayak (Kannada Saahitya Parishattu, Bangalore)
2. Novel : Bettada Jeeva-Shivarama Karanta Madhavi-Arupama Niranjana Odalaala-Devanuru Mahadeva
3. Short Story : Kannada Sanna Kathegalu, Ed. G.H. Nayak (Sahitya Academy, New Delhi).
4. Drama : Shudra Tapaswi-Kuvempu. Tughlak-Girish Karnad.
5. Vichara Saahitya : Devaru-A.N. Moorty Rao (Pub : D.V.K. Moorty, Mysore.)

B. Folk Literature

1. Janapada Swaroopa-Dr. H.M. Nayak. (Ta. Vem. Smaraka Grantha Male, Mysore.)
2. Janapada Geetaanjali-Ed.D. Javare Gowda. (Pub : Sahitya Academy, New Delhi.)
3. Kannada Janapada Kathegalu-Ed. J.S. Paramashivaiah, (Mysore University.)
4. Beedi Makkalu Beledo. Ed. Kalegowda Nagavara (Pub : Bangalore University.)
5. Savirada Ogatugalu-Ed : S.G. Imrapura.

KASHMIRI

PAPER-I

Answers must be written in Kashmiri

Section-A

1. Genealogical relationship of the Kashmiri language: various theories.
2. Areas of occurrence and dialects (geographical/social)
3. Phonology and grammar:
   (i) Vowel and consonant system;
   (ii) Nouns and pronouns with various case inflections;
   (iii) Verbs: various types and tenses.
4. Syntactic structure:
   (i) Simple, active and declarative statments;
   (ii) Coordination;
   (iii) Relativisation.

Section-B

1. Kashmiri literature in the 14th century (Socio-cultural and intellectual background with special reference to Lal Dyad and Sheikhul Alam)
2. Nineteenth century Kashmiri literature (development of various genres: vatsun; ghazal; and mathnavi).
3. Kashmiri literature in the first half of the twentieth century (with special reference to Mahjoor and Azad; various literary influences).
4. Modern Kashmiri literature (with special refernece to the development of the short story, drama, novel and nazm).

PAPER-II

Answers must be written in Kashmiri

Section-A

1. Intensive study of Kashmiri poetry upto the nineteenth century:
   (i) Lal Dyad

(ii) Sheikhul Aalam

(iii) Habba Khatoon

2. Kashmiri poetry: 19th Century

(i) Mahmood Gami (Vatsans)

(ii) Maqbool Shah (Gulrez)

(iii) Rasool Mir (Ghazals)

(iv) Abdul Ahad Nadim (N'at)

(v) Krishanjoo Razdan (Shiv Lagun)

(vi) Sufi Poets (Text in Sanglaab, published by the Deptt. of Kashmiri, University of Kashmir)

3. Twentieth Century Kashmiri poetry (text in Azich Kashir Shairi, published by the Deptt. of Kashmiri, University of Kashmir)

4. Literary criticism and research work: development and various trends.

Section-B

1. An analytical study of the short story in Kashmiri.

(i) *Afsana Majmu'a*, published by the Deptt. of Kashmiri, University of Kashmir.

(ii) *Kashur Afsana Az*, published by the Sahitya Akademi

(iii) *Hamasar Kashur Afsana*, published by the Sahitya Akademi.

The following short story writers only: Akhtar Mohi-ud-Din, Kamil, Hari Krishan Kaul, Hraday Kaul Bharti, Bansi Nirdosh, Gulshan Majid.

2. Novel in Kashmiri:

(i) Mujrim by G.N. Gowhar

(ii) Marun-Ivan Ilyichun, (Kashmiri version of Tolstoy's The Death of Ivan Iiyich (Published by Kashmiri Deptt).

3. Drama in Kashmiri

(i) Natuk Kariv Band, by Hari Krishan Kaul

(ii) Qk Angy Natuk, ed. Motilal Keemu published by Sahitya Akademi.

(iii) Razi Oedipus, tr. Naji Munawar, published by Sahitya Akademi.

4. Kashmiri Folk Literature:

(i) Kashur Luki Theatre by Mohammad Subhan Bhagat, published by Deptt. of Kashmiri, University of Kashmir.

(ii) Kashiry Luki Beeth (all volumes) published by the J & K Cultural Academy.

KONKANI

PAPER-I

Answers must be written in Konkani

Section-A

History of the Konkani Language:

(i) Origin and development of the language and influences on it.

(ii) Major variants of Konkani and their linguistic features.

(iii) Grammatical and lexicographic work in Konkani, including a study of cases, adverbs, indeclinables and voices.

(iv) Old Standard Konkani, new Standard and standardisation problems.

Section-B

History of Konkani literature:

Candidates would be expected to be wellacquainted with Konkani literature and its social and cultural background and consider the problems and issues arising out of them.

(i) History of Konkani literature from its probable source to the present times, with emphasis on its major works, writers and movements.

(ii) Social and cultural background of the making of Konkani literature from time to time.

(iii) Indian and Western influences on Konkani literature from the earliest to modern times.

(iv) Modern literary trends in the various genres and regions including a study of Konkani folklore.

PAPER-II

Answers must be written in Konkani

Textual Criticism of Konkani Literature

The paper will be designed to test the canidate's critical and analytical abilities. Candidates would be expected to be wellacquainted with Konkani Literature and required to have a first-hand reading of the following texts:

Section-A

Prose

1. (a) Konkani Mansagangotri (excluding poetry) ed. by Prof. Olivinho Gomes.

   (b) Old Konkani language and literature-the Portuguese Role.

2. (a) Otmo Denvcharak-a novel by A.V. da Cruz.

   (b) Vadoll ani Varem-A novel by Antonio Pereira.

   (c) Devache Kurpen-a novel by V J P Saldanha.

3. (a) Vajralikhani-Shenoy Goem-bab-An anthology-ed. by Shantaram Varde Valavalikar
   (b) Konkani Lalit Niband-Essays-ed. By Shyam Verenkar
   (c) Teen Dasakam-An lAnthology-ed. by Chandrakant Keni.
4. (a) Demand-Drama-by Pundalik Naik
   (b) Kadambini- A miscellany of modern Prose-ed. by Prof. OJF Gomes & Smt. P.S. Tadkodkar.
   (c) Ratha Tujeo Ghudieo-by Smt. Jayanti Naik.

Section-B

Poetry

1. (a) Ev ani Mori: Poetry by Eduardo Bruno de Souza.
   (b) Abravanchem Yadnyadan-by Luis Mascarenhas.
2. (a) Godde Ramayan-ed.by R.K. Rao
   (b) Ratnahar I &II-collection of poems ed. R.V. Pandit.
3. (a) Zayo Zuyo-poems-Manohar L. Sardessai.
   (b) Kanadi Mati Konkani Kavi-Anthology of Poems-ed. Pratap Naik.
4. (a) Adrushatache Kalle-Poems by Pandurang Bhangui.
   (b) Yaman-Poems by Madhav Borkar

MAITHILI

PAPER-I

History of Maithili Language and its Literature

Answer to be written in Maithili

Part-A

History of Maithili Language

1. Place of Maithili in Indo-European language family.
2. Origin and development of Maithili language. (Sanskrit, Prakrit, Avhatt, Maithili)
3. Periodic division of Maithili Language. (Beginning, Middle era, Modern era)
4. Maithili and its different dialects.
5. Relationship between Maithili and other Eastern languages (Bengali, Assamese, Oriya).
6. Origin and development of Tirhuta Script.
7. Pronouns and Verbs in Maithili Language.

Part-B

History of Maithili Literature

1. Background of Maithili Literature (Religious, economic, social, cultural).
2. Periodic division of Maithili literature.
3. Pre-Vidyapati Literature.
4. Vidyapati and his tradition.
5. Medieval Maithili Drama (Kirtaniya Natak, Ankai Nat, Maithili dramas written in Nepal).
6. Maithili Folk Literature (Folk Tales, Folk Drama, Folk Stories, Folk Songs).
7. Development of different literary forms in modern era.
   - (a) Prabandh-kavya
   - (b) Muktak-kavya
   - (c) Novel
   - (d) Short Story
   - (e) Drama
   - (f) Essay
   - (g) Criticism
   - (h) Memoirs
   - (i) Translation
8. Development of Maithili Magazines and Journals.

PAPER-II

Answers must be written in Maithili

The paper will require first-hand reading of the prescribed texts and will test the critical ability of the candidates.

Part-A

1. Vidyapati Geet-Shati-Publisher: Sahitya Akademi, New Delhi (Lyrics-1 to 50)
2. Govind Das Bhajanavali-Publisher: Maithili Academy, Patna (Lyrics-1 to 25).
3. Krishnajanm – Manbodh
4. Mithilabhasha Ramayana – Chanda Jha (only Sunder-Kand)
5. Rameshwar Charit Mithila Ramayan - Lal Das (only Bal-kand)
6. Keechak-Vadh-Tantra Nath Jha.
7. Datta-Vati-Surendra Jha 'Suman' (only 1st and 2nd Cantos).
8. Chitra-Yatri
9. Samakaleen Maithili Kavita – Publisher : Sahitaya Akademi, New Delhi.

Part-B

10. Varna Ratnakar - Jyotirishwar (only 2nd Kallol)
11. Khattar Kakak Tarang - Hari Mohan Jha.
12. Lorik-Vijaya-Manipadma
13. Prithvi Putra-Lalit
14. Bhaphait Chahak Jinagi-Sudhanshu 'Shekar' Choudhary.
15. Kirti Rajkamlak-Publisher : Maithili Academy, Patna (First Ten Stories only).
16. Katha-Sangrah-Publisher : Maithili Academy, Patna.

MALAYALAM

PAPER-I

Answers must be written in Malayalam

Section-A

Unit 1-Early phase of Malayalam Language

1.1 Various theories: origin from proto Dravidian, Tamil, Sanskrit.

1.2 Relation between Tamil and Malayalam: Six nayas of A.R. Rajarajavarma.

1.3 Pattu school-definition, Ramacharitam, later pattu works-Niranam works and Krishnagatha.

Unit 2-Linguistic features of:

2.1 Manipravalam-definition. Language of early manipravala works-Champu, Sandesakavya, Chandrotsava, minor works. Later Manipravala works-medieval Champu and Attakkatha.

2.2 Folklore-Southern and Northern ballads, Mappila songs.

2.3 Early Malayalam prose-Bhashakautaliyam, Brahmandapuranam, Attaprakaram, Kramadipika and Nambiantamil.

Unit 3-Standardisation of Malayalam:

3.1 Peculairities of the language of Pana, Kilippattu and Tullal.

3.2 Contributions of indigenous and European missionaries to Malayalam.

3.3 Characteristics of contemporary Malayalam : Malayalam as administravie language. Language of scientific and technical literature-media language.

Section-B

Literary History

Unit-4 Ancient and Medieval Literature

4.1 Pattu-Ramacharitam, Niranam works and Krishnagatha.

4.2 Manipravalam-early and medieval manipravala works including attakkatha and champu.

4.3 Folk literature.

4.4 Kilippattu, Tullal and Mahakavya.

Unit 5-Modern Literature-Poerty

5.1 Venmani poets and contemporaries.

5.2 The advent of Romanticism-Poerty of Kavitraya i.e., Asan, Ulloor and Vallathol

5.3 Poetry after Kavitraya.

5.4 Modernism in Malayalam poetry.

Unit 6-Modern Literature-Prose

6.1 Drama

6.2 Novel

6.3 Short story

6.4 Biography, travelogue, essay and criticism.

PAPER-II

Answers must be written in Malayalam

This paper will require first hand reading of the texts prescribed and is designed to test the candidate's critical ability.

Section-A

Unit 1

1.1 Ramacharitam-Patalam 1.

1.2 Kannassaramayanam-Balakandam first 25 stanzas.

1.3 Unnunilisandesam-Purvabhagam 25 slokas including Prastavana

1.4 Mahabharatham Kilippattu-Bhishmaparvam.

Unit 2

2.1 Kumaran Asan-Chintavisthayaya Sita.

2.2 Vailoppilli-Kutiyozhikkal.

2.3 G. Sankara Kurup-Perunthachan.

2.4 N.V. Krishna Variar-Tivandiyile Pattu.

Unit 3

3.1 ONV -Bhumikkoru Charamagitam

3.2 Ayyappa Panicker-Kurukshetram.

3.3 Akkittam-Pandatha Messanthi

3.4 Attur Ravivarma-Megharupan.

Section-B

Unit 4

4.1 O. Chanthu Menon-Indulekha

4.2 Thakazhy-Chemmin.

4.3 O V Vijayan-Khasakkinte Ithihasam.

Unit 5

5.1 MT Vasudevan Nair-Vanaprastham (Collection).

5.2 N S Madhavan-Higvitta (Collection).

5.3 C J. Thomas-1128-il Crime 27.

Unit 6

6.1 Kuttikrishna Marar-Bharataparyatanam

6.2 M. K Sanu-Nakshatrangalute snehabhajanam

6.3 V.T. Bhattathirippad-Kannirum Kinavum.

MANIPURI

PAPER-I

Answers must be written in Manipuri

Section-A

Language

(a) General characteristics of Manipuri Language and history of its development; its importance and status among the TibetoBurman Languages of North-East India; recent development in the study of Manipuri language; evolution and study of old Manipuri script.

(b) Significant features of Manipuri language :

(i) Phonology-Phoneme-vowels, consonants juncture, tone, consonant cluster and its occurrence, syllable-its structure, pattern and types.

(ii) Morphology : Word-class, root and its types; affix and its types; grammatical categories-gender, number, person, case, tense and aspects, process of compounding (samas and sandhi).

(iii) Syntax : Word order : types of sentences, pharse and clause structures.

Section-B

(a) Literary History of Manipuri:

Early period (upto 17th century)-Social and cultural background; Themes, diction and style of the works.

Medieval period (18th and 19th century) Social, religious and political background; Themes, diction and style of the works.

Modern period-Growth of major literary forms; change of Themes, diction and style.

(b) Manipuri Folk Literature: Legend, Folktale, Folksong, Ballad, Proverb and Riddle.

(c) Aspects of Manipuri Culture: Pre-Hindu Manipuri Faith; Advent of Hinduism and the process of syncreticism.

Performing arts-Lai Haraoba, Maha Ras; Indegenous games-Sagol Kangjei, Khong Kangjei, Kang.

PAPER II

Answers must be written in Manipuri

This paper will require first hand reading of the texts prescribed and will be designed to test the candidate's critical ability to assess them.

Section-A

Old and Medieval Manipuri Literature

(a) Old Manipuri Literature

(i) O. Bhogeswar Singh (Ed.) : Numit Kappa

(ii) M. Gourachandra Singh (Ed.) : Thawanthaba Hiran

(iii) N. Khelchandra Singh (Ed.) : Naothingkhong Phambal Kaba

(iv) M. Chandra Singh (Ed.) : Panthoibi Khonggul

(b) Medieval Manipuri Literature :

(i) M. Chandra Singh (Ed.) : Samsok Ngamba

(ii) R.K.Snahal Singh (Ed.) : Ramayana Adi Kanda

(iii) N. Khelchandra SIngh (Ed.) : Dhananjoy Laibu Ningba

(iv) O. Bhogeswar Singh (Ed.) : Chandrakirti Jila Changba

Section-B

Modern Manipuri Literature

Poetry and Epic

1. Poetry:

(a) Manipuri Sheireng (Pub) Manipuri Sahitya Parishad, 1988 (ed.)
Kh. Chaoba Singh : Pi Thadoi, Lamgi Chekla Amada, Loktak
Dr. L. Kamal Singh: Nirjanata, Nirab Rajani
A. Minaketan Singh : Kamalda, Nonggumlakkhoda
L. Samarendra Singh : Ingagi Nong, Mamang Leikai Thambal Satle
E. Nilakanta Singh : Manipur, Lamangnaba
Shri Biren : Tangkhul Hui Th. Ibopishak : Anouba Thunglaba Jiba

(b) Kanchi Sheireng. (Pub) Manipur University 1998 (ed.)
Dr. L. Kamal Singh: Biswa-Prem
Shri Biren : Chaphadraba Laigi Yen
Th. Ibopishak : Norok Patal Prithivi

2. Epic:

(a) A. Dorendrajit Singh : Kansa Bodha

(b) H. Anganghal Singh : Khamba-Thoibi Sheireng (SanSenba, Lei Langba, Shamu Khonggi Bichar)

3. **Drama:**

(a) S. Lalit Singh : Areppa Marup

(b) G.C. Tongbra : Matric Pass

(c) A. Samarendra : Judge Sahebki Imung

(b) Novel, Short-story and Prose

1. **Novel**

(a) Dr. L. Kamal Singh : Madhabi

(b) H. Anganghal Singh : Jahera

(c) H. Guno Singh : Laman

(d) Pacha Meetei : Imphal Amasung, Magi Ishing, Nungsitki Phibam

2. **Short-story**

(a) Kanchi Warimacha (Pub) Manipur University 1997 (ed.)

R.K. Shitaljit Singh : Kamala Kamala

M.K. Binodini : Eigi Thahoudraba Heitup Lalu

Kh. Prakash : Wanom Shareng

(b) Parishadki Khangatlaba Warimacha (Pub) Manipuri Sahitya Parishad 1994 (ed.)

S. Nilbir Shastri : Loukhatpa

R.K. Elangba : Karinunggi

(c) Anouba Manipuri Warimacha (Pub) The Cultural Forum Manipur 1992 (ed.)

N. Kunjamohon Singh : Ijat Tanba

E. Dinamani : Nongthak Khongnang

3. **Prose**

(a) Warenggi Saklon [Due Part (Pub) The Cultural Forum Manipur 1992 (ed.)

Kh. Chaoba Singh : Khamba-Thoibigi Wari Amasung Mahakavya

(b) Kanchi Wareng (Pub) Manipur University 1998 (ed.)

B. Manisana Shastri : Phajaba

Ch. Manihar Singh : Lai-Haraoba

(c) Apunba Wareng. (Pub) Manipur University, 1986 (ed.)

Ch. Pishak Singh : Samaj Amasung, Sanskriti

M.K. Binodini : Thoibidu Warouhouida

Eric Newton : Kalagi Mahousa (translated by I.R. Babu)

(d) Manipuri Wareng (Pub) The Cultural Forum Manipur 1999 (ed.)
S. Krishnamohan Singh : Lan

MARATHI

PAPER-I

Answers must be written in Marathi

Section-A

Language and Folk-lore

(a) **Nature and Functions of Language** (with reference to Marathi) Language as a signifying system : Langue and Parole; Basic functions; Poetic language; Standard Language and dialect; Language variations according to social parameters. Linguistic features of Marathi in thirteenth century and seventeenth century.

(b) Dialects of Marathi: Ahirani; Varhadi; Dangi

(c) Marathi Grammar: Parts of Speech; Case-system; Prayog-vichar (Voice)

(d) **Nature and kinds of Folk-lore** (with special reference to Marathi): Lok-Geet, Lok Katha, Lok Natya

Section-B

History of Literature and Literary Criticism

(a) History of Marathi Literature

1. From beginning to 1818 AD, with special reference to the following : The Mahanubhava writers, the Varkari poets, the Pandit poets, the Shahirs, Bakhar literature.
2. From 1850 to 1990, with special reference to developments in the following major forms : Poetry, Fiction (Novel and Short Story), Drama; and major literary currents and movements, Romantic, Realist, Modernist, Dalit Gramin, Feminist.

(b) Literary Criticism

1. Nature and function of Literature;
2. Evaluation of Literature;
3. Nature, Objectives and Methods of Criticism;
4. Literature, Culture and Society.

PAPER-II

Answers must be written in Marathi

Textual study of prescribed literary works

The paper will require first-hand reading of the texts prescribed and will be designed to test the candidate's critical ability.

Section-A

Prose

1. 'Smritishala'
2. Mahatma Jotiba Phule "Shetkaryacha Asud; 'Sarvajanik Satyadharma'
3. S.V. Ketkar 'Brahmankanya;
4. P.K. Atre 'Sashtang Namaskar'
5. Sharchchandra Muktibodh 'Jana Hey Volatu Jethe'
6. Uddhav Shelke 'Shilan'
7. Baburao Bagul 'Jevha Mi Jaat Chorli Hoti'
8. Gouri Deshpande 'Ekek Paan Galavaya'
9. P.I. Sonkamble 'Athavaninche Pakshi'

Section-B

Poetry

1. Namadevanchi Abhangawani' Ed: Inamdar, Relekar, Mirajkar Modern Book Depot, Pune
2. 'Painjan' Ed : M.N. Adwant Sahitya Prasar Kendra, Nagpur
3. 'Damayanti-Swayamvar' By Raghunath Pandit
4. 'Balakvinchi Kavita' By Balkavi
5. 'Vishakha' By Kusumagraj
6. 'Mridgandh' By Vinda Karandikar
7. 'Jahirnama' By Narayan Surve
8. 'Sandhyakalchya Kavita' By Grace
9. 'Ya Sattet Jeev Ramat Nahi' By Namdev Dhasal

NEPALI

PAPER-I

Answers must be written in Nepali

Section-A

1. History of the origin and development of Nepali as one of the new IndoAryan Languages
2. Fundamentals of Nepali Grammar and phonology:
   (i) Nominal forms and categories: Gender, Number, Case, Adjectives, Pronouns, Avyayas

(ii) Verbal forms and categoriesTense, Aspects, Voice, Roots and Fixes

(iii) Nepali Swara and Vyanjana;

3. Major Dialects of Nepali

4. Standardisation and Modernisation of Nepali with special reference to language movements (viz. Halanta Bahiskar, Jharrovad etc.)

5. Teaching of Nepali language in India; its history and development with special reference to its socio-cultural aspects.

Section-B

1. History of Nepali literature with special reference to its development in India.

2. Fundamental concepts and theories of literature: Kavya/Sahitya, Kavya Prayojan, Literary genres, Shabda Shakti, Rasa, Alankara, Tragedy, Comedy, Aesthetics, Stylistics.

3. Major literary trends and movementsSwachchhandatavad, Yatharthavad, Astitwavad, Ayamik Movement, Contemporary Nepali writings, Postmodernism.

4. Nepali folklores (the following folkform only)- Sawai, Jhyaurey, Selo, Sangini, Lahari.

PAPER-II

Answers must be written in Nepali

This paper will require first hand reading of the texts prescribed below and questions will be designed to test the candidate's critical acumen.

Section-A

1. Santa Jnandil Das-Udaya Lahari

2. Lekhnath Poudyal-Tarun Tapasi: (Vishrams III, V, VI, XII, XV, XVIII only)

3. Agam Singh Giri-Jaleko Pratibimba: Royeko Pratidhwani (The following poems only - rasawako Chichy-ahatsanga Byunjheko Ek Raat, Chhorolai, Jaleko Pratibimba: Royeko Pratidhwani, Hamro Akashmani Pani Hunchha Ujyalo, Tihar).

4. Haribhakta Katuwal-Yo Zindagi Khai Ke Zindagi : (The following poems only - Jeevan : Ek Dristi, Yo Zindagi Khai Ke Zindagi, Akashka tara Ke Tara, Hamilai Nirdho Nasamjha, Khai Many-ata Yahan Atmahutiko Balidan Ko).

5. Balkrishna Sama - Prahlad

6. Manbahadur Mukhia - Andhyaroma Banchneharu (The following OneAct plays only - 'Andhyaroma Banchneharu', 'Suskera').

Section-B

1. Indra Sundas-Sahara
2. Lilbahadur Chhetri-Brahmaputrako Chheuchhau
3. Rupnarayan Sinha-Katha Navaratna (The following stories only-Biteka Kura, Jimmewari Kasko, Dhanamatiko Cinema-Swapna, Vidhwasta Jeevan).
4. Indrabahadur Rai-Vipana Katipaya (The following stories only-Raatbhari Huri Chalyo, Jayamaya Aphumatra Lekha-pani Aipugi, Bhagi, Ghosh Babu, Chhutyaiyo).
5. Sanu Lama-Katha Sampad (The following stories only-Swasni Manchhey, Khani Tarma Ekdin, Phurbale Gaun Chhadyo, Asinapo Manchhey).
6. Laxmi Prasad Devkota-Laxmi Nibandha Sangraha (The following essays only-Sri Ganeshaya Namah, Nepali Sahityako Itihasma Sarvashrestha Purus, Kalpana, Kala Ra Jeevan, Gadha Buddhiman Ki Guru).
7. Ramkrishna Sharma-Das Gorkha (The following essays only-Kavi, Samaj Ra Sahitya, Sahityama Sapekshata, Sahityik Ruchiko Praudhata, Nepali Sahityako Pragati).

ORIYA

PAPER-I

Answers must be written in Oriya

Section-A

History of Oriya Language

1. Origin and development of Oriya Language-Influence of Austric, Dravidian, Perso-Arabic and English on Oriya Language.
2. Phonetics and Phonemics: Vowels, Consonants Principles of changes in Oriya sounds.
3. Morphology: Morphemes (free, bound compound and complex), derivational and inflectional affixes, case inflection, conjugation of verb.
4. Syntax: Kinds of sentences and their transformation, structure of sentences.
5. Semantics-Different types of change in meaning Euphemism.
6. Common errors in spellings, grammatical uses and construction of sentences.
7. Regional variations in Oriya Language (Western, Southern and Northern Oriya) and Dialects (Bhatri and Desia).

Section-B

History of Oriya Literature

1. Historical backgrounds (social, cultural and political) of Oriya Literature of different periods.

2. Ancient epics, ornate kavyas and padavalis.
3. Typical structural forms of Oriya Literature (Koili, Chautisa, Poi, Chaupadi, Champu).
4. Modern trends in poetry, drama short story, novel, essay and literary criticism.

PAPER-II

Answers must be written in Oriya

Critical Study of texts

The paper will require first hand reading of the text and test the critical ability of the candidate.

Section-A

Poetry

Ancient

1. Sãralã Das-Shanti Parva from Mãhãbharãta.
2. Jaganãth Das-Bhãgãbate, XI Skandha-Jadu Avadhuta Sambãda.

Medieval

3. Dinãkrushna Dãs-Rasakallola-(Chhãndas-16 & 34)
4. Upendra Bhanja-Lãvanyabati (Chhãndas-1 & 2)

Modern

5. Rãdhãnãth Rãy-Chandrabhãgã
6. Mãyãdhãr Mãnasinha-Jeevan Chitã
7. Satchidãnanda Routray-Kabitã-1962
8. Ramãkãnta Ratha-Saptama Ritu.

Section-B

Drama

9. Manoranjan Dãs-Kãtha-Ghodã
10. Bijay Mishra-Tata Niranjanã

Novel

11. Fakir Mohan Senãpati-Chhamãna Ãthaguntha
12. Gopinãth Mohanty-Dãnãpãni

Short Story

13. Surendra Mohãnty-Marãlãra Mrityu
14. Manoj Dãs-Laxmira Abhisara

Essay

15. Chittaranjan Dãs-Taranga O Tadit (First five essays).
16. Chandra Sekhar Rath-Mun Satyadhãrma Kahuchhi (First five essays)

PUNJABI

PAPER-I

Answers must be written in Punjabi in Gurumukhi Script

Section-A

(a) Origin of Punjabi language: different stages of development and recent development in Punjabi language; characteristics of Punjabi phonology and the study of its tones : classification of vowels and consonants.

(b) Punjabi morphology: the number-gender system (animate and inanimate), prefixes, affixes and different categories of Post positions: Punjabi word formation: Tatsam. Tad Bhav, forms: Sentence structure, the notion of subject and object in Punjabi: Noun and verb phrases.

(c) Language and dialect : the notions of dialect and idiolect; major dialects of Punjabi; Pothohari, Majhi, Doabi, Malwai, Puadhi; the validity of speech variation on the basis of social stratification, the distinctive features of various dialects with special reference to tones. Language and script; origin and development of Gurmukhi; suitability of Gurmukhi for Punjabi.

(d) Classical background : Nath Jogi Sahit Medieval literature : Gurmat, Sufti, Kissa and Var Janamsakhis.

Section-B

(a) Modern Trends - Mystic, romantic, progressive and neomystic (Vir Singh, Puran Singh, Mohan Singh, Amrita Pritam, Bawa Balwant, Pritam Singh Safeer, J.S. Neki). Experimentalist (Jasbir Singh Ahluwalia, Ravinder Ravi, Ajaib Kamal) Aesthetes (Harbhajan Singh, Tara Singh). Neo-progressive (Pash, Jagtar, Patar)

Origin and Development of Genres

(b) Folk literature - Folk songs, Folk tales. Riddles, Proverbs.

Epic - (Vir Singh, Avtar Singh, Azad Mohan Singh)

Lyric - (Gurus, Sufis and Modern Lyricists-Mohan Singh Amrita Pritam, Shiv Kumar, Harbhajan Singh)

(c) Drama (I.C. Nanda, Harcharan Singh, Balwant Gargi, S.S.Sekhon, Charan Das Sidhu)

Novel (Vir Singh, Nanak Singh, Jaswant Singh Kanwal, K.S. Duggal, Sukhbir, Gurdial Singh, Dalip Kaur Tiwana, Swaran Chandan)

Short Story (Sujan Singh, K.S. Virk, Prem Parkash, Waryam Sandhu).

(d) Socio - cultural Literary influences - Sanskrit, Persian and Western.

Essay - (Puran Singh, Teja Singh, Gurbaksh Singh)

Literary Criticism - (S.S. Sekhon, Attar Singh, Kishan Singh, Harbhajan Singh, Najam Hussain Sayyad).

PAPER-II

Answers must be written in Punjabi in Gurumukhi Script

This paper will require first-hand reading of the texts prescribed and will be designed to test the candidate's critical ability.

Section-A

(a)	Sheikh Farid	The complete Bani as included in the Adi Granth.
(b)	Guru Nanak	Japu Ji Baramah, Asa di Var
(c)	Bulleh Shah	Kafian
(d)	Waris Shah	Heer

Section-B

(a)	Shah Mohammad	Jangnama (JangSinghan te Firangian)
	Dhani Ram Chatrik	Chandan Vari (Poet), Sufi Khana, Nawan Jahan
(b)	Nanak Singh (Novelist)	Chitta Lahu, Pavittar Papi, Ek Mian Do Talwaran
(c)	Gurbaksh Singh (Essayist)	Zindagi-di-Ras, Nawan Shivala, Merian Abhul Yadaan.
	Balraj Sahni (Travelogue)	Mera Roosi Safarnama Mera Pakistani Safarnama
(d)	Balwant Gargi (Dramatist)	Loha Kutt; Dhuni-di-Agg; Sultan Razia
	Sant Singh Sahityarth (Critic)	Sekhon, Parsidh Punjabi Kavi, Punjabi Kav Shiromani

SANSKRIT

PAPER-I

There will be three questions as indicated in the question paper which must be answered in Sanskrit. The remaining questions must be answered either in Sanskrit or in the medium of examination opted by the candidate.

Section-A

1. Significant features of the grammar, with particular stress on Sanjna, Sandhi, Karaka, Samasa, Kartari and Karmani vacyas (voice usages) (to be answered in Sanskrit).

2. (a) Main characteristics of Vedic Sanskrit language.
   (b) Prominent features of classical Sanskrit language.
   (c) Contribution of Sanskrit to linguistic studies.
3. General Knowledge of:
   (a) Literary history of Sanskrit,
   (b) Principal trends of literary criticism
   (c) Ramayana,
   (d) Mahabharata
   (e) The origin and development of literary geners of Mahakavya
   Rupaka (drama)
   Katha
   Akhyayika
   Campu
   Khandakavya
   Muktaka Kavya.

Section-B

4. Essentials of Indian Culture with stress on
   (a) Purusarthas
   (b) Samskaras
   (c) Varnasramavyavastha
   (d) Arts and fine arts
   (e) Technical sciences
5. Trends of Indian Philosophy
   (a) Mimansa
   (b) Vedanta
   (c) Nyaya
   (d) Vaisesika
   (e) Sankhya
   (f) Yoga
   (g) Bauddha
   (h) Jaina
   (i) Carvaka
6. Short Essay in Sanskrit
7. Unseen passage with the questions, to be answered in Sanskrit.

PAPER-II

Question from Group 4 is to be answered in Sanskrit only. Question from Groups 1, 2 and 3 are to be answered either in Sanskrit or in the medium opted by the candidate.

Section-A

General study of the following groups:

Group 1

(a) Raghuvamsam-Kalidasa
(b) Kumarasambhavam-Kalidasa
(c) Kiratarjuniyam-Bharavi
(d) Sisupalavadham-Magha
(e) Naisadhiyacaritam-Sriharsa
(f) Kadambari-Banabhatta
(g) Dasakumaracaritam -Dandin
(h) Sivarajyodayam-S.B. Varnekar

Group 2

(a) Isavasyopanisad
(b) Bhagavadgita
(c) Sundarakanda of Valmiki's Ramayana
(d) Arthasastra of Kautilya

Group 3

(a) Svapnavasavadattam- Bhasa
(b) Abhijnanasakuntalam- Kalidasa
(c) Mricchakatikam- Sudraka
(d) Mudraraksasam- Visakhadatta
(e) Uttararamacaritam- Bhavabhuti
(f) Ratnavali- Sriharshavardhana
(g) Venisamharam- Bhattanarayana

Group 4

Short notes in Sanskrit on the following:

(a) Meghadutam-Kalidasa
(b) Nitisatakam-Bhartrhari
(c) Panchtantra
(d) Rajatarangini-Kalhana
(e) Harsacaritam-Banabhatta
(f) Amarukasatakam-Amaruka
(g) Gitagovindam-Jayadeva

Section-B

Questions from Groups 1 & 2 are to be answered in Sanskrit only. (Questions from Groups 3 & 4 are to be answered in Sanskrit or in the medium opted by the candidate).

This Section will require first hand reading of the following selected texts:

Group 1

(a) Raghuvansam-CantoI, Verses 1 to 10
(b) Kumarasambhavam-Canto I, Verses 1 to 10
(c) Kiratarjuniyam-Canto I, Verses 1 to 10

Group 2

(a) Isavasyopanisad-verses-1, 2, 4, 6, 7, 15 and 18

(b) Bhagavatgita II chapter verses 13 to 25

(c) Sundarakandam of Valmiki Canto 15, Verses 15 to 30 (Geeta Press Edition)

Group 3

(a) Meghadutam-verses 1 to 10

(b) Nitisatakam-Verses 1 to 10 (Edited by D.D. Kosambi Bharatiya Vidya Bhavan Publication)

(c) Kadambari-Sukanaso-padesa (only)

Group 4

(a) Svapnavasavadattam Act VI

(b) Abhijnansakuntalam Act IV verses 15 to 30 (M.R. Kale Edition)

(c) Uttararamacharitam Act 1 verses 31 to 47 (M.R. Kale Edition)

SANTHALI

PAPER-I

Answers must be written in Santhali

Section-A

Part-I History of Santhali Language

1. Main Austric Language family, population and distribution.
2. Grammatical structure of Santhali Language.
3. Important character of Santhali Language : Phonology, Morphology, Syntax, Semantics, Translation, Lexicography.
4. Impact of other languages on Santhali.
5. Standardization of Santhali Language.

Part-II History of Santhali Literature.

1. Literary trends of the following four periods of History of Santhali Literature.
   (a) Ancient literature before 1854.
   (b) Missionary period : Literature between 1855 to 1889 AD.
   (c) Medieval period : Literature between 1890 to 1946 AD.
   (d) Modern period : Literature from 1947 AD to till date.
2. Writing tradition in History of Santhali Literature.

Section-B

Literary forms: Main characteristics, history and development of following literary forms.

Part-I: Folk Literature in Santhali-folk song, folk tale, phrase, idioms, puzzles and Kudum.

Part-II: Modern literature in Santhali

(a) Development of poetry and prominent poets.

(b) Development of prose and prominent writers.

   (i) Novels and prominent Novelists.

   (ii) Stories and prominent story writers.

   (iii) Drama and prominent Dramatist.

   (iv) Criticism and prominent critics.

   (v) Essay, sketches, memoirs, travelogues and prominent writers.

Santhali Writers

Shyam Sunder Hembram, Pandit Raghunath Murmu, Barha Beshra, Sadhu Ramchand Murmu, Narayan Soren 'Toresutam', Sarada Prasad Kisku, Raghunath Tudu, Kalipada Soren, Sakla Soren, Digambar Hansda, Aditya Mitra 'Santhali', Babulal Murmu 'Adivasi', Jadumani Beshra, Arjun Hembram, rishna Chandra Tudu, Rupchand Hansda, Kalendra Nath Mandi, Mahadev Hansda, Gour Chandra Murmu, Thakur Prasad Murmu, Hara Prasad Murmu, Uday Nath Majhi, Parimal Hembram, Dhirendra Nath Baske, Shyam Charan Hembram, Damayanti Beshra, T.K. Rapaj, Boyha Biswanath Tudu.

Part-III: Cultural Heritage of Santhali tradition, customs, festival and rituals (birth, marriage and death).

PAPER-II

Answers must be written in Santhali

Section-A

This paper will require in-depth reading of the following texts and the questions will be designed to test the candidates' criticial ability.

Ancient Literature

Prose

(a) Kherwal Bonso Dhorom Puthi-Majhi Ramdas Tudu "Rasika".

(b) Mare Hapramko Reyak Katha-L.O. Scrafsrud.

(c) Jomsim Binti Lita-Mangal Chandra Turkulumang Soren.

(d) Marang Buru Binti-Kanailal Tudu.

Poetry

(a) Karam Sereng-Nunku Soren.

(b) Devi Dasain Sereng-Manindra Hansda.

(c) Horh Sereng-W.G. Archer.

(d) Baha Sereng-Balaram Tudu

(e) Dong Sereng-Padmashri Bhagwat Murmu 'Thakur'

(f) Hor Sereng-Raghunath Murmu.

(g) Soros Sereng-Babulal Murmu "Adivasi"

(h) More Sin More Nida-Rup Chand Hansda

(i) Judasi Madwa Latar-Tez Narayan Murmu.

Section-B

Modern Literature

Part-I: Poetry

(a) Onorhen Baha Dhalwak-Paul Jujhar Soren.

(b) Asar Binti-Narayan Soren "Tore Sutam"

(c) Chand Mala-Gora Chand Tudu.

(d) Onto Baha Mala-Aditya Mitra "Santhali"

(e) Tiryo Tetang-Hari Har Hansda

(f) Sisirjon Rar-Thakur Prasad Murmu.

Part-II: Novels

(a) Harmawak Ato-R. Karstiars (Translator-R.R. Kisku Rapaz).

(b) Manu Mati-Chandra Mohan Hansda

(c) Ato Orak-Doman Hansda

(d) Ojoy Gada Dhiphre-Nathenial Murmu

Part-III: Stories

(a) Jiyon Gada-Rup Chand Hansda and Jadumani Beshra.

(b) Mayajaal-Doman Sahu, 'Samir' and Padmashri Bhagwat Murmu 'Thakur'

Part-IV: Drama

(a) Kherwar Bir-Pandit Raghunath Murmu

(b) Juri Khatir-Dr. K.C. Tudu

(c) Birsa Bir-Ravi Lal Tudu

Part-V: Biography

Santal Ko Ren Mayam Gohako-Dr. Biswanath Hansda.

SINDHI

PAPER-I

Answers must be written in Sindhi

(Arabic or Devanagari script)

Section-A

1. (a) Origin and evolution of Sindhi language-views of different scholars.

   (b) Significant linguistic features of Sindhi language, including those pertaining to its phonology, morphology and syntax.

   (c) Major dialects of the Sindhi language.

   (d) Sindhi vocabularly-stages of its growth, including those in the pre-partition and post-partition periods.

   (e) Historical study of various Writing Systems (Scripts) of Sindhi.

   (f) Changes in the structure of Sindhi language in India, after partition, due to influence of other languages and social conditions.

Section-B

2. Sindhi literature through the ages in context of socio-cultural conditions in the respective periods:

   (a) Early medieval literature upto 1350 A.D. including folk literature.

   (b) Late medicval period from 1350 A.D. to 1850 A.D.

   (c) Renaissance period from 1850 A.D. to 1947 A.D.

   (d) Modern period from 1947 and onwards (Literary genres in Modern Sindhi literature and experiments in poetry, drama, novel, short story, essay, literary criticism, biography, autobiography, memoirs, and travelogues.)

PAPER-II

Answers must be written in Sindhi

(Arabic or Devanagari script)

This paper will require the first-hand reading of the texts prescribed and will be designed to test the candidates' critical ability.

Section-A

References to context and critical appreciation of the texts included in this section.

(1) Poetry

(a) "Shah Jo Choond Shair": ed. H.I. Sadarangani, Published by Sahitya Akademi (First 100 pages)

(b) "Sachal Jo Choond Kalam" : ed. Kalyan B. Advani Published by Sahitya Akademi (Kafis only)

(c) "Sami-a-ja Choond Sloka" : ed. B.H. Nagrani Published by Sahitya Akademi (First 100 pages)

(d) "Shair-e-Bewas" : by Kishinchand Bewas ("Saamoondi Sipoon" portion only)

(e) "Roshan Chhanvro" : Narayan Shyam

(f) "Virhange Khanpoije Sindhi Shair jee Choond" : ed. H.I. Sadarangani Published by Sahitya Akademi

(2) Drama

(g) "Behtareen Sindhi Natak" (One-act Plays) : Edited by M. Kamal Published by Gujarat Sindhi Academy.

(h) "Kako Kaloomal" (Full-length Play) : by Madan Jumani

Section-B

References to context and critical appreciation of the texts included in this section.

(a) 'Pakheeara Valar Khan Vichhrya' (Novel) : by Gobind Malhi

(b) 'Sat Deenhan' (Novel) : by Krishan Khatwani

(c) 'Choond Sindhi Kahanyoon' (Short Stories) Vol. III. : Edited by Prem Prakash, Published by Sahitya Akademi.

(d) 'Bandhan' (Short Stories) : Sundari Uttamchandani

(e) 'Behtareen Sindhi Mazmoon' (Essays) : Edited by Hiro Thakur, published by Gujarat Sindhi Akademi.

(f) 'Sindhi Tanqeed' (Criticism) : Edited by Harish Vaswani : Published by Sahitya Akademi.

(g) 'Mumhinjee Hayati-a ja Sona Ropa varqa' (Autobiography) : by Popati Hiranandani

(h) "Dr. Choithram Gidwani" (Biography) : by Vishnu Sharma

TAMIL

PAPER-I

Answers must be written in Tamil

Section-A

Part: 1 History of Tamil Language

Major Indian Language Families – The place of Tamil among Indian languages in general and Dravidian in particular-Enumeration and Distribution of Dravidian languages.

The language of Sangam literature – The language of medieval Tamil: Pallava period only-Historical study of Nouns, Verbs, adjectives, adverbs Tense markers and case markers in Tamil.

Borrowing of words from other languages into Tamil-Regional and social dialects-difference between literary and spoken Tamil.

Part: 2 History of Tamil Literature

Tolkappiyam-Sangam Literatue - The division of Akam and puram-The secular characteristics of Sangam Literature-The development of Ethical literatureSilappadikaram and Manimekalai.

Part: 3 Devotional literature (Alwars and Nayanmars)

The bridal mysticism in Alwar hymns-Minor literary forms (Tutu, Ula, Parani, Kuravanji) Social factors for the development of Modern Tamil literature: Novel, Short story and New Poetry-The impact of various political ideologies on modern writings.

Section-B

Part:1 Recent trends in Tamil Studies

Approaches to criticism: Social, psychological, historical and moralistic-the use of criticism-the various techniques in literature; Ullurai, Iraicchi, Thonmam (Myth) Otturuvagam (allegory), Angadam (Satire), Meyppadu, Padimam(image), Kuriyeedu (Symbol), Irunmai (ambiguity)-The concept of comparative literature-the principle of comparative literature.

Part: 2 Folk literature in Tamil

Ballads, Songs, proverbs and riddles-Sociological study of Tamil folklore. Uses of translation. Translation of Tamil works into other languages-Development of journalism in Tamil.

Part: 3 Cultural Heritage of the Tamils

Concept of Love and War-Concept of Aramthe ethical codes adopted by the ancient Tamils in their warfare-customs, beliefs, rituals, modes of worship in the five Thinais. The cultural changes as revealed in post sangam literature-cultural fusion in the medieval period (Jainism & Buddhism). The development of arts and architecture through the ages (Pallavas, later cholas, and Nayaks). The impact of various political, social, religious and cultural movements on Tamil Society. The role of mass media in the cultural change of contemporary Tamil society.

PAPER-II

Answers must be written in Tamil

The paper will require first hand reading of the Text prescribed and will be designed to test the critical ability of the candidate.

Section-A

Part: 1 Ancient Literature

1. Kuruntokai (1-25 poems)
2. Purananurui (182-200 poems)
3. Tirukkural Porutpal : Arasiyalum Amaichiyalum (from Iraimatchi to Avaianjamai)

Part : 2 Epic Literature

1. Silappadikaram: Madhurai Kandam only.
2. Kambaramayanam: Kumbakarunan Vadhai Padalam

Part 3: Devotional Literature

1. Tiruvasagam: Neetthal Vinnappam
2. Tiruppavai: (Full Text)

Section-B

Modern Literature

Part 1: Poetry

1. Bharathiar: Kannan Pattu
2. Bharathidasan: Kudumba Vilakku
3. Naa. Kamarasan: Karuppu Malarkal

Prose

1. Mu. Varadharajanar : Aramum Arasiyalum
2. C N Annadurai : Ye!Thazhntha Tamilagame.

Part : 2 Novel, Short story and Drama

1. Akilon: Chittirappavai
2. Jayakanthan: Gurupeedam
3. Cho: Yarukkum Vetkamillai

Part: 3 Folk Literature

1. Muthuppattan Kathai Edited by Na. Vanamamalai, (Publication: Madurai Kamaraj University)
2. Malaiyaruvi, Edited by Ki. Va Jagannathan (Publication: Saraswathi, Mahal, Thanjavur)

TELUGU

PAPER-I

(Answers must be written in Telugu)

Section-A

Language

1. Place of Telugu among Dravidian languages and its antiquity-Etymological history of Telugu, Tenugu and Andhra.
2. Major linguistic changes in phonological, morphological, grammatical and syntactical levels, from Proto-Dravidian to old Telugu and from old Telugu to Modern Telugu.
3. Evolution of spoken Telugu when compared to classical Telugu-Formal and functional view of Telugu language.
4. Influence of other languages and its impact on Telugu.
5. Modernization of Telugu language.
   (a) Linguistic and literary movements and their role in modernization of Telugu.
   (b) Role of media in modernization of Telugu (Newspapers, Radio, TV etc.)
   (c) Problems of terminology and mechanisms in coining new terms in Telugu in various discourses including scientific and technical.
6. Dialects of Telugu-Regional and social variations and problems of standardization.
7. Syntax-Major divisions of Telugu sentences-simple, complex and compound sentences-Noun and verb predications-Processes of nominlization and relativization-Direct and indirect reporting-conversion processes.
8. Translation-Problems of translation, cultural, social and idiomatic-Methods of translation-Approaches to translation-Literary and other kinds of translation-various uses of translation.

Section-B

Literature

1. Literature in Pre-Nannaya Period-Marga and Desi poetry.
2. Nannaya Period-Historical and literary background of Andhra Mahabharata.
3. Saiva poets and their contribution-Dwipada, Sataka, Ragada, Udaharana.
4. Tikkana and his place in Telugu literature.
5. Errana and his literary works-Nachana Somana and his new approach to poetry.

6. Srinatha and Potana-Their woks and contribution.
7. Bhakti poets in Telugu literature-Tallapaka Annamayya, Ramadasu, Tyagayya.
8. Evolution of prabandhas-Kavya and prabandha.
9. Southern school of Telugu literature-Raghunatha Nayaka, Chemakura Vankatakavi and women poets-Literary forms like yakshagana, prose and padakavita.
10. Modern Telugu Literature and literary forms-Novel, Short Story, Drama, Playlet and poetic forms.
11. Literary Movements: Reformation, Nationalism, Neo-classicism, Romanticism and Progressive, Revolutionary movements.
12. Digambarakavulu, Feminist and Dalit Literature.
13. Main divisions of folk literature-Performing folk arts.

PAPER-II

(Answers must be written in Telugu)

This paper will require first hand reading of the prescribed texts and will be designed to test the candidate's critical ability, which will be in relation to the following approaches.

(i) Aesthetic approach-Rasa, Dhwani, Vakroti and Auchitya-Formal and Structural-Imagery and Symbolism.

(ii) Sociological, Historical, Ideological, Psychological approaches.

Section-A

1. Nannaya-Dushyanta Charitra (Adiparva 4th Canto verses 5-109)
2. Tikkana-Sri Krishna Rayabaramu (Udyoga parva -3rd Canto verses 1144)
3. Srinatha-Guna Nidhi Katha (Kasikhandam, 4th Canto, verses 76-133)
4. Pingali Surana-Sugatri Salinulakatha (Kalapurnodayamu 4 Canto verses, 60-142)
5. Molla-Ramayanamu (Balakanda including avatarika)
6. Kasula Purushothama Kavi-Andhra Nayaka Satakamu

Section-B

7. Gurajada Appa Rao - Animutyalu (Short stories)
8. Viswanatha Satyanarayana-Andhra prasasti
9. Devulapalli Krishna Sastry - Krishnapaksham (excluding Urvasi and Pravasam)
10. Sri Sri - Maha prastanam.
11. Jashuva - Gabbilam (Part I)

12. C. Narayana Reddy - Karpuravasanta rayalu.
13. Kanuparti Varalakshmamma - Sarada lekhalu (Part I)
14. Atreya - N.G.O.
15. Racha konda Visswanatha Sastry - Alpajaeevi.

URDU

PAPER-I

(Answers must be written in Urdu)

Section-A

Development of Urdu Language

(a) Development of Indo-Aryan (i) Old IndoAryan (ii) Middle Indo Aryan (iii) New Indo Aryan

(b) Western Hindi and its dialects Brij Bhasha Khadi Boli, Haryanavi Kannauji, Bundeli-Theories about the origin of Urdu Language

(c) Dakhani Urdu-Origin and development, its significant linguistic features.

(d) Social and Cultural roots of Urdu language-and its distinctive features.

Script, Phonology, Morphology, Vocabulary.

Section-B

(a) Genres and their development:
   (i) Poetry : Ghazal, Masnavi, Qasida, Marsia, Rubai, Jadid Nazm,
   (ii) Prose : Novel, Short Story, Dastan, Drama, Inshaiya, Khutoot, Biography.

(b) Significant features of:
   (i) Deccani, Delhi and Lucknow schools
   (ii) Sir Syed movement, Romantic movement, Progressive movement, Modernism.

(c) Literary Criticism and its development with reference to Hali, Shibli, Kaleemuddin Ahmad, Ehtisham Hussain, Ale-Ahmad Suroor.

(d) Essay writing (covering literary and imaginative topics)

PAPER-II

(Answers must be written in Urdu)

This paper will require first hand reading of the texts prescribed and will be designed to test the candidate's critical ability.

Section-A

1.	Mir Amman	Bagho-Babar
2.	Ghalib	Intikhab-e-Khutoot-e-Ghalib
3.	Mohd. Husain Azad	Nairang-e-Khayal
4.	Prem Chand	Godan
5.	Rajendra Singh	Apne Dukh Mujhe Bedi Dedo
6.	Abul Kalam Azad	Ghubar-e-Khatir

Section-B

1.	Mir	Intikhab-e-Kalam-e-Mir (Ed. Abdul Haq.)
2.	Mir Hasan	Sahrul Bayan
3.	Ghalib	Diwan-e-Ghalib
4.	Iqbal	Bal-e-Jibrail
5.	Firaq	Gul-e-Naghma
6.	Faiz	Dast-e-Saba
7.	Akhtruliman	Bint-e-Lamhat

MANAGEMENT

The candidate should make a study of the concept and development of management as science and art drawing upon the contributions of leading thinkers of management and apply the concepts to the real life of government and business decision making keeping in view the changes in the strategic and operative environment.

PAPER–I

1. Managerial Function and Process

Concept and Foundations of Management, Evolution of Management Thoughts; Managerial Functions – Planning, Organizing, Controlling; Decision making; Role of Manager, Managerial skills; Entrepreneurship; Management of innovation; Managing in a global environment, Flexible Systems Management; Social responsibility and managerial ethics; Process and customer orientation; Managerial processes on direct and indirect value chain.

2. Organisational Behaviour and Design

Conceptual model of organization behaviour; The individual processes – personality, values and attitude, perception, motivation, learning and reinforcement, work stress and stress management; The dynamics of organization behaviour – power and politics, conflict and negotia-tion, leadership process and styles, communication; The Organizational Processes - decision making, job design; Classical, Neoclassical and Contingency approaches to organizational design; Organizational theory and design – organizational culture, managing cultural diversity, learning organization; organizational change and development; Knowledge Based Enterprise – systems and processes; Networked and virtual organizations.

3. Human Resource Management

HR challenges; HRM functions; The future challenges of HRM; Strategic Management of human resources; Human resource planning; Job analysis; Job evaluation; Recruitment and selection; Training and development; Promotion and transfer; Performance management; Compensation management and benefits; Employee morale and productivity; Management of organizational climate and Industrial relations; Human resources accounting and audit; Human resource information system; International human resource management.

4. Accounting for Managers

Financial accounting – concept, importance and scope, generally accepted accounting principles, preparation of financial tatements with special reference to analysis of a balance sheet and measurement of business income, inventory valuation and depreciation, financial statement analysis, fund flow analysis, the statement of cash flows; Management accounting – concept, need, importance and scope; Cost accounting – records and processes, cost ledger and control accounts, reconciliation and integration between financial and cost accounts; Overhead cost and control, Job and process costing, Budget and budgetary control, Performance budgeting, Zero-base budgeting, relevant costing and costing for decision-making, standard costing and variance analysis, marginal costing and absorption costing.

5. Financial Management

Goals of finance function; Concepts of value and return; Valuation of bonds and shares; Management of working capital: Estimation and financing; Management of cash, receivables, inventory and current liabilities; Cost of capital; Capital budgeting; Financial and operating leverage; Design of capital structure: theories and practices; Shareholder value creation: dividend policy, corporate financial policy and strategy, management of corporate distress and restructuring strategy; Capital and money markets: institutions and instruments; Leasing, hire purchase and venture capital; Regulation of capital market; Risk and return: portfolio theory; CAPM; APT; Financial derivatives: option, futures, swap; Recent reforms in financial sector.

6. Marketing Management

Concept, evolution and scope; Marketing strategy formulation and components of marketing plan; Segmenting and targeting the market; Positioning and differentiating the market offering; Analyzing competition; Analyzing consumer markets; Industrial buyer behaviour; Market research; Product strategy; Pricing strategies; Designing and managing Marketing channels; Integrated marketing communications; Building customer satisfaction, Value and retention; Services and non-profit marketing; Ethics in marketing; Consumer protection; Internet marketing; Retail management; Customer relationship management; Concept of holistic marketing.

PAPER–II

1. Quantitative Techniques in Decision Making

Descriptive statistics – tabular, graphical and numerical methods, introduction to probability, discrete and continuous probability distributions, inferential statistics-sampling distributions, central limit theorem, hypothesis testing for differences between means and proportions, inference about population variances, Chisquare and ANOVA, simple correlation and regression, time series and forecasting, decision theory, index numbers; Linear programming – problem formulation, simplex method and graphical solution, sensitivity analysis.

2. Production and Operations Management

Fundamentals of operations management; Organizing for production; Aggregate production planning, capacity planning, plant design: process planning, plant size and scale of operations, Management of facilities; Line balancing; Equipment replacement and maintenance; Production control; Supply chain management – vendor evaluation and audit; Quality management; Statistical process control, Six Sigma; Flexibility and agility in manufacturing systems; World class manufacturing; Project management concepts, R&D management, Management of service operations; Role and importance of materials management, value analysis, make or buy decision; Inventory control, MRP; Waste management.

3. Management Information System

Conceptual foundations of information systems; Information theory; Information resource management; Types of information systems; Systems development – Overview of systems and design; System development management life-cycle, Designing for online and distributed environments; Implementation and control of project; Trends in information technology; Managing data resources - Organising data; DSS and RDBMS; Enterprise Resource Planning (ERP), Expert systems, e-Business architecture, e-Governance; Information systems planning, Flexibility in information systems; User involvement; Evaluation of information systems.

4. Government Business Interface

State participation in business, Interaction between Government, Business and different Chambers of Commerce and Industry in India; Government's policy with regard to Small Scale Industries; Government clearances for establishing a new enterprise; Public Distribution System; Government control over price and distribution; Consumer Protection Act (CPA) and The Role of voluntary organizations in protecting consumers' rights; New Industrial Policy of the Government: liberalization, deregulation and privatisation; Indian planning system; Government policy concerning development of Backward areas/regions;

The Responsibilities of the business as well as the Government to protect the environment; Corporate Governance; Cyber Laws.

5. Strategic Management

Business policy as a field of study; Nature and scope of strategic management, Strategic intent, vision, objectives and policies; Process of strategic planning and implementation; Environmental analysis and internal analysis; SWOT analysis; Tools and techniques for strategic analysis – Impact matrix: The experience curve, BCG matrix, GEC mode, Industry analysis, Concept of value chain; Strategic profile of a firm; Framework for analysing competition; Competitive advantage of a firm; Generic competitive strategies; Growth strategies – expansion, integration and diversification; Concept of core competence, Strategic flexibility; Reinventing strategy; Strategy and structure; Chief Executive and Board; Turnaround management; Management of strategic change; Strategic alliances, Mergers and Acquisitions; Strategy and corporate evolution in the Indian context.

6. International Business

International Business Environment: Changing composition of trade in goods and services; India's Foreign Trade: Policy and trends; Financing of International trade; Regional Economic Cooperation; FTAs; Internationalisation of service firms; International production; Operation Management in International companies; International Taxation; Global competitiveness and technological developments; Global e-Business; Designing global organisational structure and control; Multicultural management; Global business strategy; Global marketing strategies; Export Management; Export- Import procedures; Joint Ventures; Foreign Investment: Foreign direct investment and foreign portfolio investment; Cross-border Mergers and Acquisitions; Foreign Exchange Risk Exposure Management; World Financial Markets and International Banking; External Debt Management; Country Risk Analysis.

MATHEMATICS

PAPER-I

(1) Linear Algebra

Vector spaces over R and C, linear dependence and independence, subspaces, bases, dimension; Linear transformations, rank and nullity, matrix of a linear transformation. Algebra of Matrices; Row and column reduction, Echelon form, congruence's and similarity; Rank of a matrix; Inverse of a matrix; Solution of system of linear equations; Eigenvalues and eigenvectors, characteristic polynomial, Cayley-Hamilton theorem, Symmetric, skew-symmetric, Hermitian, skew-Hermitian, orthogonal and unitary matrices and their eigenvalues.

(2) Calculus

Real numbers, functions of a real variable, limits, continuity, differentiability, meanvalue theorem, Taylor's theorem with remainders, indeterminate forms, maxima and minima, asymptotes; Curve tracing; Functions of two or three variables: limits, continuity, partial derivatives, maxima and minima, Lagrange's method of multipliers, Jacobian. Riemann's definition of definite integrals; Indefinite integrals; Infinite and improper integrals; Double and triple integrals (evaluation techniques only); Areas, surface and volumes.

(3) Analytic Geometry

Cartesian and polar coordinates in three dimensions, second degree equations in three variables, reduction to canonical forms, straight lines, shortest distance between two skew lines; Plane, sphere, cone, cylinder, paraboloid, ellipsoid, hyperboloid of one and two sheets and their properties.

(4) Ordinary Differential Equations

Formulation of differential equations; Equations of first order and first degree, integrating factor; Orthogonal trajectory; Equations of first order but not of first degree, Clairaut's equation, singular solution.

Second and higher order linear equations with constant coefficients, complementary function, particular integral and general solution.

Second order linear equations with variable coefficients, Euler-Cauchy equation; Determination of complete solution when one solution is known using method of variation of parameters. Laplace and Inverse Laplace transforms and their properties; Laplace transforms of elementary functions. Application to initial value problems for 2nd order linear equations with constant coefficients.

(5) Dynamics & Statics

Rectilinear motion, simple harmonic motion, motion in a plane, projectiles; constrained motion; Work and energy, conservation of energy; Kepler's laws, orbits under central forces. Equilibrium of a system of particles; Work and potential energy, friction; common catenary; Principle of virtual work; Stability of equilibrium, equilibrium of forces in three dimensions.

(6) Vector Analysis

Scalar and vector fields, differentiation of vector field of a scalar variable; Gradient, divergence and curl in cartesian and cylindrical coordinates; Higher order derivatives; Vector identities and vector equations.

Application to geometry: Curves in space, Curvature and torsion; Serret-Frenet's formulae. Gauss and Stokes' theorems, Green's identities.

PAPER - II

(1) Algebra

Groups, subgroups, cyclic groups, cosets, Lagrange's Theorem, normal subgroups, quotient groups, homomorphism of groups, basic isomorphism theorems, permutation groups, Cayley's theorem. Rings, subrings and ideals, homomorphisms of rings; Integral domains, principal ideal domains, Euclidean domains and unique factorization domains; Fields, quotient fields.

(2) Real Analysis

Real number system as an ordered field with least upper bound property; Sequences, limit of a sequence, Cauchy sequence, completeness of real line; Series and its convergence, absolute and conditional convergence of series of real and complex terms, rearrangement of series.

Continuity and uniform continuity of functions, properties of continuous functions on compact sets. Riemann integral, improper integrals; Fundamental theorems of integral calculus. Uniform convergence, continuity, differentiability and integrability for sequences and series of functions; Partial derivatives of functions of several (two or three) variables, maxima and minima.

(3) Complex Analysis

Analytic functions, Cauchy-Riemann equations, Cauchy's theorem, Cauchy's integral formula, power series representation of an analytic function, Taylor's series; Singularities; Laurent's series; Cauchy's residue theorem; Contour integration.

(4) Linear Programming

Linear programming problems, basic solution, basic feasible solution and optimal solution; Graphical method and simplex method of solutions; Duality. Transportation and assignment problems.

(5) Partial Differential Equations

Family of surfaces in three dimensions and formulation of partial differential equations; Solution of quasilinear partial differential equations of the first order, Cauchy's method of characteristics; Linear partial differential equations of the second order with constant coefficients, canonical form; Equation of a vibrating string, heat equation, Laplace equation and their solutions.

(6) Numerical Analysis and Computer Programming

Numerical methods: Solution of algebraic and transcendental equations of one variable by bisection, Regula-Falsi and Newton-Raphson methods; solution of system of linear equations by Gaussian elimination and Gauss-Jordan (direct), Gauss-Seidel(iterative) methods. Newton's (forward and backward) interpolation, Lagrange's interpolation. Numerical integration: Trapezoidal rule, Simpson's rules, Gaussian quadrature formula. Numerical solution of ordinary differential equations: Euler and Runga Kutta-methods. Computer Programming: Binary system; Arithmetic and logical operations on numbers; Octal and Hexadecimal systems; Conversion to and from decimal systems; Algebra of binary numbers.

Elements of computer systems and concept of memory; Basic logic gates and truth tables, Boolean algebra, normal forms.

Representation of unsigned integers, signed integers and reals, double precision reals and long integers.

Algorithms and flow charts for solving numerical analysis problems.

(7) Mechanics and Fluid Dynamics

Generalized coordinates; D' Alembert's principle and Lagrange's equations; Hamilton equations; Moment of inertia; Motion of rigid bodies in two dimensions. Equation of continuity; Euler's equation of motion for inviscid flow; Stream-lines, path of a particle; Potential flow; Two-dimensional and axisymmetric motion; Sources and sinks, vortex motion; Navier-Stokes equation for a viscous fluid.

MECHANICAL ENGINEERING

PAPER-I

1. Mechanics

1.1 Mechanics of rigid bodies

Equations of equilibrium in space and its application; first and second moments of area; simple problems on friction; kinematics of particles for plane motion; elementary particle dynamics.

1.2 Mechanics of deformable bodies

Generalized Hooke's law and its application; design problems on axial stress, shear stress and bearing stress; material properties for dynamic loading; bending shear and stresses in beams;. determination of principle stresses and strains – analytical and graphical; compound and combined stresses; bi-axial stresses - thin walled pressure vessel; material behaviour and design factors for dynamic load; design of circular shafts for bending and torsional load only; deflection of beam for statically determinate problems; theories of failure.

2. Engineering Materials

Basic concepts on structure of solids; common ferrous and non-ferrous materials and their applications; heattreatment of steels; non-metals- plastics, ceramics, composite materials and nano-materials.

3. Theory of Machines

Kinematic and dynamic analysis of plane mechanisms. Cams, Gears and epicyclic gear trains, flywheels, governors, balancing of rigid rotors, balancing of single and multicylinder engines, linear vibration analysis of mechanical systems (single degree of freedom), Critical speeds and whirling of shafts.

4. Manufacturing Science

4.1 Manufacturing Process

Machine tool engineering – Merchant's force analysis; Taylor's tool life equation; conventional machining; NC and CNC machining process; jigs and fixtures.

Non-conventional machining – EDM, ECM, ultrasonic, water jet machining etc; application of lasers and plasmas; energy rate calculations.

Forming and welding processes- standard processes.

Metrology-concept of fits and tolerances; tools and gauges; comparators; inspection of length; position; profile and surface finish.

4.2. Manufacturing Management

System design: factory location- simple OR models; plant layout - methods based; applications of engineering economic analysis and break- even analysis for product selection, process selection and capacity planning; predetermined time standards.

System planning; forecasting methods based on regression and decomposition, design and balancing of multi model andstochastic assembly lines; inventory management – probabilistic inventory models for order time and order quantity determination; JIT systems; strategic sourcing; managing inter plant logistics.

System operations and control: Scheduling algorithms for job shops; applications of statistical methods for product and process quality control - applications of control charts for mean, range, percent defective, number of defectives and defects per unit; quality cost systems; management of resources, organizations and risks in projects.

System improvement: Implementation of systems, such as total quality management, developing and managing flexible, lean and agile organizations.

PAPER-II

1. Thermodynamics, Gas Dynamics and Turbine:

1.1 Basic concept of First – law and second law of Thermodynamics; concept of entropy and reversibility; availability and unavailability and irreversibility.

1.2 Classification and properties of fluids; incompressible and compressible fluids flows; effect of Mach number and compressibility; continuity momentum and energy equations; normal and oblique shocks; one dimensional isentropic flow; flow or fluids in duct with frictions that transfer.

1.3 Flow through fans, blowers and compressors; axial and centrifugal flow configuration; design of fans and compressors; single problems compresses and turbine cascade; open and closed cycle gas turbines; work done in the gas turbine; reheat and regenerators.

2. Heat Transfer

2.1 Conduction heat transfer- general conduction equation - Laplace, Poisson and Fourier equations; Fourier law of conduction; one dimensional steady state heat conduction applied to simple wall, solid and hollow cylinder & spheres.

2.2 Convection heat transfer-Newton's law of convection; free and forces convection; heat transfer during laminar and turbulent flow of an incompressible fluid over a flat plate; concepts of Nusselt number, hydrodynamic and thermal boundary layer their thickness; Prandtl number; analogy between heat and momentum transferReynolds, Colbum, Prandtl analogies; heat transfer during laminar and turbulent flow through horizontal tubes; free convection from horizontal and vertical plates.

2.3 Black body radiation - basic radiation laws such as Stefan-Boltzman, Planck distribution, Wein's displacement etc.

2.4 Basic heat exchanger analysis; classification of heat exchangers.

3. I .C. Engines

3.1 Classification, thermodynamic cycles of operation; determination of break power, indicated power, mechanical efficiency, heat balance sheet, interpretation of performance characteristics, petrol, gas and diesel engines.

3.2 Combustion in SI and CI engines, normal and abnormal combustion; effect of working parameters on knocking, reduction of knocking; Forms of combustion chamber for SI and CI engines; rating of fuels; additives; emission.

3.3 Different systems of IC engines- fuels; lubricating; cooling and transmission systems. Alternate fuels in IC engines.

4. Steam Engineering

4.1 Steam generation- modified Rankine cycle analysis; Modern steam boilers; steam at critical and supercritical pressures; draught equipment; natural and artificial draught; boiler fuels solid, liquid and gaseous fuels. Steam turbines - principle; types; compounding; impulse and reaction turbines; axial thrust.

4.2 Steam nozzles- flow of steam in convergent and divergent nozzle; pressure at throat for maximum discharge with different initial steam conditions such as wet, saturated and superheated, effect of variation of back pressure; supersaturated flow of steam in nozzles, Wilson line.

4.3 Rankine cycle with internal and external irreversibility; reheat factor; reheating and regeneration, methods of governing; back pressure and pass out turbines.

4.4 Steam power plants - combined cycle power generation; heat recovery steam generators (HRSG) fired and unfired, co- generation plants.

5. Refrigeration and air-conditioning

5.1 Vapour compression refrigeration cycle - cycle on p-H & T-s diagrams; eco-friendly refrigerants -R134a,123; Systems like evaporators, condensers, compressor, expansion devices. Simple vapour absorption systems.

5.2 Psychrometry - properties; processes; charts; sensible heating and cooling; humidification and dehumidification effective temperature; air-conditioning load calculation; simple duct design.

MEDICAL SCIENCE

PAPER-I

1. Human Anatomy

Applied anatomy including blood and nerve supply of upper and lower limbs and joints of shoulder, hip and knee.

Gross anatomy, blood supply and lymphatic drainage of tongue, thyroid, mammary gland, stomach, liver, prostate, gonads and uterus.

Applied anatomy of diaphragm, perineum and inguinal region.

Clinical anatomy of kidney, urinary bladder, uterine tubes, vas deferens.

Embryology: Placenta and placental barrier. Development of heart, gut, kidney, uterus, ovary, testis and their common congenital abnormalities.

Central and peripheral autonomic nervous system : Gross and clinical anatomy of ventricles of brain, circulation of cerebrospinal fluid; Neural pathways and lesions of cutaneous sensations, hearing and vision; Cranial nerves, distribution and clinical significance; Components of autonomic nervous system.

2. Human Physiology

Conduction and transmission of impulse, mechanism of contraction, neuromuscular transmission, reflexes, control of equilibrium, posture and muscle tone, descending pathways, functions of cerebellum, basal ganglia, Physiology of sleep and consciousness.

Endocrine system: Mechanism of action of hormones, formation, secretion, transport, metabolism, function and regulation of secretion of pancreas and pituitary gland.

Physiology of reproductive system: Menstrual cycle, lactation, pregnancy.

Blood: Development, regulation and fate of blood cells.

Cardio-vascular, cardiac output, blood pressure, regulation of cardiovascular functions;

3. Biochemistry

Organ function tests-liver, kidney, thyroid Protein synthesis.

Vitamins and minerals.

Restriction fragment length polymorphism (RFLP).

Polymerase chain reaction (PCR).

Radio - immunoassays (RIA).

4. Pathology

Inflammation and repair, disturbances of growth and cancer, Pathogenesis and histopathology of rheumatic and ischemic heart disease and diabetes mellitus. Differentiation between benign, malignant, primary and metastatic malignancies, Pathogenesis and histopathology of bronchogenic carcinoma, carcinoma breast, oral cancer, cancer cervix, leukemia, Etiology, pathogenesis and histopathology of cirrhosis liver, glomerulonephritis, tuberculosis, acute osteomyelitis.

5. Microbiology

Humoral and cell mediated immunity Diseases caused by and laboratory diagnosis of:

- Meningococcus, Salmonella
- Shigella, Herpes, Dengue, Polio
- HIV/AIDS, Malaria, E. Histolytica, Giardia
- Candida, Cryptococcus, Aspergillus

6. Pharmacology

Mechanism of action and side effects of the following drugs:

- Antipyretics and analgesics, Antibiotics, Antimalaria; Antikala-azar, Antidiabetics
- Antihypertensive, Antidiuretics, General and cardiac vasodilators, Antiviral, Antiparasitic, Antifungal, Immunosuppressants
- Anticancer

7. Forensic Medicine and Toxicology

Forensic examination of injuries and wounds; Examination of blood and seminal stains; poisoning, sedative overdose, hanging, drowning, burns, DNA and finger print study.

PAPER-II

1. General Medicine

Etiology, clinical features, diagnosis and principles of management (including prevention) of: - Tetanus, Rabies, AIDS, Dengue, Kala-azar, Japanese Encephalitis.

Etiology, clinical features, diagnosis and principles of management of: Ischaemic heart disease, pulmonary embolism.

Bronchial asthma. Pleural effusion, tuberculosis, Malabsorption syndromes, acid peptic diseases, Viral hepatitis and cirrhosis of liver.

Glomerulonerphritis and pyelonephritis, renal failure, nephrotic syndrome, renovascular hypertension, complications of diabetes mellitus, coagulation disorders, leukemia, Hypo and hyper thyrodism, meningitis and encephalitis.

Imaging in medical problems, ultrasound, echocardiogram, CT scan, MRI. Anxiety and Depressive Psychosis and schizophrenia and ECT.

2. Pediatrics

Immunization, Baby friendly hospital, congenital cyanotic heart disease, respiratory distress syndrome, broncho - pneumonias, kernicterus. IMNCI classification and management, PEM grading and management. ARI and Diarrhea of under five and their management.

3. Dermatology

Psoriasis, Allergic dermatitis, scabies, eczema, vitiligo, Stevan Johnson's syndrome, Lichen Planus.

4. General Surgery

Clinical features, causes, diagnosis and principles of management of cleft palate, harelip.

Laryngeal tumor, oral and esophageal tumors.

Peripheral arterial diseases, varicose veins, coarctation of aorta.

Tumors of Thyroid, Adrenal Glands.

Abscess, cancer, fibroadenoma and adenosis of breast.

Bleeding peptic ulcer, tuberculosis of bowel, ulcerative colitis, cancer stomach.

Renal mass, cancer Prostate. Haemothorax, stones of Gall bladder, Kidney, Ureter and Urinary Bladder.

Management of surgical conditions of Rectum, Anus and Anal canal, Gall bladder and Bile ducts.

Splenomegaly, cholecystitis, portal hypertension, liver abscess, peritonitis, carcinoma head of pancreas.

Fractures of spine, Colles' fracture and bone tumors. Endoscopy.

Laprascopic Surgery.

5. Obstetrics and Gynaecology including Family Planning

Diagnosis of pregnancy

Labour management, complications of 3rd stage, Antepartum and postpartum hemorrhage, resuscitation of the newborn, Management of abnormal lie and difficult labour, Management of small for date or premature newborn. Diagnosis and management of anemia. Preeclampsia and Toxaemias of pregnancy, Management of Post menopausal Syndrome. Intra-uterine devices, pills, tubectomy and vasectomy. Medical termination of pregnancy including legal aspects.

Cancer cervix

Leucorrhoea, pelvic pain, infertility, dysfunctional uterine bleeding (DUB), amenorrhoea, Fibroid and prolapse of uterus.

6. Community Medicine (Preventive and Social Medicine)

Principles, methods, approach and measurements of Epidemiology.

Nutrition, nutritional diseases / disorders & Nutrition Programmes.

Health information Collection, Analysis and Presentation.

Objectives, components and critical analysis of National programmes for control/ eradication of:

Malaria, Kala-azar, Filaria and Tuberculosis, HIV/AIDS, STDs and Dengue Critical appraisal of Health care delivery system.

Health management and administration: Techniques, Tools, Programme Implementation and Evaluation. Objective, Component, Goals and Status of Reproductive and Child Health, National Rural Health Mission and Millennium Development Goals.

Management of hospital and industrial waste.

PHILOSOPHY

PAPER-I

History and Problems of Philosophy

1. Plato and Aristotle: Ideas; Substance; Form and Matter; Causation; Actuality and Potentiality.
2. Rationalism (Descartes, Spinoza, Leibniz): Cartesian Method and Certain Knowledge; Substance; God; Mind-Body Dualism; Determinism and Freedom.
3. Empiricism (Locke, Berkeley, Hume): Theory of Knowledge; Substance and Qualities; Self and God; Scepticism.
4. Kant: Possibility of Synthetic a priori Judgments; Space and Time; Categories; Ideas of Reason; Antinomies; Critique of Proofs for the Existence of God
5. Hegel: Dialectical Method; Absolute Idealism
6. Moore, Russell and Early Wittgenstein: Defence of Commonsense; Refutation of Idealism; Logical Atomism; Logical Constructions; Incomplete Symbols; Picture Theory of Meaning; Saying and Showing.
7. Logical Positivism: Verification Theory of Meaning; Rejection of Metaphysics; Linguistic Theory of Necessary Propositions.
8. Later Wittgenstein: Meaning and Use; Language-games; Critique of Private Language.
9. Phenomenology (Husserl): Method; Theory of Essences; Avoidance of Psychologism.

10. Existentialism (Kierkegaard, Sartre, Heidegger): Existence and Essence; Choice, Responsibility and Authentic Existence; Being-in-the –world and Temporality.
11. Quine and Strawson: Critique of Empiricism; Theory of Basic Particulars and Persons.
12. Cârvâka : Theory of Knowledge; Rejection of Transcendent Entities.
13. Jainism: Theory of Reality; Saptabhaòginaya; Bondage and Liberation.
14. Schools of Buddhism: Pratîtyasamutpâda; Ksanikavada, Nairâtmyavâda.
15. Nyâya- Vaiúesika: Theory of Categories; Theory of Appearance; Theory of Pramâna; Self, Liberation; God; Proofs for the Existence of God; Theory of Causation; Atomistic Theory of Creation.
16. Sâmkhya: Prakrti; Purusa; Causation; Liberation.
17. Yoga: Citta; Cittavrtti; Klesas; Samadhi; Kaivalya.
18. Mimâmsâ: Theory of Knowledge.
19. Schools of Vedânta: Brahman; Îúvara; Âtman; Jiva; Jagat; Mâyâ; Avidyâ; Adhyâsa; Moksa; Aprthaksiddhi; Pancavidhabheda
20. Aurobindo: Evolution, Involution; Integral Yoga.

PAPER–II

Socio-Political Philosophy

1. Social and Political Ideals: Equality, Justice, Liberty.
2. Sovereignty: Austin, Bodin, Laski, Kautilya.
3. Individual and State: Rights; Duties and Accountability.
4. Forms of Government: Monarchy; Theocracy and Democracy.
5. Political Ideologies: Anarchism; Marxism and Socialism.
6. Humanism; Secularism; Multiculturalism.
7. Crime and Punishment: Corruption, Mass Violence, Genocide, Capital Punishment.
8. Development and Social Progress.
9. Gender Discrimination: Female Foeticide, Land and Property Rights; Empowernment.
10. Caste Discrimination: Gandhi and Ambedkar

Philosophy of Religion

1. Notions of God: Attributes; Relation to Man and the World. (Indian and Western).

2. Proofs for the Existence of God and their Critique (Indian and Western).
3. Problem of Evil.
4. Soul: Immortality; Rebirth and Liberation.
5. Reason, Revelation and Faith.
6. Religious Experience: Nature and Object (Indian and Western).
7. Religion without God.
8. Religion and Morality.
9. Religious Pluralism and the Problem of Absolute Truth.
10. Nature of Religious Language: Analogical and Symbolic; Cognitivist and Noncognitive.

PHYSICS

PAPER-I

1.

(a) **Mechanics of Particles:** Laws of motion; conservation of energy and momentum, applications to rotating frames, centripetal and Coriolis accelerations; Motion under a central force; Conservation of angular momentum, Kepler's laws; Fields and potentials; Gravitational field and potential due to spherical bodies, Gauss and Poisson equations, gravitational self-energy; Two-body problem; Reduced mass; Rutherford scattering; Centre of mass and laboratory reference frames.

(b) **Mechanics of Rigid Bodies:** System of particles; Centre of mass, angular momentum, equations of motion; Conservation theorems for energy, momentum and angular momentum; Elastic and inelastic collisions; Rigid body; Degrees of freedom, Euler's theorem, angular velocity, angular momentum, moments of inertia, theorems of parallel and perpendicular axes, equation of motion for rotation; Molecular rotations (as rigid bodies); Di and tri-atomic molecules; Precessional motion; top, gyroscope.

(c) **Mechanics of Continuous Media:** Elasticity, Hooke's law and elastic constants of isotropic solids and their inter-relation; Streamline (Laminar) flow, viscosity, Poiseuille's equation, Bernoulli's equation, Stokes' law and applications.

(d) **Special Relativity:** Michelson-Morley experiment and its implications; Lorentz transformations-length contraction, time dilation, addition of relativistic velocities, aberration and Doppler effect, mass-energy relation, simple applications to a decay process; Four dimensional momentum vector; Covariance of equations of physics.

2. Waves and Optics

(a) **Waves:** Simple harmonic motion, damped oscillation, forced oscillation and resonance; Beats; Stationary waves in a string; Pulses and wave packets;

Phase and group velocities; Reflection and Refraction from Huygens' principle.

(b) **Geometrical Optics:** Laws of reflection and refraction from Fermat's principle; Matrix method in paraxial optics-thin lens formula, nodal planes, system of two thin lenses, chromatic and spherical aberrations.

(c) **Interference:** Interference of light-Young's experiment, Newton's rings, interference by thin films, Michelson interferometer; Multiple beam interference and Fabry-Perot interferometer.

(d) **Diffraction:** Fraunhofer diffraction-single slit, double slit, diffraction grating, resolving power; Diffraction by a circular aperture and the Airy pattern; Fresnel diffraction: half-period zones and zone plates, circular aperture.

(e) **Polarization and Modern Optics:** Production and detection of linearly and circularly polarized light; Double refraction, quarter wave plate; Optical activity; Principles of fibre optics, attenuation; Pulse dispersion in step index and parabolic index fibres; Material dispersion, single mode fibres; Lasers-Einstein A and B coefficients; Ruby and He-Ne lasers; Characteristics of laser light-spatial and temporal coherence; Focusing of laser beams; Three-evel scheme for laser operation; Holography and simple applications.

3. Electricity and Magnetism

(a) **Electrostatics and Magnetostatics:** Laplace and Poisson equations in electrostatics and their applications; Energy of a system of charges, multipole expansion of scalar potential; Method of images and its applications; Potential and field due to a dipole, force and torque on a dipole in an external field; Dielectrics, polarization; Solutions to boundary-value problemsconducting and dielectric spheres in a uniform electric field; Magnetic shell, uniformly magnetized sphere; Ferromagnetic materials, hysteresis, energy loss.

(b) **Current Electricity:** Kirchhoff's laws and their applications; Biot-Savart law, Ampere's law, Faraday's law, Lenz' law; Self-and mutual-inductances; Mean and r m s values in AC circuits; DC and AC circuits with R, L and C components; Series and parallel resonances; Quality factor; Principle of transformer.

4. Electromagnetic Waves and Blackbody Radiation

Displacement current and Maxwell's equations; Wave equations in vacuum, Poynting theorem; Vector and scalar potentials; Electromagnetic field tensor, covariance of Maxwell's equations; Wave equations in isotropic dielectrics, reflection and refraction at the boundary of two dielectrics; Fresnel's relations; Total internal reflection; Normal and anomalous dispersion; Rayleigh scattering; Blackbody radiation and Planck's radiation law, StefanBoltzmann law, Wien's displacement law and Rayleigh-Jeans' law.

5. Thermal and Statistical Physics

(a) **Thermodynamics:** Laws of thermodynamics, reversible and irreversible processes, entropy; Isothermal, adiabatic, isobaric, isochoric processes and entropy changes; Otto and Diesel engines, Gibbs' phase rule and chemical potential; van der Waals equation of state of a real gas, critical constants; Maxwell-Boltzman distribution of molecular velocities, transport phenomena, equipartition and virial theorems; Dulong-Petit, Einstein, and Debye's theories of specific heat of solids; Maxwell relations and applications; Clausius- Clapeyron equation; Adiabatic demagnetisation, Joule-Kelvin effect and liquefaction of gases.

(b) **Statistical Physics:** Macro and micro states, statistical distributions, Maxwell-Boltzmann, Bose-Einstein and Fermi-Dirac distributions, applications to specific heat of gases and blackbody radiation; Concept of negative temperatures.

PAPER-II

1. Quantum Mechanics

Wave-particle dualitiy; Schroedinger equation and expectation values; Uncertainty principle; Solutions of the one-dimensional Schroedinger equation for a free particle (Gaussian wave-packet), particle in a box, particle in a finite well, linear harmonic oscillator; Reflection and transmission by a step potential and by a rectangular barrier; Particle in a three dimensional box, density of states, free electron theory of metals; Angular momentum; Hydrogen atom; Spin half particles, properties of Pauli spin matrices.

2. Atomic and Molecular Physics

Stern-Gerlach experiment, electron spin, fine structure of hydrogen atom; L-S coupling, J-J coupling; Spectroscopic notation of atomic states; Zeeman effect; FrankCondon principle and applications; Elementary theory of rotational, vibratonal and electronic spectra of diatomic molecules; Raman effect and molecular structure; Laser Raman spectroscopy; Importance of neutral hydrogen atom, molecular hydrogen and molecular hydrogen ion in astronomy; Fluorescence and Phosphorescence; Elementary theory and applications of NMR and EPR; Elementary ideas about Lamb shift and its significance.

3. Nuclear and Particle Physics

Basic nuclear properties-size, binding energy, angular momentum, parity, magnetic moment; Semi-empirical mass formula and applications, mass parabolas; Ground state of deuteron, magnetic moment and non-central forces; Meson theory of nuclear forces; Salient features of nuclear forces; Shell model of the nucleus-successes and limitations; Violation of parity in beta decay; Gamma decay and internal conversion; Elementary ideas about Mossbauer spectroscopy; Q-value of nuclear reactions; Nuclear fission and fusion, energy production in stars; Nuclear reactors.

Classification of elementary particles and their interactions; Conservation laws; Quark structure of hadrons; Field quanta of electroweak and strong interactions; Elementary ideas about unification of forces; Physics of neutrinos.

4. Solid State Physics, Devices and Electronics

Crystalline and amorphous structure of matter; Different crystal systems, space groups; Methods of determination of crystal structure; X-ray diffraction, scanning and transmission electron microscopies; Band theory of solids - conductors, insulators and semiconductors; Thermal properties of solids, specific heat, Debye theory; Magnetism: dia, para and ferromagnetism; Elements of superconductivity, Meissner effect, Josephson junctions and applications; Elementary ideas about high temperature superconductivity.

Intrinsic and extrinsic semiconductors; p-n-p and n-p-n transistors; Amplifiers and oscillators; Op-amps; FET, JFET and MOSFET; Digital electronics-Boolean identities, De Morgan's laws, logic gates and truth tables; Simple logic circuits; Thermistors, solar cells; Fundamentals of microprocessors and digital computers.

POLITICAL SCIENCE AND INTERNATIONAL RELATIONS

PAPER-I

Political Theory and Indian Politics

1. Political Theory: meaning and approaches.
2. Theories of the State: Liberal, Neoliberal, Marxist, Pluralist, Post-colonial and feminist.
3. Justice: Conceptions of justice with special reference to Rawl's theory of justice and its communitarian critiques.
4. Equality: Social, political and economic; relationship between equality and freedom; Affirmative action.
5. Rights: Meaning and theories; different kinds of rights; concept of Human Rights.
6. Democracy: Classical and contemporary theories; different models of democracy – representative, participatory and deliberative.
7. Concept of power, hegemony, ideology and legitimacy.
8. Political Ideologies: Liberalism, Socialism, Marxism, Fascism, Gandhism and Feminism.
9. Indian Political Thought : Dharamshastra, Arthashastra and Buddhist traditions; Sir Syed Ahmed Khan, Sri Aurobindo, M.K. Gandhi, B.R. Ambedkar, M.N. Roy.

10. Western Political Thought: Plato, Aristotle, Machiavelli, Hobbes, Locke, John S. Mill, Marx, Gramsci, Hannah Arendt.

Indian Government and Politics

1. Indian Nationalism
   (a) Political Strategies of India's Freedom Struggle: Constitutionalism to mass Satyagraha, Non-cooperation, Civil Disobedience; Militant and revolutionary movements, Peasant and workers' movements.
   (b) Perspectives on Indian National Movement: Liberal, Socialist and Marxist; Radical humanist and Dalit.
2. Making of the Indian Constitution: Legacies of the British rule; different social and political perspectives.
3. Salient Features of the Indian Constitution: The Preamble, Fundamental Rights and Duties, Directive Principles; Parliamentary System and Amendment Procedures; Judicial Review and Basic Structure doctrine.
4. (a) Principal Organs of the Union Government: Envisaged role and actual working of the Executive, Legislature and Supreme Court.
   (b) Principal Organs of the State Government: Envisaged role and actual working of the Executive, Legislature and High Courts.
5. Grassroots Democracy: Panchayati Raj and Municipal Government; significance of 73rd and 74th Amendments; Grassroot movements.
6. Statutory Institutions/Commissions: Election Commission, Comptroller and Auditor General, Finance Commission, Union Public Service Commission, National Commission for Scheduled Castes, National Commission for Scheduled Tribes, National Commission for Women; National Human Rights Commission, National Commission for Minorities, National Backward Classes Commission.
7. Federalism: Constitutional provisions; changing nature of centre-state relations; integrationist tendencies and regional aspirations; inter-state disputes.
8. Planning and Economic Development : Nehruvian and Gandhian perspectives; role of planning and public sector; Green Revolution, land reforms and agrarian relations; liberalilzation and economic reforms.
9. Caste, Religion and Ethnicity in Indian Politics.
10. Party System: National and regional political parties, ideological and social bases of parties; patterns of coalition politics; Pressure groups, trends in electoral behaviour; changing socio- economic profile of Legislators.
11. Social Movements: Civil liberties and human rights movements; women's movements; environmentalist movements.

PAPER–II

Comparative Politics and International Relations

Comparative Political Analysis and International Politics

1. Comparative Politics: Nature and major approaches; political economy and political sociology perspectives; limitations of the comparative method.
2. State in comparative perspective: Characteristics and changing nature of the State in capitalist and socialist economies, and, advanced industrial and developing societies.
3. Politics of Representation and Participation: Political parties, pressure groups and social movements in advanced industrial and developing societies.
4. Globalisation: Responses from developed and developing societies.
5. Approaches to the Study of International Relations: Idealist, Realist, Marxist, Functionalist and Systems theory.
6. Key concepts in International Relations: National interest, Security and power; Balance of power and deterrence; Transnational actors and collective security; World capitalist economy and globalisation.
7. Changing International Political Order:
   (a) Rise of super powers; strategic and ideological Bipolarity, arms race and Cold War; nuclear threat;
   (b) Non-aligned movement: Aims and achievements;
   (c) Collapse of the Soviet Union; Unipolarity and American hegemony; relevance of non-alignment in the contemporary world.
8. Evolution of the International Economic System: From Brettonwoods to WTO; Socialist economies and the CMEA (Council for Mutual Economic Assistance); Third World demand for new international economic order; Globalisation of the world economy.
9. United Nations: Envisaged role and actual record; specialized UN agencies-aims and functioning; need for UN reforms.
10. Regionalisation of World Politics: EU, ASEAN, APEC, SAARC, NAFTA.
11. Contemporary Global Concerns: Democracy, human rights, environment, gender justice, terrorism, nuclear proliferation.

India and the World

1. Indian Foreign Policy: Determinants of foreign policy; institutions of policy-making; continuity and change.
2. India's Contribution to the Non-Alignment Movement: Different phases; current role.

3. India and South Asia:
   - (a) Regional Co-operation: SAARC – past performance and future prospects.
   - (b) South Asia as a Free Trade Area.
   - (c) India's "Look East" policy.
   - (d) Impediments to regional co-operation: river water disputes; illegal cross-border migration; ethnic conflicts and insurgencies; border disputes.
4. India and the Global South: Relations with Africa and Latin America; leadership role in the demand for NIEO and WTO negotiations.
5. India and the Global Centres of Power: USA, EU, Japan, China and Russia.
6. India and the UN System: Role in UN Peace-keeping; demand for Permanent Seat in the Security Council.
7. India and the Nuclear Question: Changing perceptions and policy.
8. Recent developments in Indian Foreign policy: India's position on the recent crisis in Afghanistan, Iraq and West Asia, growing relations with US and Israel; vision of a new world order.

PSYCHOLOGY

PAPER-I

Foundations of Psychology

1. Introduction

Definition of Psychology; Historical antecedents of Psychology and trends in the 21st century; Psychology and scientific methods; Psychology in relation to other social sciences and natural sciences; Application of Psychology to societal problems.

2. Methods of Psychology

Types of research: Descriptive, evaluative, diagnostic and prognostic; Methods of Research: Survey, observation, case-study and experiments; Characteristics of experimental design and non-experimental design, Quasi-experimental designs; Focussed group discussions, brain storming, grounded theory approach.

3. Research Methods

Major steps in Psychological research (problem statement, hypothesis formulation, research designs, sampling, tools of data collection, analysis and interpretation and report writing) Fundamental versus applied research; Methods of data collection (interview, observation, questionnaire); Research designs (ex-post facto and experimental); Application of statistical technique (t - test, two way ANOVA correlation, regression and factor analysis); Item response theory.

4. Development of Human Behaviour

Growth and development; Principles of development, Role of genetic and environmental factors in determining human behaviour; Influence of cultural factors in socialization; Life span development Characteristics, development tasks, promoting psychological well-being across major stages of the life span.

5. Sensation, Attention and Perception

Sensation: concepts of threshold, absolute and difference thresholds, signal-detection and vigilance; Factors influencing attention including set and characteristics of stimulus; Definition and concept of perception, biological factors in perception; Perceptual organization-influence of past experiences, perceptual defencefactors influencing space and depth perception, size estimation and perceptual readiness; The plasticity of perception; Extrasensory perception; Culture and perception, Subliminal perception.

6. Learning

Concept and theories of learning (Behaviourists, Gestaltalist and Information processing models); The Processes of extinction, discrimination and generalization; Programmed learning, probability learning, selfinstructional learning, concepts; Types and the schedules of reinforcement, escape, avoidance and punishment, modeling and social learning.

7. Memory

Encoding and remembering; Short term memory, Long term memory, Sensory memory, Iconic memory, Echoic memory: The Multistore model, levels of processing; Organization and Mnemonic techniques to improve memory; Theories of forgetting: decay, interference and retrieval failure: Metamemory; Amnesia: Anterograde and retrograde.

8. Thinking and Problem Solving

Piaget's theory of cognitive development; Concept formation processes; Information processing, Reasoning and problem solving, Facilitating and hindering factors in problem solving, Methods of problem solving: Creative thinking and fostering creativity; Factors influencing decision making and judgment; Recent trends.

9. Motivation and Emotion

Psychological and physiological basis of motivation and emotion; Measurement of motivation and emotion; Effects of motivation and emotion on behaviour; Extrinsic and intrinsic motivation; Factors influencing intrinsic motivation; Emotional competence and the related issues.

10. Intelligence and Aptitude

Concept of intelligence and aptitude, Nature and theories of intelligence Spearman, Thurstone, Gullford Vernon, Sternberg and J.P; Das; Emotional Intelligence, Social intelligence, measurement of intelligence and aptitudes, concept of IQ, deviation IQ, constancy of IQ; Measurement of multiple intelligence; Fluid intelligence and crystallized intelligence.

11. Personality

Definition and concept of personality; Theories of personality (psychoanalytical, sociocultural, interpersonal, developmental, humanistic, behaviouristic, trait and type approaches); Measurement of personality (projective tests, pencil-paper test); The Indian approach to personality; Training for personality development; Latest approaches like big 5 factor theory; The notion of self in different traditions.

12. Attitudes, Values and Interests

Definition of attitudes, values and interests; Components of attitudes; Formation and maintenance of attitudes; Measurement of attitudes, values and interests; Theories of attitude change; Strategies for fostering values; Formation of stereotypes and prejudices; Changing others behaviour; Theories of attribution; Recent trends.

13. Language and Communication

Human language - Properties, structure and linguistic hierarchy, Language acquisition-predisposition, critical period hypothesis; Theories of language development Skinner and Chomsky; Process and types of communication - effective communication training.

14. Issues and Perspectives in Modern Contemporary Psychology

Computer application in the psychological laboratory and psychological testing; Artificial intelligence; Psychocybernetics; Study of consciousness-sleep-wake schedules; dreams, stimulus deprivation, meditation, hypnotic/drug induced states; Extrasensory perception; Intersensory perception Simulation studies.

PAPER-II

Psychology: Issues and Applications

1. Psychological Measurement of Individual Differences

The nature of individual differences; Characteristics and construction of standardized psychological tests; Types of psychological tests; Use, misuse and limitation of psychological tests; hical issues in the use of psychological tests.

2. Psychological well being and Mental Disorders

Concept of health-ill health; Positive health, well being; Causal factors in mental disorders (Anxiety disorders, mood disorders, schizophrenia and delusional disorders; personality disorders, substance abuse disorders); Factors influencing positive health, well being, life style and quality of life; Happiness disposition.

3. Therapeutic Approaches

Psychodynamic therapies; Behaviour therapies; Client centered therapy; Cognitive therapies; Indigenous therapies (Yoga, Meditation); Bio-feedback therapy; Prevention and rehabilitation of the mentally ill; Fostering mental health.

4. Work Psychology and Organisational Behaviour

Personnel selection and training; Use of psychological tests in the industry; Training and human resource development; Theories of work motivation – Herzberg, Maslow, Adam Equity theory, Porter and Lawler, Vroom; Leadership and participatory management; Advertising and marketing; Stress and its management; Ergonomics; consumer psychology; Managerial effectiveness; Transformational leadership; Sensitivity training; Power and politics in organizations.

5. Application of Psychology to Educational Field

Psychological principles underlying effective teaching-learning process; Learning styles; Gifted, retarded, learning disabled and their training; Training for improving memory and better academic achievement; Personality development and value education, Educational, vocational guidance and career counseling; Use of psychological tests in educational institutions; Effective strategies in guidance programmes.

6. Community Psychology

Definition and concept of community psychology; Use of small groups in social action; Arousing community consciousness and action for handling social problems; Group decision making and leadership for social change; Effective strategies for social change.

7. Rehabilitation Psychology

Primary, secondary and tertiary prevention programmes-role of psychologists; Organising of services for rehabilitation of physically, mentally and socially challenged persons including old persons, Rehabilitation of persons suffering from substance abuse, juvenile delinquency, criminal behaviour; Rehabilitation of victims of violence, Rehabilitation of HIV/AIDS victims, the role of social agencies.

8. Application of Psychology to disadvantaged groups:

The concepts of disadvantaged, deprivation; Social, physical, cultural and economic consequences of disadvantaged and deprived groups; Educating and motivating the disadvantaged towards development; Relative and prolonged deprivation.

9. Psychological problems of social integration

The concept of social integration; The problem of caste, class, religion and language conflicts and prejudice; Nature and manifestation of prejudice between the in-group and out-group; Causal factors of social conflicts and prejudices; Psychological strategies for handling the conflicts and prejudices; Measures to achieve social integration.

10. Application of Psychology in Information Technology and Mass Media

The present scenario of information technology and the mass media boom and the role of psychologists; Selection and training of psychology professionals to work in the field of IT and mass media; Distance learning through IT and mass media; Entrepreneurship through e-commerce; Multilevel marketing; Impact of TV and fostering value through IT and mass media; Psychological consequences of recent developments in Information Technology.

11. Psychology and Economic development

Achievement motivation and economic development; Characteristics of entrepreneurial behaviour; Motivating and training people for entrepreneurship and economic development; Consumer rights and consumer awareness, Government policies for promotion of entrepreneurship among youth including women entrepreneurs.

12. Application of psychology to environment and related fields

Environmental psychology-effects of noise, pollution and crowding; Population psychology: psychological consequences of population explosion and high population density; Motivating for small family norm; Impact of rapid scientific and technological growth on degradation of environment.

13. Application of psychology in other fields

(a) Military Psychology: Devising psychological tests for defence personnel for use in selection, Training, counseling; training psychologists to work with defence personnel in promoting positive health; Human engineering in defence.

(b) Sports Psychology: Psychological interventions in improving performance of athletes and sports. Persons participating in Individual and Team Games.

(c) ***Media influences on pro and antisocial behaviour.***

(d) ***Psychology of terrorism.***

14. Psychology of Gender

Issues of discrimination, Management of diversity; Glass ceiling effect, Self fulfilling prophesy, Women and Indian society.

PUBLIC ADMINISTRATION

PAPER–I

ADMINISTRATIVE THEORY

1. Introduction

Meaning, scope and significance of Public Administration; Wilson's vision of Public Administration; Evolution of the discipline and its present status; New

Public Administration; Public Choice approach; Challenges of liberalization, Privatisation, Globalisation; Good Governance: concept and application; New Public Management.

2. Administrative Thought

Scientific Management and Scientific Management movement; Classical Theory; Weber's bureaucratic model – its critique and post-Weberian Developments; Dynamic Administration (Mary Parker Follett); Human Relations School (Elton Mayo and others); Functions of the Executive (C.I. Barnard); Simon's decisionmaking theory; Participative Management (R. Likert, C. Argyris, D. McGregor).

3. Administrative Behaviour

Process and techniques of decision-making; Communication; Morale; Motivation Theories – content, process and contemporary; Theories of Leadership: Traditional and Modern.

4. Organisations

Theories – systems, contingency; Structure and forms: Ministries and Departments, Corporations, Companies, Boards and Commissions; Ad hoc and advisory bodies; Headquarters and Field relationships; Regulatory Authorities; Public – Private Partnerships.

5. Accountability and control

Concepts of accountability and control; Legislative, Executive and Judicial control over administration; Citizen and Administration; Role of media, interest groups, voluntary organizations; Civil society; Citizen's Charters; Right to Information; Social audit.

6. Administrative Law

Meaning, scope and significance; Dicey on Administrative law; Delegated legislation; Administrative Tribunals.

7. Comparative Public Administration

Historical and sociological factors affecting administrative systems; Administration and politics in different countries; Current status of Comparative Public Administration; Ecology and administration; Riggsian models and their critique.

8. Development Dynamics

Concept of development; Changing profile of development administration; 'Antidevelopment thesis'; Bureaucracy and development; Strong state versus the market debate; Impact of liberalisation on administration in developing countries; Women and development - the self-help group movement.

9. Personnel Administration

Importance of human resource development; Recruitment, training, career advancement, position classification, discipline, performance appraisal, promotion, pay and service conditions; employer-employee relations, grievance redressal mechanism; Code of conduct; Administrative ethics.

10. Public Policy

Models of policy-making and their critique; Processes of conceptualisation, planning, implementation, monitoring, evaluation and review and their limitations; State theories and public policy formulation.

11. Techniques of Administrative Improvement

Organisation and methods, Work study and work management; e-governance and information technology; Management aid tools like network analysis, MIS, PERT, CPM.

12. Financial Administration

Monetary and fiscal policies; Public borrowings and public debt Budgets – types and forms; Budgetary process; Financial accountability; Accounts and audit.

PAPER-II

INDIAN ADMINISTRATION

1. Evolution of Indian Administration

Kautilya's Arthashastra; Mughal administration; Legacy of British rule in politics and administration - Indianization of public services, revenue administration, district administration, local self-government.

2. Philosophical and Constitutional framework of government

Salient features and value premises; Constitutionalism; Political culture; Bureaucracy and democracy; Bureaucracy and development.

3. Public Sector Undertakings

Public sector in modern India; Forms of Public Sector Undertakings; Problems of autonomy, accountability and control; Impact of liberalization and privatization.

4. Union Government and Administration

Executive, Parliament, Judiciary - structure, functions, work processes; Recent trends; Intragovernmental relations; Cabinet Secretariat; Prime Minister's Office; Central Secretariat; Ministries and Departments; Boards; Commissions; Attached offices; Field organizations.

5. Plans and Priorities

Machinery of planning; Role, composition and functions of the Planning Commission and the National Development Council; 'Indicative' planning; Process of plan formulation at Union and State levels; Constitutional Amendments (1992) and decentralized planning for economic development and social justice.

6. State Government and Administration

Union-State administrative, legislative and financial relations; Role of the Finance Commission; Governor; Chief Minister; Council of Ministers; Chief Secretary; State Secretariat; Directorates.

7. District Administration since Independence

Changing role of the Collector; Unionstate-local relations; Imperatives of development management and law and order administration; District administration and democratic decentralization.

8. Civil Services

Constitutional position; Structure, recruitment, training and capacity-building; Good governance initiatives; Code of conduct and discipline; Staff associations; Political rights; Grievance redressal mechanism; Civil service neutrality; Civil service activism.

9. Financial Management

Budget as a political instrument; Parliamentary control of public expenditure; Role of finance ministry in monetary and fiscal area; Accounting techniques; Audit; Role of Controller General of Accounts and Comptroller and Auditor General of India.

10. Administrative Reforms since Independence

Major concerns; Important Committees and Commissions; Reforms in financial management and human resource development; Problems of implementation.

11. Rural Development

Institutions and agencies since independence; Rural development programmes: foci and strategies; Decentralization and Panchayati Raj; 73rd Constitutional amendment.

12. Urban Local Government

Municipal governance: main features, structures, finance and problem areas; 74th Constitutional Amendment; Globallocal debate; New localism; Development dynamics, politics and administration with special reference to city management.

13. Law and Order Administration

British legacy; National Police Commission; Investigative agencies; Role of central and state agencies including paramilitary forces in maintenance of law and order and countering insurgency and terrorism; Criminalisation of politics and administration; Police-public relations; Reforms in Police.

14. Significant issues in Indian Administration

Values in public service; Regulatory Commissions; National Human Rights Commission; Problems of administration in coalition regimes; Citizen-administration interface; Corruption and administration; Disaster management.

SOCIOLOGY

PAPER-I

Fundamentals of Sociology

1. **Sociology - The Discipline**
   (a) Modernity and social changes in Europe and emergence of sociology.
   (b) Scope of the subject and comparison with other social sciences.
   (c) Sociology and common sense.
2. **Sociology as Science**
   (a) Science, scientific method and critique.
   (b) Major theoretical strands of research methodology.
   (c) Positivism and its critique.
   (d) Fact value and objectivity.
   (e) Non- positivist methodologies.
3. **Research Methods and Analysis**
   (a) Qualitative and quantitative methods.
   (b) Techniques of data collection.
   (c) Variables, sampling, hypothesis, reliability and validity.
4. **Sociological Thinkers**
   (a) Karl Marx- Historical materialism, mode of production, alienation, class struggle.
   (b) Emile Durkheim- Division of labour, social fact, suicide, religion and society.
   (c) Max Weber- Social action, ideal types, authority, bureaucracy, protestant ethic and the spirit of capitalism.
   (d) Talcolt Parsons- Social system, pattern variables.
   (e) Robert K. Merton- Latent and manifest functions, conformity and deviance, reference groups.
   (f) Mead - Self and identity.
5. **Stratification and Mobility:**
   (a) Concepts-equality, inequality, hierarchy, exclusion, poverty and deprivation.
   (b) Theories of social stratification- Structural functionalist theory, Marxist theory, Weberian theory.
   (c) Dimensions-Social stratification of class, status groups, gender, ethnicity and race.
   (d) Social mobility-open and closed systems, types of mobility, sources and causes of mobility.

6. **Works and Economic Life:**
   (a) Social organization of work in different types of society- slave society, feudal society, industrial /capitalist society.
   (b) Formal and informal organization of work.
   (c) Labour and society.

7. **Politics and Society:**
   (a) Sociological theories of power.
   (b) Power elite, bureaucracy, pressure groups, and political parties.
   (c) Nation, state, citizenship, democracy, civil society, ideology.
   (d) Protest, agitation, social movements, collective action, revolution.

8. **Religion and Society:**
   (a) Sociological theories of religion.
   (b) Types of religious practices: animism, monism, pluralism, sects, cults.
   (c) Religion in modern society: religion and science, secularization, religious revivalism, fundamentalism.

9. **Systems of Kinship:**
   (a) Family, household, marriage.
   (b) Types and forms of family.
   (c) Lineage and descent.
   (d) Patriarchy and sexual division of labour.
   (e) Contemporary trends.

10. **Social Change in Modern Society:**
   (a) Sociological theories of social change.
   (b) Development and dependency.
   (c) Agents of social change.
   (d) Education and social change.
   (e) Science, technology and social change.

PAPER-II

Indian Society : Structure and Change

A. Introducing Indian Society

(i) **Perspectives on the study of Indian society**
   (a) Indology (GS. Ghurye).
   (b) Structural functionalism (M N Srinivas).
   (c) Marxist sociology (A R Desai).

(ii) **Impact of colonial rule on Indian society**
   (a) Social background of Indian nationalism.

(b) Modernization of Indian tradition.

(c) Protests and movements during the colonial period.

(d) Social reforms.

B. Social Structure

(i) Rural and Agrarian Social Structure:

(a) The idea of Indian village and village studies.

(b) Agrarian social structure - evolution of land tenure system, land reforms.

(ii) Caste System

(a) Perspectives on the study of caste systems: GS Ghurye, M N Srinivas, Louis Dumont, Andre Beteille.

(b) Features of caste system.

(c) Untouchability - forms and perspectives.

(iii) Tribal communities in India:

(a) Definitional problems.

(b) Geographical spread.

(c) Colonial policies and tribes.

(d) Issues of integration and autonomy.

(iv) Social Classes in India:

(a) Agrarian class structure.

(b) Industrial class structure.

(c) Middle classes in India.

(v) Systems of Kinship in India:

(a) Lineage and descent in India.

(b) Types of kinship systems.

(c) Family and marriage in India.

(d) Household dimensions of the family.

(e) Patriarchy, entitlements and sexual division of labour.

(vi) Religion and Society:

(a) Religious communities in India.

(b) Problems of religious minorities.

C. Social Changes in India

(i) Visions of Social Change in India

(a) Idea of development planning and mixed economy.

(b) Constitution, law and social change.

(c) Education and social change.

(ii) Rural and Agrarian transformation in India

(a) Programmes of rural development, Community Development Programme, cooperatives, poverty alleviation schemes.

(b) Green revolution and social change.

(c) Changing modes of production in Indian agriculture.

(d) Problems of rural labour, bondage, migration.

(iii) Industrialization and Urbanisation in India

(a) Evolution of modern industry in India.

(b) Growth of urban settlements in India.

(c) Working class: structure, growth, class mobilization.

(d) Informal sector, child labour.

(e) Slums and deprivation in urban areas.

(iv) Politics and Society

(a) Nation, democracy and citizenship.

(b) Political parties, pressure groups, social and political elite.

(c) Regionalism and decentralization of power.

(d) Secularization.

(v) Social Movements in Modern India:

(a) Peasants and farmers movements.

(b) Women's movement.

(c) Backward classes & Dalit movement.

(d) Environmental movements.

(e) Ethnicity and Identity movements.

(vi) Population Dynamics:

(a) Population size, growth, composition and distribution.

(b) Components of population growth: birth, death, migration.

(c) Population policy and family planning.

(d) Emerging issues: ageing, sex ratios, child and infant mortality, reproductive health.

(vii) Challenges of Social Transformation:

(a) Crisis of development: displacement, environmental problems and sustainability.

(b) Poverty, deprivation and inequalities.

(c) Violence against women.

(d) Caste conflicts.

(e) Ethnic conflicts, communalism, religious revivalism.

(f) Illiteracy and disparities in education.

STATISTICS

PAPER-I

1. Probability

Sample space and events, probability measure and probability space, random variable as a measurable function, distribution function of a random variable, discrete and continuous-type random variable, probability mass function, probability density function, vector-valued random variable, marginal and conditional distributions, stochastic independence of events and of random variables, expectation and moments of a random variable, conditional expectation, convergence of a sequence of random variable in distribution, in probability, in p-th mean and almost everywhere, their criteria and inter-relations, Chebyshev's inequality and Khintchine's weak law of large numbers, strong law of large numbers and Kolmogoroff's theorems, probability generating function, moment generating function, characteristic function, inversion theorem, Linderberg and Levy forms of central limit theorem, standard discrete and continuous probability distributions.

2. Statistical Inference

Consistency, unbiasedness, efficiency, sufficiency, completeness, ancillary statistics, factorization theorem, exponential family of distribution and its properties, uniformly minimum variance unbiased (UMVU) estimation, Rao-Blackwell and Lehmann-Scheffe theorems, Cramer-Rao inequality for single parameter.

Estimation by methods of moments, maximum likelihood, least squares, minimum chi-square and modified minimum chi-square, properties of maximum likelihood and other estimators, asymptotic efficiency, prior and posterior distributions, loss function, risk function, and minimax estimator. Bayes estimators.

Non-randomised and randomised tests, critical function, MP tests, Neyman-Pearson lemma, UMP tests, monotone likelihood ratio, similar and unbiased tests, UMPU tests for single parameter likelihood ratio test and its asymptotic distribution. Confidence bounds and its relation with tests. Kolmogoroff's test for goodness of fit and its consistency, sign test and its optimality. Wilcoxon signed-ranks test and its consistency, Kolmogorov-Smirnov two-sample test, run test, Wilcoxon- Mann-Whitney test and median test, their consistency and asymptotic normality.

Wald's SPRT and its properties, OC and ASN functions for tests regarding parameters for Bernoulli, Poisson, normal and exponential distributions. Wald's fundamental identity.

3. Linear Inference and Multivariate Analysis

Linear statistical models', theory of least squares and analysis of variance, Gauss-Markoff theory, normal equations, least squares estimates and their precision, test of significance and interval estimates based on least squares theory in one-way, two-way and three-way classified data, regression analysis, linear regression, curvilinear regression and orthogonal polynomials, multiple regression, multiple and partial correlations, estimation of variance and covariance components, multivariate normal distribution, Mahalanobis-D2 and Hotelling's T2 statistics and their applications and properties, discriminant analysis, canonical correlations, principal component analysis.

4. Sampling Theory and Design of Experiments

An outline of fixed-population and superpopulation approaches, distinctive features of finite population sampling, probability sampling designs, simple random sampling with and without replacement, stratified random sampling, systematic sampling and its efficacy , cluster sampling, twostage and multi-stage sampling, ratio and regression methods of estimation involving one or more auxiliary variables, two-phase sampling, probability proportional to size sampling with and without replacement, the Hansen-Hurwitz and the Horvitz- Thompson estimators, non-negative variance estimation with reference to the Horvitz-Thompson estimator, non-sampling errors.

Fixed effects model (two-way classification) random and mixed effects models (two-way classification with equal observation per cell), CRD, RBD, LSD and their analyses, incomplete block designs, concepts of orthogonality and balance, BIBD, missing plot technique, factorial experiments and 2n and 32, confounding in factorial experiments, split-plot and simple lattice designs, transformation of data Duncan's multiple range test.

PAPER-II

1. Industrial Statistics

Process and product control, general theory of control charts, different types of control charts for variables and attributes, X, R, s, p, np and c charts, cumulative sum chart. Single, double, multiple and sequential sampling plans for attributes, OC, ASN, AOQ and ATI curves, concepts of producer's and consumer's risks, AQL, LTPD and AOQL, Sampling plans for variables, Use of Dodge-Roming tables.

Concept of reliability, failure rate and reliability functions, reliability of series and parallel systems and other simple configurations, renewal density and renewal function, Failure models: exponential, Weibull, normal, lognormal.

Problems in life testing, censored and truncated experiments for exponential models.

2. Optimization Techniques

Different types of models in Operations Research, their construction and general methods of solution, simulation and Monte-Carlo methods formulation of linear programming (LP) problem, simple LP model and its graphical solution, the simplex procedure, the two-phase method and the M-technique with artificial variables, the duality theory of LP and its economic interpretation, sensitivity analysis, transportation and assignment problems, rectangular games, twoperson zero-sum games, methods of solution (graphical and algebraic).

Replacement of failing or deteriorating items, group and individual replacement policies, concept of scientific inventory management and analytical structure of inventory problems, simple models with deterministic and stochastic demand with and without lead time, storage models with particular reference to dam type.

Homogeneous discrete-time Markov chains, transition probability matrix, classification of states and ergodic theorems, homogeneous continuous-time Markov chains, Poisson process, elements of queuing theory, M/M/1, M/M/K, G/M/1 and M/G/1 queues.

Solution of statistical problems on computers using well-known statistical software packages like SPSS.

3. Quantitative Economics and Official Statistics

Determination of trend, seasonal and cyclical components, Box-Jenkins method, tests for stationary series, ARIMA models and determination of orders of autoregressive and moving average components, forecasting.

Commonly used index numbersLaspeyre's, Paasche's and Fisher's ideal index numbers, chain-base index number, uses and limitations of index numbers, index number of wholesale prices, consumer prices, agricultural production and industrial production, test for index numbers proportionality, time-reversal, factorreversal and circular. General linear model, ordinary least square and generalized least squares methods of estimation, problem of multi-collinearity, consequences and solutions of mult-icollinearity, auto-correlation and its consequences, heteroscedasticity of disturbances and its testing, test for independence of disturbances, concept of structure and model for simultaneous equations, problem of identification-rank and order conditions of identifiability, two-stage least square method of estimation.

Present official statistical system in India relating to population, agriculture, industrial production, trade and prices, methods of collection of official statistics, their reliability and limitations, principal publications containing such statistics, various official agencies responsible for data collection and their main functions.

4. Demography and Psychometry

Demographic data from census, registration, NSS other surveys, their limitations and uses, definition, construction and uses of vital rates and ratios, measures of fertility, reproduction rates, morbidity rate, standardized death rate, complete and abridged life tables, construction of life tables from vital statistics and census returns, uses of life tables, logistic and other population growth curves, fitting a logistic curve, population projection, stable population, quasi-stable population, techniques in estimation of demographic parameters, standard classification by cause of death, health surveys and use of hospital statistics.

Methods of standardisation of scales and tests, Z-scores, standard scores, T-scores, percentile scores, intelligence quotient and its measurement and uses, validity and reliability of test scores and its determination, use of factor analysis and path analysis in psychometry.

ZOOLOGY

PAPER–I

1. Non-chordata and Chordata

(a) Classification and relationship of various phyla up to subclasses: Acoelomate and Coelomate, Protostomes and Deuterostomes, Bilateria and Radiata; Status of Protista, Parazoa, Onychophora and Hemichordata; Symmetry.

(b) Protozoa: Locomotion, nutrition, reproduction, sex; General features and life history of Paramaecium, Monocystis, Plasmodium and Leishmania.

(c) Porifera: Skeleton, canal system and reproduction.

(d) Cnidaria: Polymorphism, defensive structures and their mechanism; coral reefs and their formation; metagenesis; general features and life history of Obelia and Aurelia.

(e) Platyhelminthes: Parasitic adaptation; general features and life history of Fasciola and Taenia and their pathogenic symptoms.

(f) Nemathelminthes: General features, life history, parasitic adaptation of Ascaris and Wuchereria.

(g) Annelida: Coelom and metamerism; modes of life in polychaetes; general features and life history of Nereis, earthworm and leach.

(h) Arthropoda: Larval forms and parasitism in Crustacea; vision and respiration in arthropods (Prawn, cockroach and scorpion); modification of mouth parts in insects (cockroach, mosquito, housefly, honey bee and butterfly); metamorphosis in insect and its hormonal regulation, social behaviour of Apis and termites.

(i) Mollusca: Feeding, respiration, locomotion, general features and life history of Lamellidens, Pila and Sepia, torsion and detorsion in gastropods.

(j) Echinodermata: Feeding, respiration, locomotion, larval forms, general features and life history of Asterias.

(k) Protochordata: Origin of chordates; general features and life history of Branchiostoma and Herdmania.

(l) Pisces: Respiration, locomotion and migration.

(m) Amphibia: Origin of tetrapods, parental care, paedomorphosis.

(n) Reptilia: Origin of reptiles, skull types, status of Sphenodon and crocodiles.

(o) Aves: Origin of birds, flight adaptation, migration.

(p) Mammalia: Origin of mammals, dentition, general features of egg laying mammals, pouched-mammals, aquatic mammals and primates, endocrine glands (pituitary, thyroid, parathyroid, adrenal, pancreas, gonads) and their interrelationships.

(q) Comparative functional anatomy of various systems of vertebrates (integument and its derivatives, endoskeleton, locomotory organs, digestive system, respiratory system, circulatory system including heart and aortic arches, urino-genital system, brain and sense organs (eye and ear).

2. Ecology

(a) Biosphere: Concept of biosphere; biomes, Biogeochemical cycles, Human induced changes in atmosphere including green house effect, ecological succession, biomes and ecotones, community ecology.

(b) Concept of ecosystem; structure and function of ecosystem, types of ecosystem, ecological succession, ecological adaptation.

(c) Population; characteristics, population dynamics, population stabilization.

(d) Biodiversity and diversity conservation of natural resources.

(e) Wildlife of India.

(f) Remote sensing for sustainable development.

(g) Environmental biodegradation, pollution and its impact on biosphere and its prevention.

3. Ethology

(a) Behaviour: Sensory filtering, reponsive-ness, sign stimuli, learning and memory, instinct, habituation, conditioning, imprinting.

(b) Role of hormones in drive; role of pheromones in alarm spreading; crypsis, predator detection, predator tactics, social hierarchies in primates, social organization in insects.

(c) Orientation, navigation, homing, biological rhythms, biological clock, tidal, seasonal and circadian rhythms.

(d) Methods of studying animal behaviour including sexual conflict, selfishness, kinship and altruism.

4. Economic Zoology

(a) Apiculture, sericulture, lac culture, carp culture, pearl culture, prawn culture, vermiculture.

(b) Major infectious and communicable diseases (malaria, filaria, tuberculosis, cholera and AIDS) their vectors, pathogens and prevention.

(c) Cattle and livestock diseases, their pathogen (helminthes) and vectors (ticks, mites, Tabanus, Stomoxys).

(d) Pests of sugar cane (Pyrilla perpusiella) oil seed (Achaea janata) and rice (Sitophilus oryzae).

(e) Transgenic animals.

(f) Medical biotechnology, human genetic disease and genetic counselling, gene therapy.

(g) Forensic biotechnology.

5. Biostatistics

Designing of experiments; null hypothesis; correlation, regression, distribution and measure of central tendency, chi square, student-test, F-test (one-way & two-way Ftest).

6. Instrumentation Methods

(a) Spectrophotometer, phase contrast and fluorescence microscopy, radioactive tracer, ultra centrifuge, gel electrophoresis, PCR, ELISA, FISH and chromosome painting.

(b) Electron microscopy (TEM, SEM).

PAPER-II

1. Cell Biology

(a) Structure and function of cell and its organelles (nucleus, plasma membrane, mitochondria, Golgi bodies, endoplasmic reticulum, ribosomes, and lysosomes), cell division (mitosis and meiosis), mitotic spindle and mitotic apparatus, chromosome movements, chromosome type polytene and lambrush, organization of chromatin, heterochromatin, Cell cycle regulation.

(b) Nucleic acid topology, DNA motif, DNA replication, transcription, RNA processing, translation, protein foldings and transport.

2. Genetics

(a) Modern concept of gene, split gene, genetic regulation, genetic code.

(b) Sex chromosomes and their evolution, sex determination in Drosophila and man.

(c) Mendel's laws of inheritance, recombination, linkage, multiple alleles, genetics of blood groups, pedigree analysis, hereditary diseases in man.

(d) Mutations and mutagenesis.

(e) Recombinant DNA technology; plasmid, cosmid, artificial chromosomes as vectors, transgenic, DNA cloning and whole animal cloning (principles and methods).

(f) Gene regulation and expression in prokaryotes and eukaryotes.

(g) Signal molecules, cell death, defects in signaling pathway and consequences.

(h) RFLP, RAPD and AFLP and application of RFLP in DNA finger printing, ribozyme technologies, human genome project, genomics and protomics.

3. Evolution

(a) Theories of origin of life.

(b) Theories of evolution; Natural selection, role of mutations in evolution, evolutionary patterns, molecular drive, mimicry, variation, isolation and speciation.

(c) Evolution of horse, elephant and man using fossil data.

(d) Hardy-Weinberg Law.

(e) Continental drift and distribution of animals.

4. Systematics

Zoological nomenclature, international code, cladistics, molecular taxonomy and biodiversity.

5. Biochemistry

(a) Structure and role of carbohydrates, fats, fatty acids and cholesterol, proteins and amino-acids, nucleic acids. Bioenergetics.

(b) Glycolysis and Kreb cycle, oxidation and reduction, oxidative phosphorylation, energy conservation and release, ATP cycle, cyclic AMP – its structure and role.

(c) Hormone classification (steroid and peptide hormones), biosynthesis and functions.

(d) Enzymes: types and mechanisms of action.

(e) Vitamins and co-enzymes

(f) Immunoglobulin and immunity.

6. Physiology (with special reference to mammals)

(a) Composition and constituents of blood; blood groups and Rh factor in man, factors and mechanism of coagulation, iron metabolism, acid-base balance, thermo-regulation, anticoagulants.

(b) Haemoglobin: Composition, types and role in transport of oxygen and carbon dioxide.

(c) Digestion and absorption: Role of salivary glands, liver, pancreas and intestinal glands.

(d) Excretion: nephron and regulation of urine formation; osmo-regulation and excretory product.

(e) Muscles: Types, mechanism of contraction of skeletal muscles, effects of exercise on muscles.

(f) Neuron: nerve impulse – its conduction and synaptic transmission, neurotransmitters.

(g) Vision, hearing and olfaction in man.

(h) Physiology of reproduction, puberty and menopause in human.

7. Developmental Biology

(a) Gametogenesis; spermatogenesis, composition of semen, in vitro and in vivo capacitation of mammalian sperm, Oogenesis, totipotency; fertilization, morphogenesis and morphogen, blastogenesis, establishment of body axes formation, fate map, gestulation in frog and chick; genes in development in chick, homeotic genes, development of eye and heart, placenta in mammals.

(b) Cell lineage, cell-to cell interaction, Genetic and induced teratogenesis, role of thyroxine in control of metamorphosis in amphibia, paedogenesis and neoteny, cell death, aging.

(c) Developmental genes in man, in vitro fertilization and embryo transfer, cloning.

(d) Stem cells: Sources, types and their use in human welfare.

(e) Biogenetic law.

A. TREND ANALYSIS-PRELIMS

Question Pattern of GS P-1 Prelim

Topic in UPSC Prelim GS Paper	2013	2014	2015	2016	2017	2018
Economy	18	10	21	29	29	25
Environment	17	28	22	21	14	12
Agriculture	5	8	4	5	5	4
Geography	14	10	11	4	7	4
Sci – Tech	13	9	9	10	6	13
History & Culture	15	20	14	17	14	21
International Relation, Defense, Persons in News (PIN)	0	4	7	8	3	8
Polity & Constitution	18	11	12	6	22	13
Total MCQ	**100**	**100**	**100**	**100**	**100**	**100**

You can see that number of questions in each segment has been subsequently either increased or decreased.

UPSC Civil Services aspirants are advised to give more time to topics as per analytical approach given in the above table along with the entire syllabus mentioned in the first chapter.

IMPORTANT TOPICS FROM WHICH QUESTIONS WERE ASKED (2011–18) IN CSAT P-1

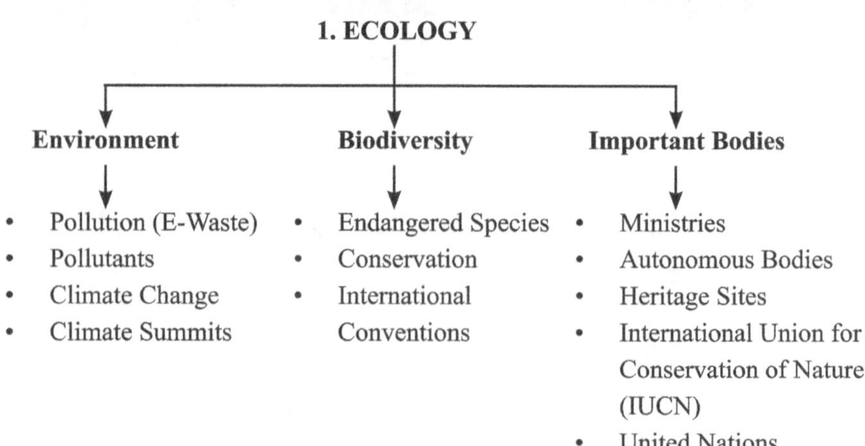

2. GENERAL SCIENCE AND SCIENCE & TECHNOLOGY

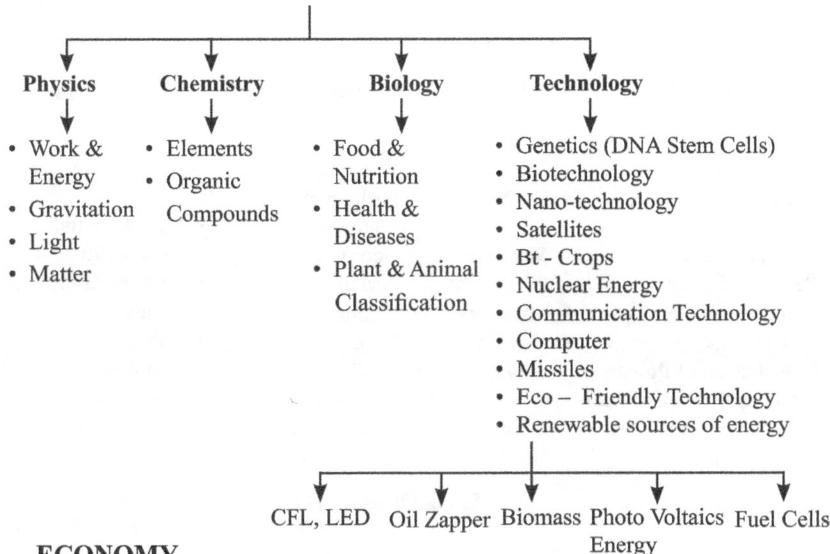

3. ECONOMY

- Taxes
- Interest Rates (Effect)
- National Income / GDP
- Growth Rate (% in 5 years)
- Banking System / Based III
- Deficit < Types / Financing
- Inflation
- FDI & FII
- Schemes / Programmes
- Budget (Concepts)
- Finance Commission (Recent)
- Five year plans
- Unemployment
- Poverty Estimation in India, Multi – dimensional Poverty Index
- Demographic Transition
- Supply & Demand of Money
- Bill of Payments
- Eight – core industries
- Monetary Policy & its Measures (CRR / SLR)
- Convertibility of Rupee
- Capital Account
- Important Items of Export & Import

4. POLITY

Important Parts of Constitution
- Fundamental Duties
- Directive Principles
- 73rd Amendment
- Passing of Bills (Ordinary & Money)
- Schedules
- Distribution of Powers between Union & States
- Various Motions
- Joint Sitting

Persons
- President
- Prime Minister
- Council of Ministers
- Governor
- Speaker
- CAG
- Attorney General

Institutions
- Parliament
- State Legislature
- Committees of Parliament
- Planning Commission
- NDC
- NITI Ayog
- Cabinet Secretariat
- Panchayati Raj

Miscellaneous
- PESA 1996
- Forest Rights ACT 2006
- Non–Proliferation Treaty
- Indian Membership in Regional Organisations

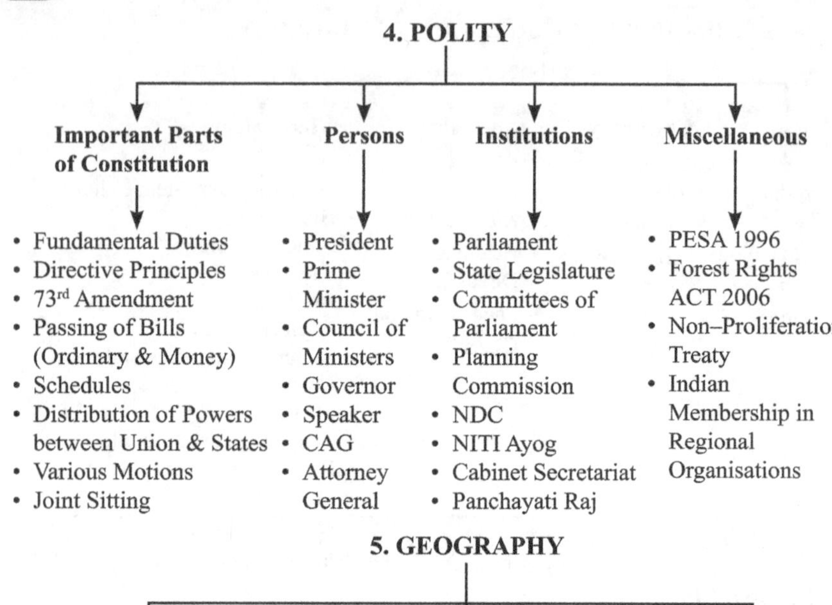

5. GEOGRAPHY

World
- Forest — Types / Features / Location
- Desert belt
- Channel
- Location of Countries between sea
- Climatic conditions in Different Regions
- Famous Mountains/ Rivers & their Locations

India
- Physiography / Mountains– Rivers Location
- Crops — Growing Season / Suitable climate / States
- Wetlands
- Monsoon
- National Parks / Wildlife Sanctuaries / Biosphere Reserves
- Drainage
- Soil–Types, Conservation Methods
- National Highways
- Forest
- Agriculture
- Farming
- Sustainable Agriculture Practices
- Tribes

Physical Factors / Universe / Earth
- Atmosphere
- Day–Night Variations
- Asteroids & Comets
- Floods / Earthquakes / Cyclones
- La Nina / El Nino
- Westerlies
- Ocean Currents
- Temperature
- Rainfall

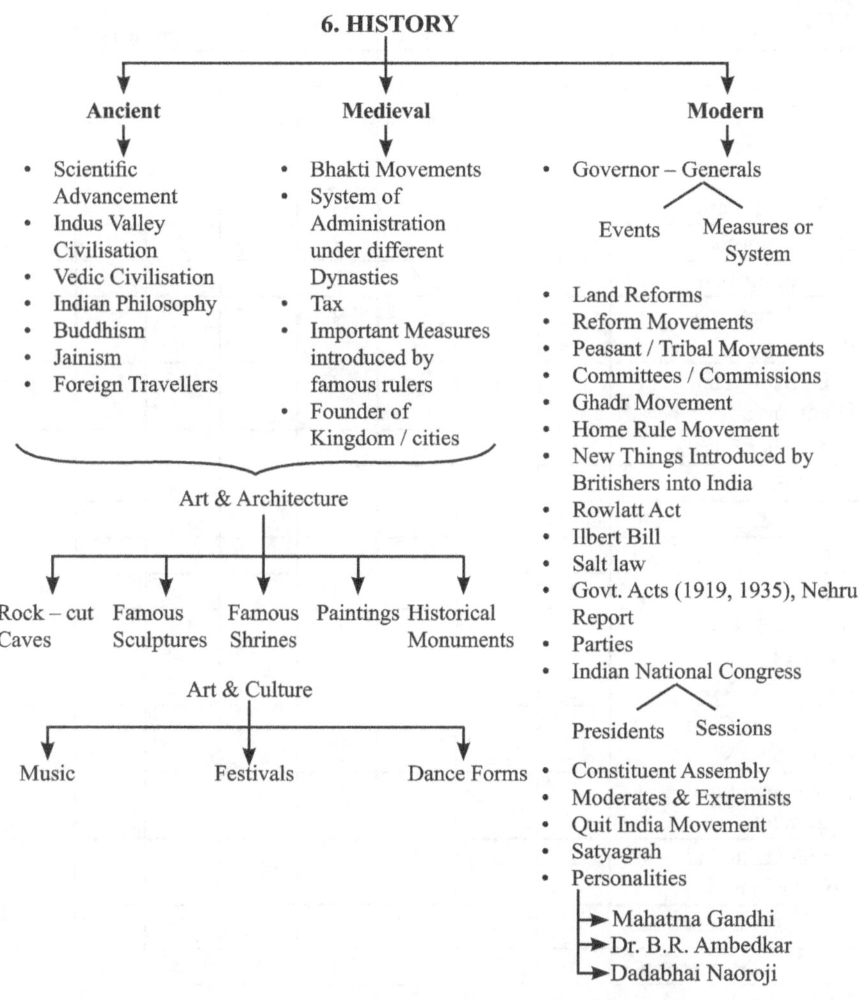

TOPIC WISE ANALYSIS - CSAT - IAS PRELIMS PAPER 2

CONTENTS	2011	2012	2013	2014	2015	2016	2017	2018
INTERPERSONAL SKILLS								
1. Interpersonal & Communication Skills	3	3	3	–	–			
MENTAL ABILITY								
1. Series				1	3			1
2. Classification or Odd One Out								

CONTENTS	2011	2012	2013	2014	2015	2016	2017	2018
3. Coding – Decoding						3	4	2
4. Analogy								
LOGICAL REASONING								
1. Blood Relation		1		3	1		2	1
2. Direction Sense	3	1		3	1	2	2	
3. Ranking Test	1	2	4	2	2			1
4. Arithmetical Reasoning				4	2	5	3	
5. Logical Venn Diagrams		1		2	–	2		
6. Number Puzzle	1		2	1	–			1
7. Syllogism					1		1	
8. Cube & Dice					1			3
9. Counting of figures					–			
10. Visual Reasoning	2	4	5	4	1			3
ANALYTICAL ABILITY/ REASONING						15	8	
1. Statement and Assumptions					–			
2. Statement and Arguments	1				–			
3. Statement and Conclusions	2	5	1		–		2	
4. Logical Deduction		4	1	–	–	1		
5. Critical Reasoning		2		4	5	14	29	
DECISION MAKING								
1. Administrative Courses of Action	2	2	1	–	–			
2. Selection Criteria				–	–			
3. Case Study		1		–	–			
4. Decision Making	3	2	2	–	–			
PROBLEM SOLVING								
1. Problem Solving	5	9	11	8	6			9

CONTENTS	2011	2012	2013	2014	2015	2016	2017	2018
COMPREHENSION								
1. General Comprehension	28	32	23	26	30	14	4	19
BASIC NUMERACY								
1. Numbers & their Relations	2		2	4	3	2	7	5
2. Percentage & Average	1		1	2	3	7	4	6
3. Orders of Magnitude	2		4	1	5			
4. Time and Work / Distance and Speed	2	1	5	2	3	3	6	2
5. Mensuration & Geometry	3				1	3	2	3
6. Advance Math	1	1	1	1	8		2	
DATA INTERPRETATION								
1. Introducing Charts and Graphs	7		1	1	2			
2. Data Interpretation	2	1	5	5	2			15
3. Data Sufficiency					–			
ENGLISH LANGUAGE COMPREHENSION SKILLS								
1. English Language Comprehension Skills	9	8	8	6	–	–		9

B. TREND ANALYSIS-MAIN (G.S.)

GSM1: Topicwise Questions since Pattern change in 2013

In 2013, UPSC changed the syllabus-pattern of Mains examination and the number of general studies papers were increased from two to four.

Category	GS Mains Paper-1	2013	2014	2015	2016	2017
History	Culture	20	40	25	25	10
History	Freedom struggle	30	30	25	37.5	65
History	World History	40	30	25	12.5	10

History	Post independence	50	0	0	0	0
Society	Religion, Region, empowerment	10	10	37.5	37.5	50
Society	Poverty, Population, Development	0	10	25	12.5	0
Society	Globalization Impact	10	0	12.5	12.5	0
Society	Women	10	30	12.5	0	0
Geography	Climate	10	20	37.5	12.5	60
Geography	Disaster	10	10	0	12.5	15
Geography	Urbanization	10	0	25	25	15
Geography	Physical	20	20	0	0	10
Geography	Resources	20	20	25	62.5	0
Geography	Industrial Location	10	30	0	0	15
	Total	250	250	250	250	250

GS2 Mains- Topicwise Questions since Syllabus change

Category	GSM-2	2013	2014	2015	2016	2017
Polity	Basic Str.	10	12.5	37.5	12.5	15
Polity	Executive	10	25	0	0	0
Polity	Legislature & Elections	10	12.5	0	12.5	40
Polity	Power Sep.	10	12.5	12.5	12.5	10
Polity	Fed-Local	30	12.5	25	37.5	10
Polity	Bodies	20	25	25	25	15
Welfare	Welfare & Protection	20	25	0	0	10
Welfare	Poverty & Hunger	10	0	12.5	0	25
Welfare	Edu,Health,HDI	20	25	25	37.5	10
Welfare	Eco.Reform	0	12.5	0	12.5	15
Governance	Accountability	20	0	25	25	10
Governance	NGO,Pressure,IAS	20	25	37.5	25	40
IR	Neighbours	50	12.5	25	12.5	10
IR	Non-Neighbours & Diaspora	10	0	12.5	12.5	30
IR	Inst., Group, Agree-ments	10	50	12.5	25	10
Total		250	250	250	250	250

GS3 Mains- Topicwise Papers since Syllabus Change

Block	GSM3	2013	2014	2015	2016	2017
1: Economy	Growth	10	25	37.5	25	35
	Budget	30	0	12.5	12.5	15
	Liberlization	20	25	0	12.5	15
	Infra, Invest	10	37.5	12.5	25	10
2: Food	land Reform	10	0	0	12.5	0
	Cropping	0	0	0	37.5	15
	MSP-PDS	20	12.5	0	0	15
	E-Tech in aid	0	0	12.5	0	10
	Food Processing	10	12.5	37.5	0	10
3: Science	Sci.Tech	40	12.5	25	0	10
	Sci.Tech (Indian)	0	25	12.5	25	25
	Environment	35	25	25	25	25
	Disaster	10	12.5	12.5	25	15
4: Crime	Develop vs Exterm.	10	0	12.5	12.5	40
	Border	10	62.5	25	25	0
	Cyber Security	25	0	25	12.5	10
	Money Laundering	10	0	0	0	0
	Total	250	250	250	250	250

Trend Analysis of GS4 Ethics Paper

Category	Sub Topic	2013	2014	2015	2016	2017
Ethics & Basics	Basic Theory	20	10	20	20	20
	EQ	30	10	0	10	10
	Thinkers	30	10	20	40	10
Family & Society	Family	0	30	35	30	0
	Social Influence	0	0	0	10	0
	Attitude	10	10	0	0	10
Job & Office	Neutrality	25	30	40	10	30
	Work Culture	60	60	25	0	10
	Compassion	25	0	20	20	20

Public Org	Theory	10	20	0	10	0
	Dilemma	0	40	20	20	0
	Code of Conduct	0	0	0	10	0
	Charter	0	0	0	0	0
	Corruption	0	10	0	25	50
	RTI	40	0	20	0	20
	IR/Funding	0	0	10	0	10
Private Org	Corporate	0	20	40	45	60
Total		**250**	**250**	**250**	**250**	**250**

SUBJECT-WISE PLANNING FOR PRELIMS

Planning for Current Events

Current Affairs questions are asked from the core disciplines or say subjects, for example, science and technology, Polity, History, Geography, Economics, and environment. So, we must give importance to current affairs from all perspectives, i.e. subjects, Prelim, Main and Personality Test.

These questions can be asked based on Government Initiatives/Policies, policies of India which have international importance– Look East Policy, International Institutions – IMF, WB, UNSC, etc. International Agreements – Non-Proliferation Treaty (NPT), etc. Human Rights Issues, Social Sector Initiatives, Sustainable Development, etc.

To bring in more clarity on this aspect, we would illustrate with a few examples.
For example:

Current Events – Geography

1 **With reference to 'Indian Ocean Dipole (IOD)' sometimes mentioned in the news while forecasting Indian monsoon, which of the following statements is/are correct? [2017]**

1. IOD phenomenon is characterized by a difference in sea surface temperature between tropical Western Indian Ocean and tropical Eastern Pacific Ocean.
2. An IOD phenomenon can influence an El Nino's impact on the monsoon.

Select the correct answer using the code given below:

(a) 1 only (b) 2 only

(c) Both 1 and 2 (d) Neither 1 nor 2

Solution: (b)

Solution: (b)

Current Events – History/Culture

2. Consider the following pairs: **(2014)**

Famous shrine	Location
1. Tabo monastery and temple complex	Spiti Valley
2. Lhotsava Lhakhang temple, Nako	Zanskar Valley
3. Alchi temple complex	Ladakh

Which of the pairs given above is/are correctly matched?

(a) 1 only (b) 2 and 3 only

(c) 1 and 3 only (d) 1, 2 and 3

Solution: (c)

Current Events – Polity/Governance

3. Which of the following can be said to be essentially the parts of Inclusive Governance? **(2012)**

1. Permitting the Non-Banking Financial Companies to do banking
2. Establishing effective District Planning Committees in all the districts
3. Increasing the government spending on public health
4. Strengthening the Mid-day Meal Scheme

Select the correct answer using the codes given below

(a) 1 and 2 only (b) 3 and 4 only

(c) 2, 3 and 4 only (d) 1, 2, 3 and 4

Solution: (c)

Current Events – Economics

Q. 4. Consider the following items: **[2018]**

1. Cereal grains hulled
2. Chicken eggs cooked
3. Fish processed and canned
4. Newspapers containing advertising material

Which of the above items is/are exempted under GST (Goods and Services Tax)?

(a) 1 only (b) 2 and 3 only

(c) 1, 2 and 4 only (d) 1, 2, 3 and 4

Solution: (a)

- Canned food (#3) and Newspaper (#4) are subject to GST. So, by elimination, we get correct answer (A)

5. **With reference to India's decision to levy an equalization tax of 6% on online advertisement services offered by non-resident entities, which of the following statements is/are correct? [2018]**
   1. It is introduced as a part of the Income Tax Act.
   2. Non-resident entities that offer advertisement services in India can claim a tax credit in their home country under the "Double Taxation Avoidance Agreements".

   Select the correct answer using the code given below:

   (a) 1 only (b) 2 only

   (c) Both 1 and 2 (d) Neither 1 nor 2

Solutions: (d) This was introduced in 2016, as a separate legislation under Finance Bill, and it doesn't provide tax credit in home country so both wrong.

6. **Which of the following statements best describes the term 'Scheme for Sustainable Structuring of Stressed Assets (S4A)', recently seen in the news? [2017]**

   (a) It is a procedure for considering ecological costs of developmental schemes formulated by the Government.

   (b) It is a scheme of RBI for reworking the financial structure of big corporate entities facing genuine difficulties.

   (c) It is a disinvestment plan of the Government regarding Central Public Sector Undertakings.

   (d) It is an important provision in 'The Insolvency and Bankruptcy Code' recently implemented by the Government.

Solution: (a)

Current Events – Science and Technology

7. **A company marketing food products advertises that its items do not contain trans-fats. What does this campaign signify to the customers?**
   1. The food products are not made out of hydrogenated oils.
   2. The food products are not made out of animal fats/oils.
   3. The oils used are not likely to damage the cardiovascular health of the consumers.

   Which of the statements given above is/are correct?

   (a) 1 only (b) 2 and 3 only

   (c) 1 and 3 only (d) 1, 2 and 3

Solution: (d)

Current Events – Environment

8. **With reference to the 'Global Alliance for Climate Smart Agriculture (GACSA)', which of the following statements is/are correct? (2018)**

1. GACSA is an outcome of the Climate Summit held in Paris in 2015.
2. Membership of GACSA does not create any binding obligations.
3. India was instrumental in the creation of GACS(A)

Select the correct answer using the code given

(a) 1 and 3 only (b) 2 only

(c) 2 and 3 only (d) 1, 2 and 3

Solution: (b)

9. The terms 'Event Horizon', 'Singularity', `String Theory' and 'Standard Model' are sometimes seen in the news in the context of [2017]

(a) Observation and understanding of the Universe

(b) Study of the solar and the lunar eclipses

(c) Placing satellites in the orbit of the Earth

(d) Origin and evolution of living organisms on the Earth

Solution: (b)

10. The term M-STRIPES' is sometimes seen in the news in the context of

(a) Captive breeding of Wild Fauna

(b) Maintenance of Tiger Reserves

(c) Indigenous Satellite Navigation System

(d) Security of National Highways

Solution: (a)

Source : The Hindu, April 2017

11. Brominated flame retardants are used in many household products like mattresses and upholstery. Why is there some concern about their use?

1. They are highly resistant to degradation in the environment.
2. They are able to accumulate in humans and animals.

Select the correct answer using the code given below.

(a) 1 only (b) 2 only

(c) Both 1 and 2 (d) Neither 1 nor 2

Solution: (c)

12. Recently there was a proposal to translocate some of the lions from their natural habitat in Gujarat to which one of the following sites ? [2017]

(a) Corbett National Park

(b) KunoPalpur Wildlife Sanctuary

(c) Mudumalai Wildlife Sanctuary

(d) Sariska National Park

Solution: (b)

Source : Indian Express

Current Events – International Organization

13. In the Indian context, what is the implication of ratifying the 'Additional Protocol' with the 'International Atomic Energy Agency (IAEA)' ?

(a) The civilian nuclear reactors come under IAEA safeguards.

(b) The military nuclear installations come under the inspection of IAE(A)

(c) The country will have the privilege to buy uranium from the Nuclear Suppliers Group (NSG).

(d) The country automatically becomes a member of the NSG.

Solution: (a)

- Under the old IAEA safeguards, all NPT signatories would specify their nuclear sites and IAEA would carry out inspections in the specified sites. Thus, IAEA, under the old safeguards, could only carry out inspection for unauthorised activities only at designated or specified sites declared by a country. This basically left an option open for states to carry out covert nuclear programmes - as it happened in case of Iraq.
- Thus, in 1993, the IAEA designed Additional Protocols (AP) to tighten the existing safeguarding regime.
- However, India specific Additional Protocols (AP) do not give IAEA the right to hinder or interfere with activities which are outside the scope of India's safeguard agreements, thus recognizing that India reserves a right to a military nuclear program outside IAEA agreement. From this description, C and D are irrelevant, and B is wrong. Thus we are left with answer (A)

Q. 14 What is the importance of developing Chabahar Port by India? [2017]

(a) India's trade with African countries will enormously increase.

(b) India's relations with oil-producing Arab countries will be strengthened.

(c) India will not depend on Pakistan for access to Afghanistan and Central Asia.

(d) Pakistan will facilitate and protect the installation of a gas pipeline between Iraq and India.

Solution: (c)

15. Which of the following organizations brings out the publication known as 'World Economic Outlook'?

(a) The International Monetary Fund

(b) The United Nations Development Programme

(c) The World Economic Forum

(d) The World Bank

Solution: (a)

Policies of India which has international ramifications

16. With reference to "Look East Policy" of India, consider the following statements:

1. India wants to establish itself as an important regional player in the East Asian affairs.
2. India wants to plug the vacuum created by the termination of Cold War.
3. India wants to restore the historical and cultural ties with its neighbours in Southeast and East Asia.

Which of the statements given above is/are correct?

(a) 1 only (b) 1 and 3 only

(c) 3 only (d) 1, 2 and 3

Solution: (c)

17. Consider the following statements: [2017]

1. The Nuclear Security Summits are periodically held under the aegis of the United Nations.
2. The International Panel on Fissile Materials is an organ of International Atomic Energy Agency.

Which of the statements given above is/are correct?

(a) 1 only (b) 2 only

(c) Both 1 and 2 (d) Neither 1 nor 2

Solution: (d)

NEWSPAPER READING FROM EXAM POINT OF VIEW

If you go through UPSC questions asked in previous years on Current Events and match the syllabus,you will find a correlation between core-subjects, such as History, Economics, Polity, Geography, Science and Tech or Environment and questions in GS Paper –I. The concept and facts asked in these questions are based on analytical aspect of contemporary issues and development in core-subjects appeared in daily newspapers. So, when you read newspaper, you should have all the core subjects in mind to note down the contemporary issues and development appearing in daily news.

Sources for Current Events:

1. **Newspapers**

   (i) *The Hindu*

   Important for:

   (a) Socio-economic and political issues,

   (b) Editorials and Opinions: An analytical view and coverage on Government programmes and policies.

(c) **Science and Technology:** Thursday Edition for scientific developments.

(d) **Environmental Issues:** Issues and policies at national and international level.

(e) **Economy:** Economic developments and policies.

(ii) ***The Indian Express***

Important for:

- Articles on International Relations.

(iii) ***Press Information Bureau***

Important for:

- Daily updates on Government Programmes and Policy.
- Articles on important personalities and their contribution.

(iv) ***PRS Legislative Research***

Important for:

- Discussion on legislative bills and policies of government.
- Summary of acts and bills.
- A monthly Policy Review.

(v) ***Institute for Defense Studies and Analysis (IDSA)***

Important For:

- India's national security, internal security and relations.
- Opinion on International Relations, Defence relations and Governments approach for national and international diplomacy.
- Paper 3 (Main)- Internal and External Security.

(vi) ***Yojana and Kurukshetra***

Important For:

- Articles on different topics- mainly on social and economic conditions of the country.
- Analysis of Government schemes and programmes.
- Social issues and policies affecting vulnerable sections.
- A very important and authentic source to generate opinion on government programmes and policies.

(vii) ***Lok Sabha and Rajya Sabha Debates***

Important For:

- Discussions on various socio-economic and political discourses.
- Opinions from experts.
- Live discussions for quality information.
- Mains Exam.

PLANNING FOR HISTORY

History is divided into 3 segments – Ancient, Medieval and Modern.

Trends of previous years questions

Year	Questions Asked
2011	13
2012	20
2013	15
2014	17
2015	13
2016	17
2017	15
2018	13

Recent trends show that number of questions asked in history segment varies from 13 to 20. So, it is better to analyse previous questions segment-wise (Ancient, Medieval, Modern & Culture) and then plan which segment should be given weightage as per analysis. More weightage is given to Modern, then to Ancient and least to medieval history as per question pattern analysis.

Modern India

Aspirants should focus on the followings:

1. Various revolts/movements/agitations (like 1857 revolt, Tebhaga Peasant Movement, Home Rule Movement, Quit India Movement, etc) based on:
   - The Purpose of the movement.
   - The Reasons which led to the movement.
   - The Consequences of the movement.
   - The people who participated in this movement.
   - Famous Personalities involved in the movement and their contribution.
   - The role of Press and Literature.

Example

Q. Which one of the following is a very significant aspect of the Champaran Satyagraha?

(a) Active all-India participation of lawyers, students and women in the National Movement

(b) Active involvement of Dalit and Tribal communities of India in the National Movement

(c) Joining of peasant unrest to India's National Movement

(d) Drastic decrease in the cultivation of plantation crops and commercial crops

Solution: (c) Option A, B and D are irrelevant to Champaran Satyagrah(a)

Q. Annie Besant was: [2013]

1. responsible for starting the Home Rule Movement
2. the founder of the Theo-sophical Society
3. once the President of the Indian National Congress

Select the correct statement/statements using the codes given below.

(a) 1 only (b) 2 and 3 only

(c) 1 and 3 only (d) 1, 2 and 3

Solution: (c)

Q. Consider the following pairs:

1. Radhakanta Deb: First President of the British Indian Association
2. GazuluLakshminarasuChetty: Founder of the Madras Mahajana Sabha
3. Surendranath Banerjee: Founder of the Indian Association

Which of the above pairs is/are correctly matched?

(a) 1 only (b) 1 and 3 only

(c) 2 and 3 only (d) 1, 2 and 3

Solution: (b)

2. Type of Administration (Revenue, Military)

- Type of Administration. Example: Mansabdari System, Jagirdhari – its significance and impact.
- The British rule. Example: Subsidiary alliance, Permanent Settlement, Mahalwari system etc. – its significance and impact.
- Similarities and Differences between the Mughal and the British Administration.
- Consolidation of the British rule in India– through enactment of various Acts/Laws (Regulation Act, 1773 to Indian Independence Act, 1947).

3. Colonial Rule in India

- Political-Administrative organization, Policies of the British India.
- Social, Economic setup like Agrarian Systems (Example: Permanent Settlement).
- Important Reports, Sessions, Acts, Committees setup during the British period.

Example

Q. After the Santhal Uprising subsided, what was/were the measure/measures taken by the colonial government? [2018]

1. The territories called 'Santhal Paraganas' were create(d)
2. It became illegal for a Santhal to transfer land to a non-Santhal.

Select the correct answer using the code given below:

(a) 1 only (b) 2 only

(c) Both 1 and 2 (d) Neither 1 nor 2

Solution (c)

Q. What was/were the object/objects of Queen Victoria's Proclamation (1858)?

1. To disclaim any intention to annex Indian States
2. To place the Indian administration under the British Crown
3. To regulate East India Company's trade with India

Select the correct answer using the code given below

(a) 1 and 2 only (b) 2 only

(c) 1 and 3 only (d) 1, 2 and 3

Solution (a)

Q. Who among the following was/were associated with the introduction of Ryotwari Settlement in India during the British rule?

1. Lord Cornwallis
2. Alexander Reed
3. Thomas Munro

Select the correct answer using the code given below:

(a) 1 only (b) 1 and 3 only

(c) 2 and 3 only (d) 1, 2 and 3

Solution (c)

Source NCERT Class VIII Part-III, Chapter-3

Q. Consider the following statements:

1. The Factories Act, 1881 was passed with a view to fix the wages of industrial workers and to allow the workers to form trade unions.
2. N.M. Lokhande was a pioneer in organizing the labour movement in British India.

Which of the above statements is/are correct?

(a) 1 only (b) 2 only

(c) Both 1 and 2 (d) Neither 1 nor 2

Solution : (b)

4. Religious and Social Reform Movements (from 1800 AD to 1947 AD)
   - The Ideological base – rationalism, humanism and universalism.
   - Reform Movements like Brahmo Samaj, Arya Samaj, Theosophical Society, Harijan Movement, etc.
   - Who started these movements?
   - What was the objective and emphasis of these movements?
   - How these movements were important in building a sense of nationalism among Indians?
   - Social reforms that had an impact on Education, Status of Women, Caste system of the society.

Example

Q. Which of the following statements is/are correct regarding BrahmoSamaj?

1. It opposed idolatry.
2. It denied the need for a priestly class for interpreting the religious texts.
3. It popularized the doctrine that the Vedas are infallible.

Select the correct answer using the codes given below :

(a) 1 only (b) 1 and 2 only

(c) 3 only (d) 1, 2 and 3

Solution: (b)

5. Important Personalities like Mahatma Gandhi, Dr B.R. Ambedkar, Subash Chandra Bose, Dadabhai Naoroji, Bal Gangadhar Tilak, Bhagat Singh, Annie Besant, etc. along with their contributions – literature, organization of movements and their role in India's Freedom Struggle should be covered.

Example

Q. He wrote biographies of Mazzini, Garibaldi, Shivaji and Shrikrishna; stayed in America for some time; and was also elected to the Central Assembly. He was

(a) Aurobindo Ghosh (b) Bipin Chandra Pal

(c) Lala Lajpat Rai (d) Motilal Nehru

Solution: (c)

Lala Lajpat Rai founded the Indian Home Rule League in the US in 1916 (TN History Class 12 book, page 150). So, he's the closest match. ICSE History textbook class 10 page 110 confirms that he indeed wrote those biographies Mazzini, Garibaldi et al.

Q. Consider the following statements:

The most effective contribution made by Dadabhai Naoroji to the cause of Indian National Movement was that he

1. exposed the economic exploitation of India by the British
2. interpreted the ancient Indian texts and restored the self-confidence of Indians
3. stressed the need for eradication of all the social evils before anything else

Which of the statements given above is/are correct?

(a) 1 only (b) 2 and 3 only

(c) 1 and 3 only (d) 1, 2 and 3

Solution: (a)

[Note: Aspirants must go through previous questions asked in Ancient &, Medieval sections to plan study]

PLANNING FOR GEOGRAPHY

Geography covers physical, Social and Economic Geography of India and the World.

You should make a Mind-Map of different topics given in the syllabus of Prelim and analyse the previous years questions asked. Your study should be based on the nature and number of questions asked from different segments year-wise.

Trends of previous years questions

Year	Questions Asked
2011	15
2012	20
2013	22
2014	26
2015	18
2016	9
2017	12
2018	9

As per the recent trend, atleast 15-20% weightage is given to Geography.

QUESTIONS ASKED IN PREVIOUS YEARS EXAM ARE BASED ON:

Q. "Momentum for Change : Climate Neutral Now" is an initiative launched by

(a) The Intergovernmentai Panel on Climate Change

(b) The UNEP Secretariat

(c) The UNFCCC Secretariat

(d) The World Meteorological Organisation

Solution: (c) UNFCCC secretariat launched its Climate Neutral Now initiative in 2015. The following year, the secretariat launched a new pillar under its Momentum for Change initiative focused on Climate Neutral Now, as part of larger efforts to showcase successful climate action around the worl(d) (Ref: "Organization's About US Page")

1. Co-relation between Geography & Current Events/Environment

We would illustrate with an example:

Q. With reference to micro-irrigation, which of the following statements is/ are correct?

1. Fertilizer/nutrient loss can be reduced
2. It is the only means of irrigation in dry land farming.
3. In some areas of farming, receding of ground water table can be checked.

Select the correct answer using the codes given below:

(a) 1 only (b) 2 and 3 only

(c) 1 and 3 only (d) 1, 2 and 3

Solution: (c)

This question, though basically forms part of current affair section, has a direct correlation with Geography.

Q. Which of the following can be threats to the biodiversity of a geographical area?

1. Global warming
2. Fragmentation of habitat
3. Invasion of alien species
4. Promotion of vegetarianism

Select the correct answer using the codes given below :

(a) 1, 2 and 3 only (b) 2 and 3 only

(c) 1 and 4 only (d) 1, 2, 3 and 4

Solution: (a)

2. Clarity of Concepts

Q. Consider the following statements:

1. The Earth's magnetic field has reversed every few hundred thousand years.
2. When the Earth was created more than 4000 million years ago, there was 54% oxygen and no carbon dioxide.
3. When living organisms originated, they modified the early atmosphere of the Earth.

Which of the statements given above is/are correct?

(a) 1 only (b) 2 and 3 only

(c) 1 and 3 only (d) 1, 2 and 3

Solution: (a)

- On the scale of a million years, the earth's magnetic fields has been found to reverse its direction. So, first statement is right.
- There are three stages in the evolution of the present atmosphere.... The early atmosphere largely contained water vapour, nitrogen, carbon

dioxide, methane, ammonia and very little of free oxygen. There was no atmosphere on early earth. Water vapour, methane, carbondioxide and ammonia released from molten mass covered the surface. So, CO2 was present, So, #2 wrong.

- Early atmosphere of earth had no free oxygen, the (life) forms until then could at best be only "anaerobic". Chlorophyll-bearing organisms later released free oxygen which gave greater possibilities for life to evolve. The first non-cellular forms of life could have originated 3 billion years back....(then) About 2000 million years ago the first cellular forms of life appeared on earth. Some of these cells had the ability to release Oxygen. It means early atmosphere of the earth was (mainly) modified by solar winds. When living organisms originated, it was beyond their capacity to modify the early atmosphere, since they couldn't synthesize oxygen at that time. This eliminates Statement#3, Thus we are left with answer "A: Only 1".

While studying Geography, clarity of concepts and it should be substantiated with appropriate facts.

Q. The Narmada river flows to the west, while most other large peninsular rivers flow to the east. Why? (2013)

1. It occupies a linear rift valley.
2. It flows between the Vindhyas and the Satpuras.
3. The land slopes to the west from Central India.

Select the correct answer using the codes given below.

(a) 1 only (b) 2 and 3

(c) 1 and 3 (d) None

Solution: (a)

Think & Learn

- Why do some rivers flow West, while majority flows in the East direction?
- Why do rivers flowing in the East direction form Deltas?
- A general awareness on which 'States' they flow and 'Hydro-electrical Projects' and 'Dams' constructed across these rivers.

Aspirants must take into account the followings:

- Importance of Geography
- Clarity of Concepts
- Significance of facts
- Level of Difficulty of Questions

Indian Geography

1. Physiography

India's physiography can be divided into:

- The Himalayas: The Greater Himalayas(Himadri), Lesser Himalayas (Himachal), Sub-Himalayas (Shivalik Range)

- Peninsular Plateau and Peninsular Mountains
- The North Plains and the Coastal plains
- Indian Desert
- Islands

Important Segments:

- Characteristics – Example: Himalayas are young, weak, flexible
- How were they formed? Example: The peninsula block was formed by various vertical movements and block faulting
- Climate and Rainfall in these regions
- Vegetation or Type of Forests found
- Soil along the slopes
- Biodiversity in the region

Example

Q. When you travel in Himalayas, you will see the following:

1. Deep gorges
2. U-turn river courses
3. Parallel mountain ranges
4. Steep gradients causing land-sliding

Which of the above can be said to be the evidences for Himalayas being young fold mountains?

(a) 1 and 2 only (b) 1, 2 and 4 only

(c) 3 and 4 only (d) 1, 2, 3 and 4

Solution: (d)

2. *River System in India*

- Indian River System can be broadly classified into 2 Major systems:
  - Himalayas River system consist of -Indus, Ganga, Brahamaputra,
  - Peninsular River Systems

Important Segments:

- Evolution of the drainage (river) system.
- Characteristics of the River system. Example: Peninsular river system is older than the Himalayan river system. They are non-perennial rivers.
- The states they flow through.
- Comparison between the Himalayas and the Peninsular river system.
- Hydro-Power projects, other Power plants and Major Dams built on these rivers. Example: Salal project on River Chenab.
- West flowing rivers in India. Why do these rivers flow West, while majority rivers flow in the East direction?

- Why do east flowing rivers form deltas?

Q. With reference to river Teesta, consider the following statements: (2012)

1. The source of river Teesta is the same as that of Brahmaputra but it flows through Sikkim.
2. River Rangeet originates in Sikkim and it is a tributary of river Teesta.
3. River Teesta flows into Bay of Bengal on the border of India and Bangladesh.

Which of the statements given above is/are correct?

(a) 1 and 3 only (b) 2 only
(c) 2 and 3 only (d) 1, 2 and 3

Solution: (b)

Source: India Year Book 2017, Chapter-1

Example

Q. The Brahmaputra, Irrawady and Mekong rivers originate in Tibet and flow through narrow and parallel mountain ranges in their upper reaches. Of these rivers, Brahmaputra makes a "U" turn in its course to flow into India. This "U" turn is due to

(a) Uplift of folded Himalayan series
(b) Syntaxial bending of geologically young Himalayas
(c) Geo-tectonic disturbance in the tertiary folded mountain chains
(d) Both (a) and (b) above

Solution: (b)

3. Minerals

Important Segments:

- Major areas where they are found
- Characteristics of the minerals
- It's Uses and Environmental impact.

Example

Q. Consider the following statements:

1. Natural gas occurs in the Gondwana beds.
2. Mica occurs in abundance in Kodarma.
3. Dharwars are famous for petroleum.

Which of the statements given above is/are correct?

(a) 1 and 2 (b) 2 only
(c) 2 and 3 (d) None

Solution: (b)

Example

Q. With reference to two non-conventional energy sources called 'coal bed methane' and 'shale gas', consider the following 'statements:

1. Coal bed methane is the pure methane gas extracted from coal seams, while shale gas is a mixture of propane and butane only that can be extracted from fine-grained sedimentary rocks.
2. In India abundant coal bed methane sources exist, but so far no shale gas sources have been found.

Which of the statements given above is/are correct?

(a) 1 only (b) 2 only

(c) Both 1 and 2 (d) Neither 1 nor 2

Solution: (d)

4. Climate

Important Segments:

- Factors determining the Climate of India
- Indian Monsoon
- It's nature/characteristics, significance and impact
- Upper Air circulation- Jet streams, Westerlies
- Cyclones – tropical and temperate
- El-Nino, La-Nino (More Emphasis should be given)
- How is it developed?
- How does this effect Indian climate and vegetation
- Related concepts like upwelling and its advantages

Example

Q. La Nina is suspected to have caused recent floods in Australia. How is La Nina different from El Nino?

1. La Nina is characterised by unusually cold ocean temperature in equatorial Indian Ocean whereas El Nino is characterised by unusually warm ocean temperature in the equatorial Pacific Ocean.
2. El Nino has adverse effect on south-west monsoon of India, but La Nina has no effect on monsoon climate.

Which of the statements given above is/are correct?

(a) 1 only (b) 2 only

(c) Both 1 and 2 (d) Neither 1 nor 2

Solution: (d)

Example

Q. Consider the following statements:

1. The duration of the monsoon decreases from southern India to northern India.

2. The amount of annual rainfall in the northern plains of India decreases from east to west.

Which of the statements given above is/are correct?

(a) 1 only (b) 2 only

(c) Both 1 and 2 (d) Neither 1 nor 2

Solution: (c)

PLANNING FOR POLITY

Polity covers Constitution of India, Indian Political System, Panchayati Raj, Public Policy, Rights, Issues, etc. First you prepare the Mind-Map of each Chapter given in the syllabus and then analyse the nature and number of questions asked in previous years GS Paper-I from Polity. If your study follows the trend analysis, your success is assured.

Trends of previous years questions

Year	Questions Asked
2011	14
2012	20
2013	18
2014	15
2015	21
2016	06
2017	22
2018	11

Strategy for Polity

How to Prepare Polity?

Questions from Polity cover both static (basic) as well as the dynamic (current events) part. For example in 2014, Judicial Appointment Bill was in news very frequently.

So, one must know the **basics of Judiciary** – its mode of appointment, powers and its autonomy granted by the Constitution of India. **Issue** related to Judiciary's autonomy comes under the dynamic part whereas the mode of appointment and powers of Judiciary comes under the static part.

This is the best way to go about reading Polity. If you can read this way, then many myths about Polity (like mugging-up all the articles, everything and anything about Constitution) can be dealt with easily.

Example

Q. Consider the following statements :

1. The Parliament of India can place a particular law in the Ninth Schedule of the Constitution of Indi(a)
2. The validity of a law placed in the Ninth Schedule cannot be examined by any court and no judgement can be made on it.

Which of the statements given above is/are correct ?

(a) 1 only (b) 2 only

(c) Both 1 and 2 (d) Neither 1 nor 2

Solution. (a)

Q. Democracy's superior virtue lies in the fact that it calls into activity

(a) the intelligence and character of ordinary men and women.

(b) the methods for strengthening executive leadership.

(c) a superior individual with dynamism and vision.

(d) a band of dedicated party workers.

Solution : (a)

Source : NCERT (New), Class-VIII, Civics, Chapter-3, pg-32

In 2014, two questions had come from Judiciary, based on the current issues. These were of static nature:

Q. The power to increase the number of judges in the Supreme Court of India is vested in

(a) The President of India (b) The Parliament

(c) The Chief Justice of India (d) The Law Commission

Solution: (b)

Example

Q. In India, Judicial Review implies

(a) the power of the Judiciary to pronounce upon the constitutionality of laws and executive orders.

(b) the power of the Judiciary to question the wisdom of the laws enacted by the Legislatures.

(c) the power of the Judiciary to review all the legislative enactments before they are assented to by the President.

(d) the power of the Judiciary to review its own judgements given earlier in similar or different cases

Solution : (a)

Source : NCERT (New), Class-XI, Chapter-6, Pg-139

Q. The power of the Supreme Court of India to decide disputes between the Centre and the States falls under its

(a) Advisory jurisdiction (b) Appellate jurisdiction.

(c) Original jurisdiction (d) Writ jurisdiction

Solution: (c)

Similarly when Comptroller and Auditor General (CAG) was in news (in 2012) with regard to exposing 2G Scam and Coal Scam), one has to go back to basics (static part) in understanding the powers and functions of CAG, mode of appointment and removal. Current events should always be prepared along with its basics.

For example:

Q. In India, other than ensuring that public funds are used efficiently and for intended purpose, what is the importance of the office of the Comptroller and Auditor General (CAG)? (2012)

1. CAG exercises exchequer control on behalf of the Parliament when the President of India declares national emergency/financial emergency.
2. CAG reports on the execution of projects or programmes by the ministries are discussed by the Public Accounts Committee.
3. Information from CAG reports can be used by investigating agencies to press charges against those who have violated the law while managing public finances.
4. While dealing with the audit and accounting of government companies, CAG has certain judicial powers for prosecuting those who violate the law.

Which of the statements given above is/are correct?

(a) 1, 3 and 4 only (b) 2 only

(c) 2 and 3 only (d) 1, 2, 3 and 4

Solution: (c)

Current events related to new Bills, Acts, Policies and related provisions should be noted down. One should try to relate current happenings with provisions of Indian Constitution.

For example:

Q. The National Green Tribunal Act, 2010 was enacted in consonance with which of the following provisions of the Constitution of India?

1. Right to healthy environment, construed as a part of Right to life under Article21

2. Provision of grants for raising the level of administration in the Scheduled Areas for the welfare of Scheduled Tribes under Article 275(1)
3. Powers and functions of Gram Sabha as mentioned under Article 243(A)

Select the correct answer using the codes given below:

(a) 1 only (b) 2 and 3 only

(c) 1 and 3 only (d) 1, 2 and 3

Solution: (a)

Questions at times are tricky, as the options given in the questions are very close to the correct choice. This creates ambiguity in the mind of the aspirant often leaving them confused.

For example:

Q. With reference to the election of the President of India, consider the following statements:

1. The value of the vote of each MLA varies from State to State.
2. The value of the vote of MPs of the Lok Sabha is more than the value of the vote of MPs of the Rajya Sabh(a)

Which of the statements given above is/are Correct?

(a) 1 only (b) 2 only

(c) Both 1 and 2 (d) Neither 1 or 2

Solution: (c) Both 1 and 2

- Statement 1 - Correct. Value of 1 MLA's vote is based on total population of state to be divided by the total MLAs. Hence it ought to vary from state to state.
- While the value of an MLA's vote depends on the population of the state he or she belongs to, the value of an MP's vote remains the same at 708. So, #2 is wrong. [Ref: IndianExpress coverage of Ramnatha Kovind's election, 2017-July]

Q. Which of the following are associated with 'Planning' in India?

1. The Finance Commission
2. The National Development Council
3. The Union Ministry of Rural Development
4. The Union Ministry of Urban Development
5. The Parliament

Select the correct answer using the code given below.

(a) 1, 2 and 5 only (b) 1, 3 and 4 only

(c) 2 and 5 Only (d) 1, 2, 3, 4 and 5

Solution: (c)

[Note: Here, though Finance Commission is involved in devolution of money it is not involved in Planning process. Many would have chosen (a) as the answer. Neither are the Ministries of Rural or Urban Development involved.]

Q. 'Economic Justice' the objectives of Constitution has been as one of the Indian provided in:

(a) the Preamble and Fundamental Rights

(b) the Preamble and the Directive Principles of State Policy

(c) the Fundamental Rights and the Directive Principles of State Policy

(d) None of the above

Solution: (b)

PLANNING FOR ECONOMICS

It covers Economic and Social Development-Sustainable Development, Poverty, Inclusion, Demographics, Social Sector Initiatives, etc.

Questions asked in this segment are based on your **conceptual understanding of macro-economics**. So, conceptual clarity is the most important factor to understand any topic, policy, data, etc. in Economics.

Your analysis of previous years questions will help you to know about the nature and types of questions asked from the Economic segment. If you apply your analysis in your preparation, you feel confident in your strengths to crack the exam.

Trends of previous years questions

Year	Questions Asked
2011	21
2012	15
2013	18
2014	11
2015	16
2016	29
2017	29
2018	20

For Example:

1. Current Affairs/Economics

Example

Q. Consider the following statements (2018)

1. The Fiscal Responsibility and Budget Management (FRBM) Review Committee Report has recommended a debt to GDP ratio of 60% for the general (combined) government by 2023, comprising 40% for the Central Government and 20% for the State Governments.

2. The Central Government has domestic liabilities of 21% of GDP as compared to that of 49% of GDP of the State Governments.
3. As per the Constitution of India, it is mandatory for a State to take the Central Government's consent for raising any loan if the former owes any outstanding liabilities to the latter.

Which of the statements given above is/are correct?

(a) 1 only (b) 2 and 3 only

(c) 1 and 3 only (d) 1, 2 and 3

Solution (c)

As per Economic Survey, first statement is right but Central Government's domestic liability is ~46% so #2 is wrong. By elimination, we get (C)

Q. With reference to the 'National Intellectual Property Rights Policy', consider the following statements:

1. It reiterates India's commitment to the Doha Development Agenda and the TRIPS Agreement.
2. Department of Industrial Policy and Promotion is the nodal agency for regulating intellectual property rights in India.

Which of the above statements is/are correct?

(a) 1 only (b) 2 only

(c) Both 1 and 2 (d) Neither 1 nor 2

Solution: (c)

Source:www.thehindu.com/news/national/cabinet-approves-national-intellectual-properly-rights-policy/article8594387.ece

Q. If the interest rate is decreased in an economy, it will

(a) decrease the consumption expenditure in the economy

(b) increase the tax collection of the Government

(c) increase the investment expenditure in the economy

(d) increase the total savings in the economy

Solution: (c)

Q. Under which of the following circumstances may 'capital gains' arise?

1. When there is an increase in the sales of a product
2. When there is a natural increase in the value of the property owned
3. When you purchase a painting and there is a growth in its value due to increase in its popularity

Select the correct answer using the codes given below:

(a) 1 only (b) 2 and 3 only

(c) 2 only (d) 1, 2 and 3

Solution: (b)

2. Introduction to Economics

Important Segments:

Understanding the basic concepts of:

- **Macro Economics:** Poverty, Growth, Employment, etc.
- **Microeconomics:** Decisions/choices made at a company, household or an individual level
- Difference between **Growth and Development**; indicators used to measure.

Example: To measure Growth- GDP is used and for Development – HDI (Human Development Index)

- **National Income Accounting:** Gross National Product (GNP), Gross Domestic Product (GDP), Gross National Income (GNI), Factor cost, Market Price, Purchasing power parity(PPP), Per-Capita Income (PCI) – a general understanding on how they are calculated and what all factors go into their calculation

Example: GDP is calculated using either of the following 3 methods- production method, expenditure method, income method.

- **Primary, Secondary, Tertiary Sectors:** What constitutes each sector? What are their contributions to the GDP?

Example: Primary Sector covers agriculture and allied activities, mining. It contributes 13.7% to India's GDP.

- **Capitalist State, Mixed Economic System:** Which type of Economic system India has adopted and why?

Example

Q. Consider the following statements: **(2018)**

1. Capital Adequacy Ratio (CAR) is the amount that banks have to maintain in the form of their own funds to offset any loss that banks incur if the account-holders fail to repay dues.
2. CAR is decided by each individual bank.

Which of the statements given above is/are correct?

(a) 1 only (b) 2 only

(c) Both 1 and 2 (d) Neither 1 nor 2

Solution: (a) CAR is decided by the benchmarks set by BASEL-III Committee on Banking supervision and implemented by the central bank of individual country. So, #2 is right, whereas #1 is correct.

Q. The national income of a country for a given period is equal to the:

(a) total value of goods and services produced by the nationals

(b) sum of total consumption and investment expenditure

(c) sum of personal income of all individuals

(d) money value of final goods and services produced

Solution: (a)

3. Growth & Development

Important Segments:

- Poverty– concepts like Below Poverty line (BPL), Poverty Gap, Poverty estimates by National Sample Survey Organisation (NSSO), which Institution in India decides on Poverty line- Planning Commission
- Different Committees set-up to measure poverty, methodology used – Alag committee, Lakadwala, Suresh Tendulkar Committee, NC Saxena Committee, Rangarajan Committee – A general understanding of how each committee differed in their measurement.

Example: Rangarajan Committee was set-up by Planning Commission in 2012; Methodology used is 'Monthly Expenditure of family of five'. According to the estimates- poverty per day per person in urban area is ₹ 47 and in rural area it is ₹ 32.

- **Inequality** – how is it measured – Gini co-efficient, Lorenz Curve; concepts like relative inequality, absolute inequality.
- **Issues with employment**, different types of unemployment like disguised unemployment, underemployment, etc; Globalization and its impact on labour.
- **Demographic Dividend, Skill Development**
- **Development Indicators** from International organisations like HDI, MPI (Multiple Poverty Index), Millennium Development Goals, etc.

Example

Q. Increase in absolute and per capita real GNP do not connote a higher level of economic development, if

(a) industrial output fails to keep pace with agricultural output.

(b) agricultural output fails to keep pace with industrial output.

(c) poverty and unemployment increase.

(d) imports grow faster than exports.

Solution: (c)

Economic development includes not only economic growth but also various other economic changes that improve the quality of life or standard of living of people in a country. If with economic growth, a country experiences various economic changes such as reduction in poverty and unemployment, reduction in income and wealth inequality, increase in literacy rate, improvement in health and hygiene, etc, that improve the quality of life then that is economic development. (NIOS Economics Textbook Page 32). So, C is the fitting choice.

Q. Disguised unemployment generally means

(a) large number of people remain unemployed

(b) alternative employment is not available

(c) marginal productivity of labour is zero

(d) productivity of workers is low

Solution: (c)

Q. What is the aim of the programme 'Unnat Bharat Abhiyan'?

(a) Achieving 100% literacy by promoting collaboration between voluntary organizations and government's education system and local communities.

(b) Connecting institutions of higher education with local communities to address development challenges through appropriate technologies.

(c) Strengthening India's scientific research institutions in order to make India a scientific and technological power.

(d) Developing human capital by allocating special funds for health care and education of rural and urban poor, and organizing skill development programmes and vocational training for them.

Solution: (a)

Source : Press information Bureau

Q. Economic growth in country X will necessarily have to occur if (2013)

(a) there is technical progress in the world economy

(b) there is population growth in X

(c) there is capital formation in X

(d) the volume of trade grows in the world economy

Solution: (c)

4. Inflation and Business Cycle

Important Segments:

- **Inflation**, **Depression**, **Recession** and related terms and concepts like deflation, disinflation, reflation, stagflation, Philip's curve.
- **Types of Inflation – based on the rate of growth of the prices**– creeping, trotting, galloping, hyper-inflation.

- **Types of Inflation – based on the causes**– Demand-pull, Cost-push, Structural, Speculation.
- **Impact of Inflation** on Indian Economy, different stakeholders in the economy. Is a minimum inflation necessary? If so why?
- **Inflation measurements** like CPI, WPI, GDP deflator:
  - Composition or what constitutes these indicators
  - Their merits and demerits
  - Which measurement is better indicator of inflation and why? Which index is used to measure inflation in India currently?
- Base year from which it's calculated:
  - What is this Base year?
  - Why does Government change the Base Year?
  - What impact it has on the economic growth or inflation?

Example: In WPI there are totally 676 items, out of that 20% weightage is given to Food, 14% to Power and Fuel, 66% to Manufactured goods. It does not include Services. Base year for WPI is 2010-11. It is published by Ministry of Commerce and Industry

- **Role of Government and RBI in controlling inflation**

Example

Q. Consider the following statements: **(2013)**

1. Inflation benefits the debtors.
2. Inflation benefits the bond-holders. Which of the statements given above is/are correct?

(a) 1 only (b) 2 only

(c) Both 1 and 2 (d) Neither 1 nor 2

Solution: (a)

Q. A rise in general level of prices may be caused by:

1. an increase in the money supply
2. a decrease in the aggregate level of output
3. an increase in the effective demand.

Select the correct answer using the codes given below.

(a) 1 only (b) 1 and 2 only

(c) 2 and 3 only (d) 1, 2 and 3

Solution: (d)

5. Money and Banking Systems

Important Segments:

- **Role and functions of RBI**
- **Monetary Policy/measures** taken by RBI like Bank rate, repo rate,

reverse repo rate, Statutory Liquidity Ratio (SLR), Cash reserve Ratio (CRR), Liquidity Adjustment Facility (LAF), Marginal Standing Facility (MSF)

— Why are these measures taken?

— What impact it has on the Supply of money, Inflation and the Economy?

- **Different types of Banks and their functioning**– Commercial Banks, RRB's, Development banks, NABARD, Co-operative Banks, Development Banks, Merchant Banks, Non-Banking Financial Company's (NBFC's), Regional Rural Banks (RRBs) etc.

  — Functions of these Banks, to whom do they lend?

  — How are these Banks regulated? Concepts like priority sector lending

Example: NBFC's are regulated by RBI, unlike the normal banks, NBFC cannot accept demand deposits (DD); NBFCs do not form part of the payment and settlement system and cannot issue 'cheques' drawn on itself.

- **Banking reforms** like Bank Nationalisation (1969, 1980) Base, Norms, etc.

  — Why were/are these reforms needed?

  — What was/is the Purpose of these reforms?

- **Understand Key-Terms**– Financial Inclusion, Fiscal Consolidation, Narrow Banking, Non-Performing Assets, Shadow Banks, Weak Bank, Core Banking, Bank Run, Priority Sector lending, Capital to Risk Weighted Assets (CRAR) etc., and other related concepts related to Banking – what steps have been taken by the Government and RBI in this regard.

- **Steps taken by government** with regard to Financial Inclusion.

  Example: Introduction of Business Correspondent model in rural areas or Woman only banks, Jan Dan Yojana, Micro-finance, Mudra Bank, etc

- Recent **Committee's setup** with regard to Banking Reforms and its important recommendations

Example

Q. If the interest rate is decreased in an economy, it will

(a) decrease the consumption expenditure in the economy

(b) increase the tax collection of the Government

(c) increase the investment expenditure in the economy

(d) increase the total savings in the economy

Solution: (c)

Example

Q. Which one of the following links all the ATMs in India?

(a) Indian banks' Association

(b) National Securities Depository Limited

(c) National Payments Corporation of India

(d) Reserve Bank of India

Solution: (c)

Till 2009, RBI's Institute for Development and Research in Banking Technology (IDRBT) provided the linkages to ATM network in India but afterwards, it was taken over by NPCi's National Financial Switch (NFS).

Q. Which of the following statements is/are correct regarding the Monetary Policy Committee (MPC)?

1. It decides the RBI's benchmark interest rates.
2. It is a 12-member body including the Governor of RBI and is reconstituted every year.
3. It functions under the chairmanship of the Union Finance Minister.

Select the correct answer using the code given below:

(a) 1 only (b) 1 and 2 only

(c) 3 only (d) 2 and 3 only

Solution: (a)

Q. The Reserve Bank of India regulates the commercial banks in matters of

1. liquidity of assets
2. branch expansion
3. merger of banks
4. winding-up of banks.

Select the correct answer using the codes given below.

(a) 1 and 4 only (b) 2, 3 and 4 only

(c) 1, 2 and 3 only (d) 1, 2, 3 and 4

Solution: (d)

Q. What is/are the facility/facilities the beneficiaries can get from the services of Business Correspondent (Bank Saathi) in branchless areas?

1. It enables the beneficiaries to draw their subsidies and social security benefits in their villages.
2. It enables the beneficiaries in the rural areas to make deposits and withdrawals.

Select the correct answer using the code given below.

(a) 1 only (b) 2 only

(c) Both 1 and 2 (d) Neither 1 nor 2

Solution: (c)

6. **Schemes/Yogana**

Example

Q. Recognition of Prior Learning Scheme' is sometimes mentioned in the news with reference to

(a) Certifying the skills acquired by construction workers through traditional channels.

(b) Enrolling the persons in Universities for distance learning programmes.

(c) Reserving some skilled jobs to rural and urban poor in some public sector undertakings.

(d) Certifying the skills acquired by trainees under the National Skill Development Programme.

Solution: (a)

Source : http://indianexpress.com/article/india

Q. What is the purpose of Vidyanjali Yojana'?

1. To enable the famous foreign educational institutions to open their campuses in India.
2. To increase the quality of education provided in government schools by taking help from the private sector and the community.
3. To encourage voluntary monetary contributions from private individuals and organizations so as to improve the infrastructure facilities for primary and secondary schools.

Select the correct answer using the code given below:

(a) 2 only (b) 3 only

(c) 1 and 2 only (d) 2 and 3 only

Solution: (a)

Source : Indianexpressjune2016

PLANNING FOR CULTURE

India is a country of diverse culture. So, it covers various cultural aspects from ancient, medieval to modern times. Indian culture comprises of Art, Paintings, Miniature, Architecture and Literature.

To cover the topics in easy way, you should analyse the previous year questions and make Mind-Map, Charts and tables of topics in chronological order to keep in memory.

Sources to Prepare from:

- Class 11th NCERT (Old)- Textbook on fine arts-Specific book on Art and Culture

- New NCERT-Class 12th-Themes in Indian History

Q. With reference to the religious history of India, consider the following statements:

1. Sautrantika and Sammitiya were the sects of Jainism.
2. Sarvastivadin held that the constituents of phenomena were not wholly momentary, but existed forever in a latent form.

Which of the statements given above is/are correct?

(a) 1 only (b) 2 only

(c) Both 1 and 2 (d) Neither 1 nor 2

Solution: (b)

Example

Q. Lord Buddha's image is sometimes shown with the hand gesture called 'Bhumisparsha Mudra'. It symbolizes

(a) Buddha's calling of the Earth to watch over Mara and to prevent Mara from disturbing his meditation

(b) Buddha's calling of the Earth to witness his purity and chastity despite the temptations of Mara

(c) Buddha's reminder to his followers that they all arise from the Earth and finally dissolve into the Earth, and thus this life is transitory

(d) Both the statements (a) and (b) are correct in this context

Solution: (b)

Example

Q. Some Buddhist rock-cut caves are called Chaityas, while the others are called Viharas. What is the difference between the two?

(a) Vihara is a place of worship, while Chaitya is the dwelling place of the monks

(b) Chaitya is a place of worship, while Vihara is the dwelling place of the monks

(c) Chaitya is the stupa at the far end of the cave, while Vihara is the hall axial to it

(d) There is no material difference between the two

Solution: (b)

1. **Architecture**

   Important Segments:

   - **Famous Temples** constructed during the reign of different Empires
   - Their location

- Different **styles of Temples** like Dravida, Nagara, Vesara, Panchayatan
- **Rock cut temples**, specific features of temples- Garbgriha, Shikhara etc.
- **Gupta Era**– Golden age of Indian Architecture- Caves- Ajanata and Ellora- Religious aspects of these caves
- **Temple Architecture in South India**– Nayaka, Vesara, Dravidian and Vijayanagara, etc
- **Sculpture**– Chola- Nataraja, etc.
- **Other school of arts**– Pala, Rashtrakuta and Hosala, etc. Their religious themes
- **Indo-Islamic Architecture**– Decoration, Dome, etc. Difference between Indo-Islamic and ancient architecture

Example

Q. With reference to the cultural history of India, the term 'Panchayatan' refers to

(a) an assembly of village elders

(b) a religious sect'

(c) a style of temple construction

(d) an administrative functionary

Solution: (c)

2. Post Mauryan Art

Important Segments:

- School of Art- Gandhara, Mathura, Gupta, Amravati
- Difference and similarities among them
- Significant features associated with each School

3. Paintings

Important Segments:

- Prehistoric Paintings like Bhimbetka Rock paintings
- Wall Paintings
- Mural Paintings (Badami)
- Cave Paintings at Ajanta and Ellora
- Themes associated with these paintings
- Special features/styles associated with different
- Their locations

Q. The well-known painting "Bani Thani" belongs to the

(a) Bundi school (b) Jaipur school

(c) Kangra school (d) Kishangarh school

Solution: (d)

Q. The painting of Bodhisattva Padmapani is one of the most famous and oft-illustrated paintings at

(a) Ajanta (b) Badami

(c) Bagh (d) Ellora

Solution: (a)

Source : NCERT(New),class-XI, Pg. 54

4. Miniature Painting

Important Segments:

- Pala School of Painting
- Western Indian Paintings (Rajasthan, Gujrat and Malwa)
- Mughal School of Painting
- Deccan School of Painting (Tanjore, Ahemadnagar, Bijapur etc)
- Pahari School of Paintings (Basholi, Kangra and Guler etc)
- Special features/styles associated with different paintings
- Similarities and Differences
- Their Location

5. Modern Painting

Important Segments:

- Bengal School of Painting
- Santiniketan school
- Specific personalities like Raja Ravi Verma, Rabindranath Tagore's, Amrita Shergil and their works, etc.

Examples

Q. Consider the following historical places:

1. Ajanta Caves
2. Lepakshi Temple
3. Sanchi Stupa

Which of the above places is / are also known for mural paintings?

(a) 1 only (b) 1 and 2 only

(c) 1, 2 and 3 (d) None

Solution: (b)

Q. Ibadat Khana at Fatehpur Sikri was

(a) the mosque for the use of Royal Family

(b) Akbar's private prayer chamber

(c) the hall in which Akbar held discussions with scholars of various religions.

(d) the room in which the nobles belonging to different religions gathered to discuss religious affairs.

Solution: (c)

PLANNING FOR ENVIRONMENT

Recent trends show that the UPSC is constantly giving importance to 'Environment Section'. There can be various reasons for it from inclusion of Indian Forest Services (IFoS) to increasing worldwide environmental concern.

Trends of previous years questions

Year	Questions Asked
2011	15
2012	10
2013	08
2014	13
2015	11
2016	21
2017	14
2018	9

Areas of Coverage

Analysis of Previous year questions shows the following topics coverage in CSAT Paper-I:

Issues related to Environmental Ecology, e.g. ecological terms like Ecotone, Ecological niche, ecosystem, effects of environmental deterioration, how it affects human being, food chain in the ecosystem.

- **Pollution:** Air, Water & Sound pollution; Acid rain, Photochemical smog, Green House Gases, Ozone hole, algal bloom.
- **Bio-diversity** includes different human races, International Union for Conservation of Nature and Natural Resources (IUCN) – Red Data Book, Biodiversity, Hotspots.
- **Conservation:** Conservation of natural resources, National Parks, Wildlife Conservations, Wetlands, Biosphere Reserves, etc. – internationally recognized Wetlands and Biosphere Reserves of India.
- **Sustainable Development:** Renewable energy, Biotechnology (bio-fertilizers, bio-pesticides), Biomass gasification.
- **Ecologically sensitive areas:** Western Ghats, Himalayas.
- **Climate Change:** Different measures taken to control climate change at national and international level (Kyoto Protocol, Montreal Protocol) held at various climate change summits.
- **Laws, Regulatory Bodies and Policies at national and international level:** Environment Protection Act, Forest Right Act, National Biodiversity Authority, Protocols and Summits like Cartanega Protocol, Nagoya Protocol and Lima Conference, etc.

- **Intergovernmental Organizations, Treaties and Conventions related to climate change, biodiversity:** Ramsar Convention, Montreux Record, The three Rio Conventions—Convention on Biological Diversity(CoB), United Nations Framework Convention on Climate Change (UNFCCC) and United Nations Convention to Combat Desertification – from the 1992 Earth Summit),UNEP, FAO, UNESCO, etc.

Sources for Study

NCERT books: Geography from 6th and 12th and Biology, 12th (Old and New)

ICSE books: Class 10th and 11th

Newspaper: The Hindu

Magazine: Science Reporter

Example

Q. Which of the following has/have shrunk immensely/dried up in the recent past due to human activities ?

1. Aral Sea
2. Black Sea
3. Lake Baikal

Select the correct answer using the code given below :

(a) 1 only (b) 2 and 3

(c) 2 only (d) 1 and 3

Solution (a)

- The Aral Sea, in Central Asia, used to be the fourth largest lake in the world, after the Caspian Sea, and Lakes Superior and Victori(a) Now barely 10% of it is left. BBC-2014.
- Lake Baikal's has been crippled by a series of detrimental phenomena.... They include the disappearance of the omul fish, rapid growth of putrid algae and the death of endemic species of sponges across its vast 3.2 million-hectare are(a) [TheHindu 2017-Oct], but there is no mention of immensely drying up. Hence answer A: 1 only.

Q. Consider the following statements:

1. The definition of "Critical Wildlife Habitat" is incorporated in the Forest Rights Act, 2006.
2. For the first time in India, Baigas have been given Habitat Rights.
3. Union Ministry of Environment, Forest and Climate Change officially decides and declares Habitat Rights for Primitive and Vulnerable Tribal Groups in any part of Indi(a)

Which of the statements given above is/are correct ?

(a) 1 and 2 only (b) 2 and 3 only

(c) 3 only (d) 1, 2 and 3

Solution (a)

- Baigas are considered as a particularly vulnerable tribal group (PVTG) in the Indian Constitution and rely mostly on shifting cultivation, forest produce and fishing for sustenance, spread over forested areas of Madhya Pradesh and Chhattisgarh. In 2016, they became India's first community to get habitat rights. Ref: Downtoearth-2016 So, #2 is right.
- Under FRA Act, district level Committees have to adjudicate the rights, whereas Tribal ministry only issues guidelines. That makes #3 wrong / irrelevant. By elimination, we are left with answer A: only 1 and 2.

Q. Due to some reasons, if there is a huge fall in the population of species of butterflies, what could be its likely consequence/consequences? (2017)

1. Pollination of some plants could be adversely affected.
2. There could be a drastic increase in the fungal infections of some cultivated plants.
3. It could lead to a fall in the population of some species of wasps, spiders and birds.

Select the correct answer using the code given below:

(a) 1 only (b) 2 and 3 only
(c) 1 and 3 only (d) 1, 2 and 3

Solution: (c)
Source : NCERT, Class-12, Biology, Pg. 30

Q. Biological Oxygen Demand (BOD) is a standard criterion for

(a) Measuring oxygen levels in blood
(b) Computing oxygen levels in forest ecosystems
(c) Pollution assay in aquatic ecosystems
(d) Assessing oxygen levels in high altitude regions

Solution: (c)
Source : NCERT, Class-11, Chemistry, Chapter-14, Page-407

Q. Consider the following pairs:

1. Dampa Tiger Reserve : Mizoram
2. Gumti Wildlife Sanctuary : Sikkim
3. Saramati Peak : Nagaland

Which of the above pairs is /are correctly matched?

(a) 1 only (b) 2 and 3 only
(c) 1 and 3 only (d) 1, 2 and 3

Solution: (c)

Q. In the context of solving pollution problems, what is/are the advantage/ advantages of bioremediation technique?

1. It is a technique for cleaning up pollution by enhancing the same biodegradation process that occurs in nature.
2. Any contaminant with heavy metals such as cadmium and lead can be readily and completely treated by bioremediation using micro-organisms.
3. Genetic engineering can be used to create microorganisms specifically designed for bioremediation.

Select the correct answer using the code given below:

(a) 1 only (b) 2 and 3 only

(c) 1 and 3 only (d) 1, 2 and 3

Solution: (c)

PLANNING FOR SCIENCE & TECHNOLOGY

Prelim syllabus gives a wide coverage to Science and Technology. As per trend analysis of previous year questions asked recently, **UPSC gives importance to dynamic-cum-analytical aspect of Science and Technology**. The questions asked are based on basic scientific concept and facts related to latest development in research focused on **issues, phenomena, their application, scope, merits, demerits, in day to day life of human beings, animals, plants, physical changes, etc.** Nature of questions is based on static scientific laws and dynamic ones. Static nature of concepts and facts are covered in NCERT books- VI to XII, but dynamic nature of concepts and facts can be searched out in Newspapers, magazines, and on different sites of NET.

Trends of previous years questions

Year	Questions Asked
2011	19
2012	14
2013	19
2014	16
2015	12
2016	10
2017	06
2018	15

Approach of Study

Go through the syllabus and make MIND-MAP of each chapter and main topics in detail. Then analyse the previous year questions to keep in mind, both syllabus and types of questions during reading the text in books and coverage in newspaper & magazines.

Let us proceed and start with Basic Science. Concentrate on following explanations:

1. **Physical Science and Current Events:** Questions from this section are basic and deal more with current happening or some phenomenon in news. There is no need to study physics as a core subject.

   Important Segments:

   Current aspects of Physics can be broadly understood under following headings which are directional that you will find while reading newspapers.

   - *Graphene:* It was asked in UPSC because in 2010, Nobel Prize in Physics was awarded on the work of Graphene. The question was on its properties rather than other facts.
   - *Higg's Boson:* A buzz for quite a long time because of its ground breaking research hence asked by UPSC. Always concentrate on properties and reasons on which the news is based on. Do not go in deep research.
   - *Big Bang Theory:* Reason for continuous expansion of the Universe, the reasons behind it and the proof available.
   - *Dark Energy and Dark Matter:* Quite often in news. Scientists are still trying to solve the mystery behind its existence.

Examples

Q. Consider the following phenomena :

1. Light is affected by gravity.
2. The Universe is constantly expanding.
3. Matter warps its surrounding space-time.

Which of the above is/are the prediction/predictions of Albert Einstein's General Theory of Relativity, often discussed in media ?

(a) 1 and 2 only (b) 3 only

(c) 1 and 3 only (d) 1, 2 and 3

Solution (d)

- 2010: International Team of Astronomers confirmed Albert Einstein's theory of general relativity and that the expansion of the universe is accelerating after looking at data from the Hubble Space Telescope. There is an unknown source of energy in the universe which is causing the cosmic expansion to speed up. 2016: Japanese researchers' study finds that the expansion of the universe could be explained by a cosmological constant, as proposed by Einstein in his theory of general relativity. So second statement is right. This eliminates B and (C)
- 2018: Hubble Space Telescope captured image of a phenomenon called Einstein Ring. Einstein in his theory of general relativity, had suggested that a massive object would warp space and time. So, statement3 is right. Hence we are left with correct answer "D": 1, 2 and 3 all correct. [Ref: TheHindu Newspaper]

Q. Graphene is frequently in news recently. What is its importance?

1. It is a two-dimensional material and has good electrical conductivity.
2. It is one of the thinnest but strongest materials tested so far.
3. It is entirely made of silicon and has high optical transparency.
4. It can be used as 'conducting electrodes' required for touch screens, LCDs and organic LEDs.

Which of the statements given above are correct?

(a) 1 and 2 only (b) 3 and 4 only

(c) 1, 2 and 4 only (d) 1, 2, 3 and 4

Solution: (c)

Recently there was news related to 'Indian Neutrino Observatory' to be set in Tamil Nadu.

Example

Q. India-based Neutrino Observatory is included by the Planning Commission as a mega science project under the 11th five-Year Plan. In this context, consider the following statements:

1. Neutrinos are chargeless elementary particles that travel close to the speed of light.

2. Neutrinos are created in nuclear reactions of beta decay.
3. Neutrinos have a negligible, but nonzero mass.
4. Trillions of Neutrinos pass through human body every second.

Which of the statements given above are correct?

(a) 1 and 3 only (b) 1, 2 and 3 only

(c) 2, 3 and 4 (d) 1, 2, 3 and 4

Solution: (d)

An articles in 'The Hindu' about scientists discussing their experience and discoveries about Dark Energy and Dark Matter. Here UPSC may be interested in.

Q. Consider the statements about 'Dark Energy and Dark Matter'.

1. Dark energy attracts while Dark matter repels.
2. While dark energy shows itself only on the largest cosmic scale, dark matter exerts its influence on individual galaxies as well as the universe at large.

Correct statement(s) is/are

(a) Only 1 (b) Only 2

(c) Both(d) None

Solution: (b) Only 2

2. Concepts: Forces in Nature and Naturally Occurring Phenomenon

Important Segments:

- **Gravitational Force:** Basic concept, its impact on earth and on other heavenly bodies. Its relation and reaction with other known forces, etc. Try to simplify your learning process. There is lot to learn in less time.
- **Electromagnetic Force and Energy:** Same as above
- **Rotation and Revolution of Earth:** Its effects on other natural phenomenon, How they are responsible for any change on Earth? Whether they are inclusive or exclusive of other changes?
- **Recent phenomenon in news:** Solar Flares, etc.

Example

Q. Consider the following: **(2013)**

1. Electromagnetic radiation
2. Geothermal energy
3. Gravitational force
4. Plate movements
5. Rotation of the earth
6. Revolution of the earth

Which of the above are responsible for bringing dynamic changes on the surface of the earth?

(a) 1, 2, 3 and 4 only (b) 1, 3, 5 and 6 only

(c) 2, 4, 5 and 6 only (d) 1, 2, 3, 4, 5 and 6

Solution: (d)

*[**Note:** Recent trend suggests that a question can be put in geography, environment as well as Science domain depending on various dimensions. For example, above question is evidently asking for physical forces that we learnt in Physics but then the scope of the question also covers geographical aspect as well. Do not get puzzled over such points whether the question is from Physics or Geography or anything. Basically, UPSC is framing questions on concepts and a single question can have one concept or five concepts at the same time. If you are weak in any of the given concept then it becomes quite difficult to solve the question, unless the 'technique of elimination' can come to your rescue.]*

Another issue from Current Affairs is Solar Flares in news.

Q. "A solar flare is a sudden flash of brightness observed over the Sun's surface or the solar limb, which is interpreted as a large energy release". Consider the statements with reference to it:

1. They are always followed by a colossal mass ejection.
2. The flare ejects clouds of neutrons, ions, and atoms through the corona of the sun into space.
3. They produce radiation across electromagnetic spectrum at all wavelength except visible

Correct code is/are

(a) 1 and 2 (b) 1, 2 and 3

(c) Only 3 (d) None

Solution: (d) None

3. Natural Processes

Important Segments: While going through NCERTS or any source, pay more attention on concepts explaining any natural phenomenon. For instance:

- What causes a Rainbow?
- Dispersion in nature, Spectrum, Total Internal Reflection, Refraction and
- Concepts like why the sky is blue in colour?
- Why does the sun appear Red during sunrise and sunset (the physics behind it needs to be known)
- Why do stars twinkle?
- What is a Pole Star? Where/which direction it is visible also needed.
- Surface tension and capillary actions
- Phenomenon related to heat and light
- Similarly you should know the reason behind what causes lightning, thunderstorms and the various types of clouds (also is given in Geography texts of NCERT)

Q. During a thunderstorm, the thunder in the skies is produced by the

1. Meeting of cumulonimbus clouds in the sky
2. Lightning that separates the nimbus clouds
3. Violent upward movement of air and water particles

Select the correct answer using the codes given below.

(a) 1 only
(b) 2 and 3
(c) 1 and 3
(d) None of the above produces the thunder

Solution: (c)

Q. Consider the following phenomena:

1. Size of the sun at dusk
2. Colour of the sun at dawn
3. Moon being visible at dawn
4. Twinkle of stars in the sky
5. Polestar being visible in the sky

Which of the above are optical illusions?

(a) 1, 2 and 3 (b) 3, 4 and 5
(c) 1, 2 and 4 (d) 2, 3 and 5

Solution: (c)

4. Chemical Science: Chemistry and Current Events

Important Segments:

- General phenomenon of chemistry or chemical change like anomalous expansion of water, density of water.
- Elements in nature: radioactive (Ex: Thorium, Uranium) and non-radio active, Carbon Dating, Lead- its harmful effects and uses (Ex: is it used in Petrol and pencils?)
- Nuclear Energy- Focus on Neutrons, use of Heavy Water, controlled and uncontrolled chain reaction and nuclear reactors. Locations of Nuclear reactors in India
- Properties of elements and compounds that you encounter in news like Ethanol, Methanol, etc.
- Terms like Antioxidant, Isotopes and Artificial Rains, etc.

Example

Q. The surface of a lake is frozen in severe winter, but the water at its bottom is still liquid. What is the reason?

(a) Ice is a bad conductor of heat

(b) Since the surface of the lake is at the same temperature as the air, no heat is lost

(c) The density of water is maximum at 4°C

(d) None of the statements (a), (b) and (c) given above is correct

Solution: (c)

Q. Which of the following is/are the example/examples of chemical change?

1. Crystallization of sodium chloride
2. Melting of ice
3. Souring of milk

Select the correct answer using the code given below.

(a) 1 and 2 only (b) 3 only

(c) 1, 2 and 3 (d) None

Solution: (b)

5. Biological Sciences: Botany, Zoology, Medical Sc. & Current Affairs

Aspirants can plan this segment like physics & chemistry...

Q. With reference to the Genetically Modified mustard (GM mustard) developed in India, consider the following statements :

1. GM mustard has the genes of a soil bacterium that give the plant the property of pest-resistance to a wide variety of pests.
2. GM mustard has the genes that allow the plant cross-pollination and hybridization.
3. GM mustard has been developed jointly by the IARI and Punjab Agricultural University.

Which of the statements given above is/are correct ?

(a) 1 and 3 only (b) 2 only

(c) 2 and 3 only (d) 1, 2 and 3

Solution (b)

- GM Mustard is a perfect flower so it 'self-pollinates'. Therefore Delhi University's then VC Dr. Deepak Pental created GM mustard so that he could cross-pollinate Indian variety with European variety to make new hybrid called DMH-11. Hence #2 is right and #3 is wrong. And by elimination, we are left with answer B: Only 2.

Q. Consider the following pairs:

Commonly used material vs. Unwanted or controversial chemicals found in them

1. Lipstick: Lead
2. Soft drinks: Brominated vegetable oils
3. Chinese fast food: Monosodium glutamate

Which of the pairs given above is/are correctly matched?

(a) 1 only (b) 2 and 3 only

(c) 1 and 3 only (d) 1, 2 and 3

Solution : (d)

Source : Newspaper-Articles&News coverage

Sources of Reading

Book: NCERT – VI to XII (For Static GK)

Newspaper: THE HINDU (For Dynamic GK)

Magazine: Science Reporter (For Dynamic GK)

Management of Time, Syllabus & Study

As you know the IAS exam is a marathon and not a sprint. For this you need to develop some routine to be able to concentrate for long hours and cover the syllabus within the time at hand. Study two or at most three subjects a day with predefined time limits so that you cover the most scoring part of the Prelims syllabus within the time you allotted to those subjects.

Routine will also help you develop a focused approach for Mains and will help you to prepare for most scoring parts of IAS Prelims syllabus early, so you can put in at least one revision before the Prelims. Preparing for IAS this way will surely boost your chances of clearing the Prelims in the first attempt itself.

So, first calculate how many days do you have to prepare for both Prelim and Main IAS Exams.

Divide the syllabus of Prelim and Main as per time you have. But, first emphasis should be on Prelim.

HOW TO MANAGE TIME

The IAS is a hard nut to crack thus time management is a very crucial part of the preparation for IAS Examination. This is because the time is limited and the IAS Syllabus is very vast. So the candidates need to make the best possible utilization of time. Also, if you do not manage your time properly, you'll end up wasting time on irrelevant things, while leaving the essential things uncovered. The first thing to bear in mind is to question whether you have a personal sense of time or a time log. This helps you to keep track of how you spend each hour.

Here are some tips for time management:

- Make a schedule: divide your day.
- Keep at least 8 - 10 hours a day for studies (if attending coaching, you'll be able to give only 6 - 8 hours a day).
- While studying for prelims, divide the study time into two parts: General Studies Paper I and General Studies Paper II (CSAT). If you are from Mathematics and English background, or are generally good in Aptitude, then you can keep only 2 hours a day for General Studies (CSAT) Paper II and devote the rest of the time to General Studies Paper I. If you are not very comfortable with the topics of (CSAT) Paper II , then you need to devote 3-4 hours for its practice.

- Devote around 1.5 hrs. for reading newspaper and making its notes. Don't skip newspapers, nor postpone reading them. You will never find time to complete them later.
- Keep 1 hour for reading current affairs magazine and other competitive magazines like **Pratiyogita Darpan**, **Yojana** and **Kurukshetra**.
- Setting deadlines and targets that are small and realistic will help you complete the syllabus in time.
- Get a proper sleep for 6 - 8 hours a day.
- You must spend 1- 2 hours for some **physical activities** like **jogging**, **cycling**, **yoga** or **playing a sport** and leisure activities like music, dance, painting, etc. (i.e. *health management*)
- Stop studying thoroughly at least 24 hours before the exam as studying now will only make you more anxious. You can go through Mind-Maps of subjects and topics. Just relax yourself for this day.

Fixing Time for an Answer

The Civil Services Main Exam consists of descriptive type of questions thus focusing on testing the candidate at various levels. Since time is the biggest constraint, it becomes necessary to answer the questions not only quickly but effectively in minimum words. The time limit for the essay, G.S. and optional papers is 3 hrs with a word limit.

PLANNING FOR PREPARATION

Planning is important because it tells us how to reach our destination or goal. In the context of the CSE, planning acquires greater significance because one has to cover a comprehensive syllabus in a limited period of time. Good planning really implies maximum results with minimum efforts. And effective planning means that you work out your own mechanism for checking whether you are spending your time effectively or not. Thus, you must focus on the following for success in Civil Services Examinations:

Master the Basics

As you are aware that UPSC has brought changes to the Civil Services Mains examination in both the pattern and the syllabus, one must keep in mind the following statement given by UPSC:

"The questions are likely to test the candidate's basic understanding of all relevant issues, and ability to analyze, and take a view on conflicting socio economic goals, objectives and demands. The candidates must give relevant, meaningful and to the point answers."

Thus, you don't have to master the topics, all you need is BASIC UNDERSTANDING (at least for Prelims) and the ability to analyze. Basic understanding comes from reading and re-reading. Ability to analyze what you have understood from reading comes from WRITING PRACTICE.

Start From Weak Areas

There is no syllabus in detail or specific for subject or areas for prelim point of view. Any question in CS prelims can be asked from anywhere, so aspirants must begin their planning and study for subject area which they are weak in or afraid the most from. When the weak areas can be overcome, a new confidence will develop that will motivate to cover up other areas/subjects easily and quicker.

Apply Intelligent Meditation in Preparation

It is very important to analyse previous questions asked in IAS Prelims and Main Exams and then think over all the aspects and diamensions on which questions can be formed and asked from particular topic or heading.

Prepare Your Own Notes & Mind-Map

Writing notes is very helpful in preparing for the examination, particularly when you study from different sources. Firstly, while writing notes you focus your attention in a more concentrated manner and many of these points remain in your memory if you put them on a Mind Map. Secondly, notes help you in quick revision.

For writing effective notes, do not start in a hurry, i.e. when you are reading the material for the first time. Without understanding what you read, you are likely to write down too much which may amount to simply reproduction of the material. After understanding the text look for the main points and sub-points. Try to write in your own words rather than using the same language. When you do this exercise get sincerely involved and write short notes preferably in points, one liner, short sentence, one or two words, short names, or abbreviations. These notes will help in revising the chapters or topics easily in lesser time.

REVISION IS THE KEY TO SUCCESS

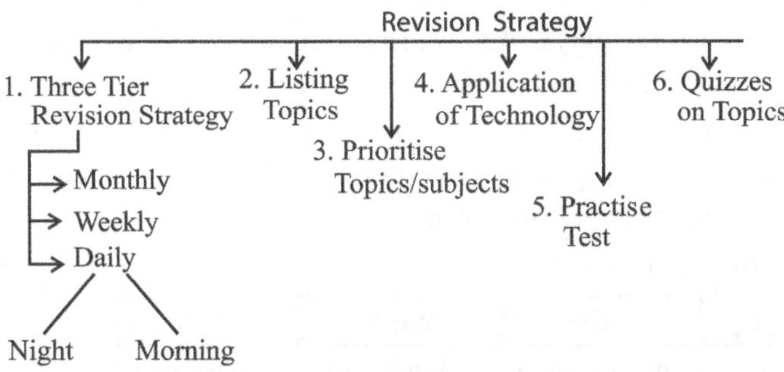

* **Revision** is the most important aspect of preparation for any exam, whether it is academic or competitive. But it plays a greater role in selection when an IAS aspirant follows it, because of complexity of syllabus and subjects for IAS exam.

Like study strategy, there is no fixed revision format that will suit each and every aspirant. Aspirants should think over which format can be best and suit them in revision. They can go through others revision techniques before making their own. But revision strategy should be prepared in such a way that help the aspirants to achieve their study goals in the best possible way.

We have given some guide lines below that will help the aspirants in making best suited revision strategy for IAS exam preparation.

1. **Three Tier Revision Strategy**

The most suited and successful revision strategy for any exam, particularly Civil Services Exam preparation is

Three Tier Strategy. This formate is based on three labels, i.e. day wise, week-wise and month-wise.

Daily revision is divided into two stages, morning and late-night. In the morning, aspirants should revise quickly all the subjects, chapters and topics they have studied previous day, thereafter, they start studying new subject/chapter or topic for the day. Before going to sleep in the late night after study, they must revise all the points they have studied the whole day.

Weekly Revision: It is second stage of revision which covers all the topics, chapters and subjects an aspirant has studied in a week, i.e. from Monday to Saturday. It is mostly fixed on Sunday.

Monthly Revision: Like wise weekly revision, monthly revision is the third stage of revision of the same topics and chapters which an aspirant have already revised weekly and daily in a month. This model of revision strategy will help the aspirants not to forget what ever they studied in a month.

The next revision can be after three and six months to freshen up your memory of three and six months studies. It will help the aspirants in building their confidence in preparation and cracking the exam.

Three Tier Revision Strategy

	Subject	Chapter	Topic
Daily	Subject name	Chapter name	Topic name
Weekly	—do—	—do—	—do—
Monthly	—do—	—do—	—do—

2. **Listing of Topics for Revision**

   Aspirants study many topics from different subjects and chapters in a day, week and month. But all the topics are not equally relevant and important from exam point of view. So they must list those topics which are important for revision according to their relevance, complexity and marks allocated for the exam. It will help aspirants to keep a check and complete their revision tasks within the time limit.

3. **Prioritise Subject and Topic**

   Aspirants list many more topics and chapters for revision. But, due to lack of time for weekly and monthly revision, they are unable to revise all the listed topics. So, they should prioritise topics for revision according to their importance in the examination and revise as per order.

4. **Application of Technology in Revision**

   Important points of a topic or chapter should be noted down on Memopad of a mobile phones or tablets to revise during going to coaching and coming back.

5. **Practice Tests**

   After completing a chapter or topic during preparation aspirants should test their learning through Practice Test based on that particular topic or chapter. These practice tests are designed on the same examination pattern as followed by UPSC to prepare the CSE paper. These practice tests will help in evaluating the aspirants preparation. These tests are a mode of revision for the topic or chapter.

6. **Solve the Topic's Quizzes**

   When you finish the topic during preparation, solve the quizzes or questions prepared on that particular topic so that you can assess your preparation and list the topic for revision accordingly.

Solve previous year question paper at regular intervals

As preparation for IAS prelims requires at least 10 months time it is easy to lose focus or go off target. To stay on the right path or get yourself on track quickly keep testing yourself against the previous IAS papers to know the effectiveness of your preparation and identify and overcome your weak points. For this grab the previous 5 year's solved section-wise Prelims Question Paper Set.

Go for Online Mock Test

After completing your syllabus and revision, you can go for a mock test. Conducted in a proper way, a mock test makes you feel the environment and experience of the real exam. It is useful in reviewing your knowledge of the subjects and judging your weak and strong areas of preparation. Through mock test you can also test your ability of time management. Do not miss the opportunity as and when any institute conducts mock test. You can take mock test online.

Choice of the Optional Subject

Choosing a right optional subject is a crucial step in your preparation for the UPSC Civil Services Exam. Select optional Subject on the basis of aptitude that you have for the subject and not because a certain subject is perceived to be more scoring than the others. Preferably, the subject must be scoring. It is better to choose a subject, in which your base is strong. While choosing the optional subject, remember that:

The subject should...

- excite you,
- make you know more about it,
- not put you to sleep,
- make you think out of the box,
- have books available easily.

Following are the important steps you should follow before you finalize a subject as your optional:

1. Go through the list of all the optional subjects thoroughly.
2. Now go back to your school and college days. Think about your favourite subjects then. Think hard in which subject you excelled, in which subject you showed more interest, in which subject you got good marks.
3. Now come to the present. See which areas of news you are more interested in. Think of short-listing them as your optional subject.
4. Based on above criteria, make a list of 4-5 subjects that you think you have interest in.
5. Now go through the syllabus of each optional subject. Read all topics carefully. Underline/highlight the topics that you think you know something about or have some interest in the syllabus of each shortlisted Optional subject.
6. Now go through the Previous Year Question papers (3 - 4 years) of the shortlisted subjects. Read all the questions. Again gauge yourself the level of interest you have or residual knowledge you possess to answer each question. It's just to know yourself how comfortable you are with a subject, don't worry if you don't know answer to any question.
7. Finally, the availability of materials and guidance in the form of coaching matters a lot. For some subjects it is difficult to get standard books, for some coaching may not be available. Non-technical subjects can be prepared by doing self-study provided you regularly practise writing.
8. By now you will have a clear picture about choosing between 2-3 subjects.

Planning For Prelim Preparation

Tips & Planning for GS Paper-1

For facing Preliminary Examination Paper 1, i.e. **General Studies**, you need to be well aware and well informed as being updated is going to help you in attempting a large number of questions. It involves both clarity about the basics as well as abreast of current affairs and contemporary developments. It includes areas like **Indian National Movement, Indian Polity, Basic Economic Understanding, Geography, Science and Technology**, etc. While the dynamic part includes **Current Affairs, GK** has no proper definition and syllabus making it quite vast subject.

Since the syllabus does not give much detail of the topics to be studied under each subject it is expected to gain knowledge of them that should be slightly below the graduation level but definitely above the high school level.

There are about 100 questions to be answered in two hours, each question carries two marks. It means there is about 80 seconds to answer each question. So speed and accuracy is essential to tackle this examination. While the correct answer will fetch 2 marks, a wrong answer means a loss of 0.66 marks.

The 100 questions in Paper 1 can be grouped into three categories:

(i) Multiple Choice Questions - Single response correct

(ii) Multiple Choice Questions - Multiple response correct

(iii) Multiple Choice Questions - Matching type

The number of questions asked from different sections varies each time and there is no fixed rule for this. **The nature of questions asked are generally on basic principles, their application, factual information and current affairs.** Some questions are based on applied aspects of principles and factual information. It has been found that many of the questions overlap with more than one section of the syllabus.

The answer to the question requires analytical bend of mind. So mere reading of NCERT high school text books is now insufficient for the preparation of the prelim examination and in depth reading is required to handle such questions. The best way should be to adopt an integrated approach for preparation combining it with Mains, and one should make efforts to understand the principles and then strive to find their applications in daily life. The new addition in the syllabus since 2011 is on *Environmental Ecology*, *Bio-diversity* and *Climate Change*. So it is wise to prepare these areas from the view-point of the Main Examination.

Considering the nature of the examination the tactics must be to focus on greater rather than intensive coverage. One is expected to know everything at the same time. However, only basics of each of the discipline are needed, so one master as many basic concepts and facts as possible, avoiding the element of over-kill in the preparations at Prelims stage.

Tips & Strategies for CSAT Paper 2

The Preliminary Examination Paper 2 (CSAT) assesses **comprehension, abstract reasoning, analysis competency, problem solving ability, judgment and decision making ability of the candidates**. Unlike paper 1 where quantity of questions is a major determinant for the static section, paper 2 cannot be tamed without solving dynamic questions that requires on the spot mental ability.

Paper-II Syllabus comprises of seven subjects and is in the nature of Aptitude Test.

1. Comprehension,
2. Interpersonal skills including communication skills,
3. Logical reasoning and analytical ability,
4. Decision making and problem solving,
5. General mental ability,
6. Basic numeracy (numbers and their relations, orders of magnitude, etc.),
7. Data interpretation (charts, graphs, tables, data sufficiency etc.).

The following are simple preparation tips to score well in the CSAT (Prelims) - PAPER 2:

- Identify your strong areas of comprehension and aptitude.
- Solve these questions first to ensure that you get the answers right.
- Do not waste too much time if you get stuck in a particular question.

- You should at least be 70% sure of the answer if you do not want to lose too many marks in negative marking.
- Practise as many mock tests as possible to be aware of what kind of mistakes you make while solving different kind of problems or aptitude questions.
- Practise questions on Permutations & Combinations, Logical Reasoning and Probability.

Planning For IAS Main Preparation

FACING THE MAIN EXAM

The IAS Main Exam happens to be a vital part of Civil Services Exam. One has to be vigilant of all the dimensions involved while appearing for the IAS Main. Revolutionary changes were introduced during this very year, i.e. 2013, in both pattern and syllabus of examination. And in August, UPSC has introduced one more change that is profoundly going to change the way Main Exam has been attempted and maneuvered by candidates so far.

Below is presented the text that has been introduced in the Civil Service Main (CSM). Instruction document that is released by the UPSC after result of Preliminary paper that contains important instructions regarding the filling of Main form.

"Candidates should note that instead of separate Question Paper and Answer Book, a consolidated Question Paper-cum-Answer Book, having space below each part/sub part of a question shall be provided to them for writing the answers. Candidates shall be required to attempt answer to the part/sub-part of a question strictly within the pre-defined space. Any attempt outside the pre-defined space shall not be evaluated."

First important thing will be how you manage your time, thoughts and writing style. Somebody who writes in *larger font size* will be at a disadvantage because of the lesser number of words he can fit in the space. At the same time, we would caution not to indulge in *micro-lettering* that can frustrate and irritate the evaluator. Rather an optimum *letter size is suggested*, the same can be decided based on your *flair of writing*. So, one should practise lots of writing.

WRITING A GOOD ESSAY & G.S. QUESTION'S ANSWER

Since it's a subjective paper, one must keep in mind two components: '*process*' and '*content*'. *Process includes how to write a good essay* and *content involves what to write in a good essay that is subject matter*. Writing essay in a right way requires a multipronged strategy. One must consider following points:

1. Proper, simple and grammatically correct language must be used.
2. Ordering of essay should be done. Essay has three parts **introduction, main body**, and **conclusion**. All three are equally important. A good conclusion can fetch 10 to 20 more marks.
3. Correct information with daily life experiences to give personal touch and uniqueness to the essay.
4. Proper time management should be there. Each and every minute should be utilized. Time should be allotted to each section in a rational manner.
5. One should have a clear understanding of topic on which he is writing. Always stay close to the topic and avoid deviating from it.
6. Don't enter the examination hall with a particular mindset as it can restrict the flow of ideas.

Interdisciplinary Approach in Study

In order to answer holistic nature of questions asked in IAS exam, specially in Main, aspirants are advised to develop interdisciplinary approach in study different subjects and topics. It will help to understand all dimensions associated with the topic.

The interdisciplinary approach is a method of integrating different informations from different subjects, headings topics to answer different nature of questions asked in the IAS Exam. For example topic can be studied or analysed on **political, economic**, **social** or **scientific ground** or parameters. It can also be based on its **problems, issues, application, impacts**, etc.

For instance, Government decision in changing previous economic policy has short and long term implication. Its impacts can be social, economic, political, demographic or scientific.

In developing interdisciplinary approach in study, aspirants need to develop and expand their outlook towards topics keeping in mind all aspects and dimensions of the topic. For this, topics can be related with different happening and changes that occur around in society, environment, polity, etc.

HOW TO READ, PREPARE NOTES, & DISCUSS IN GROUP

How to Read

Aspirants often face trouble when see the extensive syllabus of Main exam. So various points should be followed:

* One should be objective and try to focus on syllabus as per analysis of trend of questions asked in recent years.
* The next thing to be kept in mind is the choice of *study material*. Be wise and just refer few *standard books* to get a deep insight of the subject. Reading from too many books will do more harm than good.

- ♦ Lastly it is good to be selective while preparing for a given topic, to list all the important points and the relevant information in a logical framework.
- ♦ It is important to remember that studying for the exam involves purposeful reading which is basically reading with a certain focus on the given topic and preparing for the possible questions accordingly.
- ♦ Before starting on any topic, it is a wise move to go through the questions asked in the past about the given topic and jot down the probable questions for the current year. It gives an idea to the kind of material one need to study to be able to answer such questions effectively.
- ♦ Mentally analyze all that you have read and try to logically link all the points and see if you have understood everything. Such a kind of periodical revision will help in the long run as it ensures to increase your understanding, improves and enhances memory thus making you more confident so that you give your best performance.

How to Prepare Notes

You might have heard a hundred times about the importance of taking small or micro notes for the IAS exam. But how do you do it in a manner that the notes are concise, effective, readable in a short time, all at once. After all you will need to go through these small notes for IAS exam before the preliminary and/or the Main in just a few days or even hours.

There are several good reasons for making your own notes:

1. Helps you to understand any given topic, pick out the important points and to summarize them.
2. Writing down any information helps you to remember the whole topic's content matter better.
3. It makes a good practice for thinking and writing easy.
4. It prompts you to revise your work since it does not take a long time to go through a set of well made notes.
5. Also helps you in your final revision by reminding you of the most important points of each topic.

Methods

There are different methods of making notes and one should decide which method suits you the best. Two common methods of making notes are:

Linear Method: It is a method in which you condense the material you have read using *headings* and *sub headings* and jotting down the most *important points*. This method works best when making notes from a book where the material is already properly organized. But one disadvantage of this method is that you end up copying a lot of material from the book which defeats the very purpose of condensing.

Pattern Method: For this, begin the topic at the centre of the page. Each line radiating from it represents a branch of the main idea. Each point is written as briefly as possible using a key word or **a phrase**. It is a **better method** to adopt because.

- It is more flexible than making linear notes. One can add extra information to it at any point without any problem.

- We can see the whole pattern at one go without actually turning the pages.
- Thirdly we can indicate the links between different topics more easily than we can do in a linear method.

But this method has some disadvantages as well. If there are too many facts and too much of information, your pattern becomes messy and over-crowded. Using key words can remind you of basic ideas but when it comes to remembering details, this method cannot be sufficient.

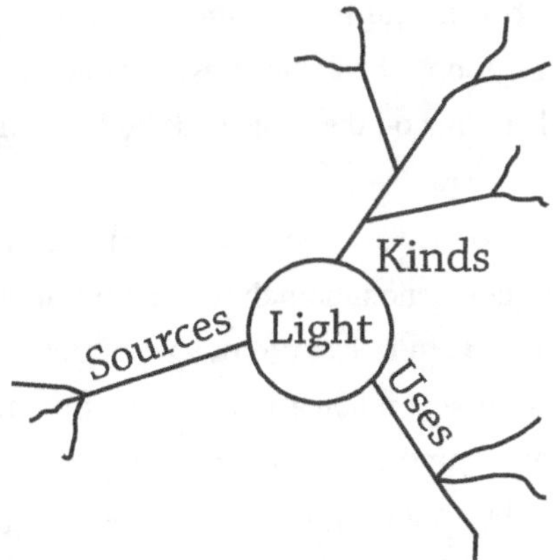

Therefore the most effective way of making good notes from the sources available is to use a combination of these two linear and pattern methods. One important thing to remember is that for many subjects your **notes will have to include diagrams, charts, tables** and **mind-maps.** They must be accurate and well labelled.

Group Discussions to clear concept

For effective learning for the UPSC Civil Services Main Exam, Group Discussion is very important. Study with a fellow or a group of friends who are also preparing for the CSE. Regular discussions with such friends are very helpful. This way you not only revise what you have studied but also learn many points which you might not have covered or did not know. Such a company happens to be of supplementing nature to each other. Besides, it makes your study more interesting, competitive and crystalised.

Some skills that are generated in a Group Discussion are:

Communication Skills: In a Group Discussion there is fair possibility that you improve your communication skills. Communication skills are considered as necessary to do well in the UPSC civil Services Exam. In a group while sharing your opinions and exchanging views with others you will automatically improve your communication skills.

Divergent Thinking: Group Discussion enables a participating candidate to think in divergent directions to generate more points and a good presentation of the topic in the group. In a group when you present your points you would think and consider all possible points on the topic and thus you improve your thinking process also.

Analytical skills: In the Group Discussion you have to be careful about the points you discuss. You should have enough analytical ability to analyse the topic and the points and then present them in front of others for discussion. You need to be careful so that there is no logical inconsistency in your points. Thus, while doing Group Discussion you get to improve your analytical skills.

Group Discussions should be polite and friendly. There should not be any attitude of hard competition, as it will not bring the desired benefit for the participating members. Group Discussions should be held with the intention of learning well and improve more.

What The Toppers Say

Success belongs only to those who are willing to work harder than anyone else.

If you are serious about being successful in your career then you can do nothing better than educating yourself about the inspirational stories of successful candidates of IAS exam.

INTERVIEW OF IAS TOPPER 2015– TINA DABI

By- Dr. Md. Usmangani Ansari

Dr. Ansari: **How did you feel when you got the news about your first position?**

Tina Dabi: I felt really happy and content that my hardwork had paid off.

Dr. Ansari: **Why did you choose IAS as a professional career?**

Tina Dabi: Civil Services provide a unique platform where one can contribute something to society, get immense job satisfaction along with a decent standard of living.

Dr. Ansari: **Who is the driving force behind your success and position in CSE?**

Tina Dabi: My mother is the reason behind my success, her constant motivation and support have been invaluable for my preparation.

Dr. Ansari: **When did you start preparing for civil services?**

Tina Dabi: I began thinking and planning my preparation since Class XI in school. But my full fledged preparation began only after my graduation.

Dr. Ansari: **How did Disha's 21 Years Previous Years Questions Book help you?**

Tina Dabi: The book proved to be a good ready reference during revision and all the questions gave a good practice. It helped understand the pattern and demand of the exam.

Dr. Ansari: **How did Disha's "101 Speed Test" for practicing CSAT Paper 1?**

Tina Dabi: Its very helpful for quick revisions.

Dr. Ansari: **Did you start preparation for CS-Main after Prelims Test or wait for the result?**

Tina Dabi: I had begun studying Mains side by side, however stopped studying for Mains three months before Prelims. I resumed Mains Preparation after Prelims exam.

Dr. Ansari: **Which strategy did you adopt for GS (Main) Papers?**

Tina Dabi: I strictly followed the Mains Test Series schedule so that with each section I prepared, I got myself tested on that section through the Test Series.

Dr. Ansari: **How did you prepare GS Paper (Mains) with the help of newspapers?**

Tina Dabi: Newspapers play a very important role. Nearly 80% of the exam paper is current affairs oriented. There were direct questions from the newspaper in the exam. I used to maintain a notebook where I only noted down the very important topics (not all) and kept a record of any new updates that occurred related to that topic.

Dr. Ansari: **How did you prepare for interview?**

Tina Dabi: I took as many mock interviews as I could. I read three newspapers and studied my graduation and optional subject.

Dr. Ansari: **What messages and tips would you like to give to IAS aspirants?**

Tina Dabi: I would like to tell them that they work hard on a consistence basis, stick to their study plans, keep themselves patient and motivated. With focus and discipline, anything is achieveable.

Dr. Ansari: Once again very very congratulations for your success. And I wish you to reach on the top of your career and get satisfaction in your life.

Tina Dabi: Thank you so much. It was really nice interacting with you Sir.

www.ingramcontent.com/pod-product-compliance
Lightning Source LLC
LaVergne TN
LVHW050537160826
845677LV00011B/2078

* 9 7 8 9 3 8 8 2 4 0 1 3 0 *